MANUFACTURING
The Formidable
Competitive Weapon

MANUFACTURING
The Formidable
Competitive Weapon

WICKHAM SKINNER
Harvard University Graduate School of Business Administration

JOHN WILEY & SONS

New York · Chichester · Brisbane · Toronto · Singapore

Library of Congress Cataloging in Publication Data:

Skinner, Wickham.
    Manufacturing, the formidable competitive weapon.

    Includes index.
    1. Production management.   I. Title.
TS155.S553   1985   658.5   85-3290
ISBN 0-471-81739-2

TO

My Colleagues
at the Harvard Business School,
Past and Present

Preface

Since the publication of *Manufacturing in the Corporate Strategy* in 1978, manufacturing in the United States has been in a state of extraordinary turmoil. Change in the manufacturing area comes about slowly— ordinarily it is ponderous and slow moving because of its immense capital requirements and the long period of time required for changing equipment or process technologies and redirecting the efforts of multitudes of workers. Now, suddenly, we find manufacturing in the grip of forces that seem to be producing an unprecedented flood of pressures on this rusty old institution, resulting in a management scene of frenetic self-criticism and questioning, experimentation, fervent rededication to old values, and great personal risk and uncertainty.

That the manufacturing sector began to boil up with such turbulence at about the same time as the publication of the earlier volume was, of course, coincidence. I had been writing about U.S. manufacturing since the early 1960s, but the cause of the cyclone had nothing to do with anybody's book or articles. Professors don't start revolutions. Ideas may be important, but the roots of major industrial change lie in economics and technology.

What has been happening in the economic and technological environment surrounding manufacturing makes the current maelstrom of pressures appear nearly inevitable. By the late 1970s it was clear that the United States had lost its century-old dominance in manufacturing in dozens of industries. Our competitive edge was destroyed by lower costs, better quality, and product and process technologies of global competitors. Imports were surging into the country from Japan, Korea, Singapore, Taiwan, and many countries of Western Europe. Manufacturing employment dropped off rapidly. Union membership declined. The auto industry was especially hard hit. Chrysler nearly went bankrupt. The giant steel industry was a disaster area. The industrial Midwest, with its concentration in heavy industry, was staggered. The area began to be called, sadly, the Rust Bowl, and similar problems occurred in textiles, consumer electronics, and high technology industries such as machine tools, electrical equipment, and instrumentation all over the country. Even the computer industry and microprocessor chip making began to feel debilitating competition.

The age of U.S. industrial supremacy had clearly ended, and a new period of head-to-head competition had begun. The economics were against us: our labor was usually more costly, financing more difficult, interest rates higher, labor unions reluctant to freeze or reduce wage rates. Relative to Asian competitors, the economic factors were particularly severe. Asian and European competitors often produced products of better quality, with equal or better delivery and service levels, and through superb organization, coordination, and cooperation developed entirely new products in half the time of U.S. competitors.

Worst of all, American productivity, which had risen steadily at 2–3% per year in most years for over a century, leveled off and in recession periods in fact declined. This caused a rash of analysis, finger-pointing, and criticism of industry from all quarters. Clearly we were in trouble and something had to be done.

Magazines ran dozens of articles focusing on industrial problems and the need for "reindustrialization." The factory was being "rediscovered." Economists probed into causes for the "productivity problem," while engineers focused on new, labor-saving mechanization of operations and computer-based automation.

Within industrial firms the pressure for better industrial performance was often severe, and in some industries the issue was one of plain survival. After years of neglect, top management's attention had been captured. Manufacturing executives received not only attention but personal pressure, and in some cases funds for anything that could conceivably help productivity and begin to restore a competitive edge became more readily available than in decades.

So the action in manufacturing has been extraordinary in these last five years. In my own experience I have never seen such frenetic, energetic, or determined efforts. Sleepy plants and organizations have bounded up with hard-charging, revitalized attempts to produce better products at lower cost and with shorter deliveries. But in many companies the pressure for improvement has been so great that a potpourri of diverse programs have been seized upon and hastily organized, often with little overall understanding and direction, and generally with more energy than analysis.

The far greatest effort has been in "productivity" programs, with productivity committees, czars, laboratories, and staff groups popping up everywhere. Some companies have turned to "quality" as a new paradigm for performing better in all corners of the organization and lifting up every employee's effort toward "excellence." Hundreds of work force management experiments have been set up, with approaches ranging from "quality circles" to "nonsupervised work groups" to totally new concepts of job content, compensation, and problem solving.

A major new emphasis has proceeded in quite another direction, the promise of new, computer-based manufacturing technologies. Computer-aided design, computer-aided manufacturing, computer/integrated manufacturing, flexible machinery systems, robots and lasers, all hold forth great promise of the "factory of the future" indeed becoming a reality.

In fact, there is today a large amount of wheelspinning and uncertainty, and many managements are floundering about in the middle of these potentially fundamental changes in manufacturing with conflicting approaches and a good deal of confusion. In fact, the situation *is* confusing. For "the productivity approach" seems to focus too much on the labor element of cost while neglecting overheads and other approaches to rebuilding competitive advantage. And the human resource experiments often fail and clearly work uphill against deep-seated management mindsets and natural proclivities. The new technologies, the third approach, are extremely capital intense, usually do not work well for several years, and are highly risky.

So in total, while many approaches to restoring a competitive edge are being tried, nothing is working so well as to demonstrate a road to survival as an industrial nation, and we are still deep in trouble. Nevertheless, our new energy and determination and experimentation with promising new approaches to manufacturing bode well. For while we are floundering and uncertain and only a few companies seem to be coping effectively with innovative responses to adversity, manufacturing people are inventive and persistent and recently extraordinarily motivated. Answers will be found. But time is a scarce resource in this competition, and there is a sense of urgency today that we need to make wise decisions quickly. But to do this companies need a long-range approach to manufacturing policy decisions, and better ways to sort out and understand their choices and opportunities.

It was for these reasons that in the spring of 1984 my publisher and I decided to publish an updated book. The objective is to offer top corporate officers and manufacturing managers an orderly and purposeful way of looking at their problems and opportunities amidst the fermentation and pressures and struggle going on today. Manufacturing executives need to get off the defensive and onto a proactive, aggressive practice of management. The approach offered in this book is to forge manufacturing into a competitive weapon by formulating a manufacturing strategy focused around the competitive needs and strategic plans of the institution. With the use of this concept the appropriate forms of productivity improvement, equipment and process technology, improved human resource management, Japanese management techniques and the myriad of other "fixes" for the factory can all become "prioritized" and much more clear. Without a clear manufacturing strategy all these fixes or levers are being jumbled together in nearly random disorder. We have too many "band-aid" solutions aimed at symptoms, chosen according to fad and the fancy of dominant managers.

So this book, it appeared to me, should focus less on trying to recapture management attention to manufacturing (a primary purpose of the earlier publication) and more on bringing some order and strategy to the scene. Since 1978 management's attention has clearly been captured; the question now is what to do, how to develop a manufacturing strategy and the place of the new technologies and other structural ingredients in it.

For these reasons more than half of the earlier book has been completely changed. I have removed the extensive case studies and several international production chapters and replaced them with ten chapters focusing on three key aspects of the situation in manufacturing today: (1) the impacts of new manufacturing technology, (2) manufacturing as a competitive resource, and (3) the need for a "new breed" of manufacturing manager, in the end analysis an absolutely key resource to effective change.

The first nine chapters have been carried over from *Manufacturing in the Corporate Strategy* to provide the basic fundamentals of manufacturing strategy, ranging from the need for such an approach to its fundamental concepts, and finally, to how it may be operationalized and implemented. Hence the major change from the earlier work is that ten of the last eleven chapters are new and focus on sorting out the principal elements in the situation as it has changed since 1978.

As before, I am grateful to many colleagues, to the Harvard Business School for financial support, to Dean John McArthur, and Director of Research Raymond Corey.

As an educational institution, the Harvard Business School is unique not only in its support of faculty research, largely financed by corporate associates and alumni, but in its tradition of a strong focus and concern with industrial management. During the 1960s and 1970s the School's substantial allocation of resources to production and operations management (POM) was a rare phenomenon in business education and decidedly unfashionable. Deans Fouraker and McArthur never wavered on this issue, and the emphasis on POM continues. This educational policy has made possible the field research and subsequent development of the ideas around which this book was written. For a student of manufacturing, there could not have been a better place to have been working than the Harvard Business School.

WICKHAM SKINNER

St. George, Maine
March 1985

Acknowledgments

I am grateful to my wife, Alice, for her enthusiasm and ever-willing availability to react to my experiences and their significance with perceptive questions and encouragement.

To the Harvard Business School, Deans George Baker, Lawrence Fouraker, and John McArthur, the Division of Research, and the Associates Program of the School, I acknowledge with gratitude the financial support that made this research possible. Suzanne Tyrer, Carole Whittemore, Kathleen Miller, Ruth Band and Vic Burford provided production and editorial services with great skill. The Harvard Business Review graciously released a number of my articles for use in this book.

I have been enormously influenced by the ideas and frequent interplay of discussion and reactions to drafts by my colleagues at the Harvard Business School. I am especially indebted to the following colleagues: Professors Franklin Folts, Arch R. Dooley, Philip Thurston, Richard Rosenbloom, Robert Hayes, Steven Wheelwright, Stanley Miller, Alfred Chandler, George Lodge, David Rogers, Joel Goldhar, Curtis Jones, Robert Ackerman, Edward Davis, Lawrence Benningson, John Rosenblum, Earl Sasser, Chris Argyris, Roger Schmenner, William Abernathy, William Fulmer, Jeffrey Miller, Duncan McDougall, Alice Amsden, Robert Stobaugh, Richard Walton, Raymond Vernon and Bert Wood. The length of this list attests to the emphasis on production and operating management at the Harvard Business School, an emphasis that has created an environment that is marvelous for writing a book on manufacturing. While I take full responsibility for the conclusions reached and judgments made, each of the above contributed significantly to the development of my thinking.

I acknowledge with great thanks the contributions of the large number of exciting and vital people in manufacturing management who cooperated with me in research and case-writing endeavors and in many exchanges of ideas. Too numerous to mention individually, they are well remembered for their stimulation, ideas, and accomplishments.

I thank the publishers who have granted me permission to reprint or adapt my articles for this book.

W.S.

Credits

Contents

Manufacturing as a Competitive Resource

Wanted: A New Breed of Manufacturing Manager

MANUFACTURING
The Formidable
Competitive Weapon

INTRODUCTION

The initial two chapters introduce the reader to what the book is about and how it came to be written. They describe some of the author's concerns about manufacturing and how it is generally managed. The second chapter makes the point that, beginning about 1965, production in the United States began to experience new and mounting pressures that made much of the art and science of manufacturing obsolete. During the past two decades the necessity of new approaches to its management became more and more evident but, in fact, significant changes have only recently begun to take place. This book suggests new approaches to the management of manufacturing which can transform that corporate function to become a formidable competitive resource.

CHAPTER 1

Manufacturing
in
Corporate Strategy

The American production system has been hailed in the United States and around the world for nearly 100 years because of its productivity, capacity, innovations, and contributions to our amazing standard of living. In the early 1960s, the picture began to change. Our number one position in world industrial capability began to erode. Comparative proportions of the world's manufacturing output, leadership in technological and process innovation, ability to compete in world markets, and many sick industries signaled that somehow U.S. industry was slipping. With few exceptions we are no longer clearly outstanding.

Cracks in our industrial base are now being blamed in part for high costs, high imports, trade imbalances, and heavy unemployment. Stagnant productivity, labor unrest, and consumer complaints over shoddy workmanship and sometimes unsafe products have caused a loss in prestige and credibility for our industrial establishment. As a place to work, the factory can hardly rank lower in its appeal to most of our young. Even the unemployed young hesitate before factory gates because they see factories as an entry into a regimented, subhuman quality of working life.

Whether fair or rational, these criticisms reflect the fact that somehow things are not working as well in industry as they once did. This book is written as the result of concern over these problems. Are our premises, our tools, our approaches, our basic concepts in industrial management realistic and adequate? These are questions pursued in this book.

In the middle 1960s, I became increasingly aware of the growing difficulties and frustrations of manufacturing executives in the United States.

As I visited companies, I became gradually aware of a new set of circumstances surrounding and invading the world of manufacturing and making a successful manufacturing operation increasingly difficult. The primary cause seemed to be a new environment—an environment in which there was more competition, more pressure from management, labor, stockholders, consumers, and the public. The environmental changes were characterized by growing foreign competition, an accelerating rate of technological change, and new modes of competition. Competition was resulting in more advertising, narrower profit margins, a flood of new products, pressures toward integrating forward and backward, and broadening product lines. Amid this frenetic background, the manufacturer was being hit with new forms of federal regulation and threatened with drastic exposure by the courts' new interpretations of company liabilities for product failures.

Controlling the old, conventional problems—to produce at lower cost, to achieve satisfactory quality constantly, to meet delivery promises, to cut down the time necessary to deliver each order, to get new products into production more quickly, and to maintain investment, facilities, and inventories at low levels while adjusting flexibly to changes in volume—became ever more difficult. This set of conflicting requirements intensified the fact that no matter what manufacturing managers attempted to do, they were always susceptible to criticism by top management. This is inherent in the nature of the manufacturing function. The successful manufacturer must produce quickly and deliver on schedule a quality product at a minimum of cost and investment.

Under added pressures from outside, the management tools available for coping with these problems proved inadequate. Manufacturing vice-presidents felt that not only were their management tools impotent and weak, but they were always being criticized for unacceptable costs, delivery, quality, or investment and cut off from top management.

Their impressions of being cut off were accurate, for during the 1950s and 1960s the typical major emphasis was on growth in sales and market share, and top management seemed to be dominated and influenced more by executives who were especially competent in marketing and finance and less by those with a manufacturing point of view. Manufacturing people felt that they were being asked to "do their duty and perform as good soldiers," doing what was asked without complaint. In spite of the fact that they were entrusted with responsibility for typically 75% of the firm's investment, 80% of the firm's personnel, and 85% or more of the firm's expenditures for materials and equipment, manufacturing issues were often treated by top management as perfunctory and operational rather than strategic. Manufacturing was considered essential, but seemed to offer little intellectual or managerial challenge.

Conceptually, manufacturing was considered a management area in which adequate theory and techniques had long been available and in which the complex problems of planning and control that had challenged management science pioneers had been solved. Paradoxically, in the very field in which scientific management had started—that is, with Frederick Taylor in industrial engineering—professional management had somehow apparently run out its string and developed itself to the point where successful manufacturing required only doing what the book prescribed. Manufacturing was perceived by many top managers and most professors in well-known schools of business as relatively routine, standardized, and unexciting. The function was no longer attracting many of the most able members of the young generation as workers, technicians, or managers.

Clearly something was basically wrong. The old tools did not seem to work in a new environment. Able, highly professional, experienced managers felt themselves unfairly criticized no matter what they did, and their whole function seemed cut off from the enterprise as a whole. The enigma was that it was out of the mainstream of communication and management of the enterprise, yet its impact on the enterprise was as pronounced as ever—if not more—in the new competitive world. Manufacturing had drifted into becoming a necessary evil in the corporation; it had become a function that was more often than not holding back the entire corporation.

In the middle of this research into what was going on in U.S. industry, of course I came across some companies whose manufacturing functions were extraordinarily well managed. The outstanding feature of these companies seemed to be that in some way or another they had forged manufacturing into a major and formidable competitive weapon. They competed not only with new products, marketing, advertising, and skillful financing, but also with unique approaches to achieving competence in manufacturing. Manufacturing became a competitive resource because they had exceptionally short deliveries, or remarkable low costs, or could move fast in developing new products, or produced the same volume with lower investment than their competitors.

I ran across some of these situations while teaching a course at the Harvard Business School. I asked students to study a group of companies within a single industry, comparing them and their performance over the industry as a whole, and then looking at the ways they structured and operated their manufacturing enterprises. Somewhat to my surprise, we found that within a given industry, companies would have entirely different approaches to manufacturing. For example, different companies could employ quite different technologies in their equipment and process decisions; or one company would have a number of small plants, whereas another would concentrate its manufacturing in one or two big plants. The organizational structure or the scheduling, inventory management, or management of work force differed among companies. So we discovered that in spite of common technology, a common set of competitors, a common industry structure, and common market practices, different companies often would have developed quite different manufacturing policies.

The next step was to analyze which manufacturing policies seemed to work best. After thorough study, it became clear that there was no principle or formula that would suggest which worked best in a given industry. The surprising fact was that the company's corporate competitive strategy was the salient factor. If the manufacturing policy was consistent with and supported the company's competitive corporate strategy, it worked well and became a competitive weapon. If the policy was not consistent with the corporate competitive strategy, it became a negative influence in the company's performance.

About this time I had a telephone call from the president of a medium-sized manufacturing firm. He asked me if I could help him with his manufacturing operations. I asked him what the trouble was, and he replied, "Everybody here is upset, disappointed, and frustrated with manufacturing. Sales are mad at them for poor deliveries, and the marketing people are angry because they are so slow at getting new products in production. The treasurer is put out with them because they seem to require so much in the way of inventories and capital equipment. The personnel manager feels that they do a lousy job with their people. No matter whom you talk with, no one is very happy with our manufacturing."

I asked him why he thought this was happening and what was the basic trouble. He hesitated a moment and then said, "I think it's because we don't have a manufacturing philosophy." I said, "A manufacturing philosophy? What's that?" His reply was, "Professor Skinner, I don't know what it is. All I know is we don't have one."

A "manufacturing philosophy"—that was a new term for me. But after visiting his operation, I came to agree that indeed they did not have a manufacturing philosophy. Instead of a consistent set of manufacturing policies that were all focused in one direction and were mutually supportive, their approaches were conflicting and at cross purposes internally. Their equipment, for example, promoted low costs but made product changeover difficult. Their production control system favored short deliveries on standard items at the cost of high inventories. Their workforce management approaches made flexibility for volume changes difficult. Across the whole span of the decisions they had made one by one, almost everything in their manufacturing pulled a different way. In fact, they were attempting to serve five markets, five technologies, and five strategic requirements within one factory.

All of these events led me to write—usually for the *Harvard Business Review*—a series of articles in which I cited the basic problems in American manufacturing and offered some ways of solving them. The articles led me from analysis of what seemed to be going wrong to a different way of looking at manufacturing from within the corporation. Essentially, what I discovered is an approach to manufacturing from the top down that is based on the recognition that manufacturing can become a major corporate competitive weapon. These articles started with problems and led into some broad new ways of looking at them, and subsequently to specific management techniques. This book follows such a sequence, moving from problems to "theory" to techniques for reforming manufacturing into a competitive, strategic resource, and ending with several chapters on the "new managers" now needed.

This book offers a new way for top management to perceive and manage manufacturing. It does not demean the conventional, from the bottom up, detailed type of tools, which in most cases are just as useful as ever. These old tools—for example, time and motion studies, operation research techniques, and the more traditional approaches in industrial engineering—are useful for optimizing one facet or another of a manufacturing operation. They cannot be thrown away, and indeed, they must be used more than ever. But top management in manufacturing must decide which tools to use and which facets of their operations to attempt to optimize, because in a technologically based system, it is almost virtually impossible to optimize one tool or facet of business without penalizing another. The better the management, the less the penalty; but some type of penalty always takes place. The new approach starts with the role of manufacturing in the corporate strategy, a link that had been missing, and it leads to a strategy for making consistent and focused basic policy decisions in the design and management of manufacturing operations.

This book is submitted with profound and heartfelt respect to my hundreds of friends in manufacturing. These are the men and women who have the difficult job of managing resources in our factories: people, capital assets, and logistics. It is exciting work. This book is offered to them with great admiration in the hope that it might make their lives even more exciting by making explicit the links between their work, the success of their enterprises, and the productive lives of the millions who spend their working lives in manufacturing to produce goods for their people.

This second edition is about five-eighths new compared to the first edition. I have chopped the cases and chapters on international production because of the need to focus on two new elements in the situation today: (1) the new technologies crowding on the scene—robots, lasers, and microprocessor-based, computer-integrated manufacturing, and (2) the increasing evidence that the major impediment to needed change in manufacturing is shifting to rest on the manager. We need new skills and attitudes in factory management and there seems to be emerging, albeit slowly, a kind of new breed that is much needed.

These new elements in manufacturing management have major corporate strategic implications and it is on these that the bulk of the new edition concentrates its attention.

CHAPTER 2

Production
Under
Pressure

There is little complacency about manufacturing in the United States today. Production managers—attempting to cope with pressures from the marketing and engineering departments, the union, the treasurer, and the controller—give an impression of being on the defensive, plagued by recurrent crises. Our position as the world leader in industrial technology has badly deteriorated. In many industries we have lost much ground to foreign competition. We are doing no better than a mediocre job of coping with and taking advantage of automation. Inferior product quality and lack of reliability are astoundingly common, considering our proven accomplishments in space technology. Are not strikes and serious industrial conflicts ordinary events?

As I examine the U.S. manufacturing scene, it appears to me that these obvious and immediate concerns are symptomatic of an underlying process of change that has major significance. The fact is, we have begun the painful process of replacing the techniques, skills, facilities, and the managers of an already outmoded concept of production, which I call, for want of a better name, "mass production".

NEW DEMANDS

The concept of mass production was characterized by certain factors:

- Long runs.
- Stabilized engineering designs.
- Concise product lines.

- Repetitive operations by each worker.
- A high proportion of the total costs spent for direct labor.
- Intensive use of labor standards and incentives.
- Many identical machines in the factory.
- Batch processes, job-shop layouts, disconnected flows, and a substantial amount of materials handling done by employees.
- Industrial engineering based on breaking a job down into its parts.
- Production management selected and promoted largely on the basis of experience and proven supervisory talents.

These factors are changing, with the extent and rate of change varying with the industry and the company. Increased competition, social change, and new technology are transforming both the factory and the job of the production manager. These changes are increasing the demands on managers and expanding the complexity and risk of their decisions.

One consequence is that many manufacturing departments are on the defensive. Another result, interestingly enough, is that the potential role of the production function in corporate strategy is being *enlarged*. The production function no longer has the relatively routine assignment of prior years: Turn out the product in volume at a reasonable quality level, and keep costs down. In most industries such an elementary definition of this task is fast becoming insufficient for corporate success.

In visits to plants and in discussions with manufacturing managers from many industries, I have observed the following:

1. Many top managements and many production managers appear unaware of the scope, nature, and significance of the changes.
2. Production managers are under increasing stress, and too many are not coping adequately with growing pressures and demands.
3. Educators and researchers are only partially effective in meeting the needs of production managers for improved knowledge and practical skills.
4. The kind of people who are needed in U.S. manufacturing are not being attracted in sufficient numbers.

What seems to be the trouble? To distinguish cause from effect is difficult, but one thing that stands out is the variety of *new* problems that are making the production manager's job more complex. These problems fall into three classes:

1. New pressures from outside the firm.
2. New problems within the firm.
3. The impacts of accelerating technology.

Let's look at each of these categories:

PRESSURES FROM OUTSIDE

One of the most noticeable sources of problems is new trends in the industry and marketplace. Their impact on corporate planners and marketing strategists has been dramatized many times. Not so widely recognized is the fact that they have a profound effect on production management.

Increasing Competition

In most U.S. industries, competition has become more severe during the past 20 years. Overcapacity has been the cause in some industries, and in other industries competition has been intensified by a management emphasis on growth and diversification as a corporate objective. Companies in the defense industry diversify into consumer products; consumer goods producers see advantages in military contracts. New products and materials capture consumer dollars from older, established products. Aluminum fights steel; plastics threatens aluminum.

Foreign competition, originally based primarily on price, has added quality in function and style to its advantages. The initial lack of distribution and service facilities has been overcome in many industries. Once established—as in textiles, typewriters, bicycles, and watches—the foreign-made product competes on an equal basis in a marketing sense, often with the advantage of lower production costs due to lower wages. Such trends are putting production executives under even more pressure to produce efficiently than in the past.

Marketing Pressures

Increased competition has naturally brought greater pressures from the marketing side of the business. "Our competition is offering 10-day delivery," states a Midwestern plastics manufacturer. "It is taking us three weeks to deliver. We've got to revise completely our production planning and control system." New products and new models are introduced more often; product life is shorter; product changes are more frequent and more drastic as research and competition combine to thwart the factory manager's traditional goal: uninterrupted long runs.

The marketing manager also insists on improved quality because the company's quality image depends in large part on the service record of its product. Higher quality in appearance and function is demanded. Tolerances are shrinking as specifications grow more exacting under demands for better performance and longer, trouble-free product life.

In many industries the manufacturing facility has been forced to produce more "specials"—short-run, special-purpose, or customer-designated items necessary to make the sale. A paper manufacturer in Ohio has added 30% to the number of products in his line in the past five years. These products all involve special setups, paperwork, control, and the conversion of a mammoth paper-making machine to special short runs. Special runs, of course, require more setups, different worker skills, special purpose tools, unique processes and equipment, and quality and production control techniques that are quite different from those used for the long, continuous runs of the mass production era.

The insistence on shorter lead times and more immediate deliveries is a sales demand that seldom can be ignored. But how to accomplish it without further increasing costs and inventories is the production manager's dilemma. These outside-generated problems represent trends that may be expected to continue, bringing further pressure on the production system to produce more products better, cheaper, often in shorter runs, and with less time allowed for delivery.

PROBLEMS FROM WITHIN

A second set of problems is complicating life in the factory. By and large they are actually old problems made critical by the outside pressures and the accelerating rate of technology. Their urgency makes them new.

Reevaluating Cost Control

Increased mechanization, shorter runs, and higher quality generally result in a higher proportion of indirect labor and fixed costs relative to direct labor and variable costs. How does a production manager cope with "stickier," less variable costs? How are indirect labor costs evaluated? Not long ago a time-study department could provide the tools and information necessary for appraisal and effective action regarding the productivity of the bulk of the work force. Today this is often not so. More direct labor time is machine controlled. Many jobs are less repetitive. Financial incentives are generally less effective in motivating workers. More technicians, maintenance men, material handlers, and paperwork personnel are required to service a shrinking direct labor group. The old concepts and techniques of job measurement, time standards, and control are becoming progressively more inadequate.

Manning the Operation

The U.S. factory labor force is tending to divide into two divergent classes: (1) the highly skilled "knowledge workers" who handle setups, equipment adjustment and overhaul, daily scheduling, and quality inspection; and (2) the relatively unskilled, trained workers who perform routine assembly work or are trained to "push the red button" if the automatic machine starts to make a strange noise. Fewer semiskilled workers are needed.

The changing mix of jobs brought about by mechanization is combining with changes in both employee qualifications and expectations. The availability of low-cost college education and widespread recognition of its advantages is drawing off the cream of the potential candidates for highly skilled positions in maintenance, toolmaking, and machine setup at the very time that automation requires increasing numbers of people with such skills.

The handling of "knowledge workers" in relation to the unskilled workers has brought problems and unanswered questions to personnel management and labor relations. For example, what skill level is needed to run a tape-controlled machine? How should the operator be paid? Are incentives useful? How can capable "knowledge workers" be found and trained? (One appliance manufacturer in the Midwest, whose apprentice program had dwindled almost to oblivion, has found a new source of candidates in college dropouts. These people are proving to be able and enthusiastic trainees for the kind of factory jobs that demand highly skilled operators.)

Production management's answers must revolve around the achievement of higher productivity, but the factory world by no means agrees on the best approaches to this objective. The market, the product, the equipment, the job, the people—all are changing. Work-force management must change in response.

Handling Paperwork

The growing volume of paperwork and of employees associated with paperwork is a common phenomenon, involving enormous costs. Planned, integrated data processing systems have begun to attack the paper monster created by shorter runs, product diversification, and the clamor for better deliveries and quality, but they have necessarily upset many traditional approaches and procedures. The resultant systems and communications problems in the factory further change the nature of the production manager's job. It is no longer a question of "men, machines, and material" as the classic definition runs; the job now requires the management of an increasingly complex information system. In fact, with increasing automation of worker jobs, the factory is turning more and more into an information processing operation while less and less employee time is spent on actual production.

ACCELERATING TECHNOLOGY

Finally, a whole set of new problems has been produced by invention and product development.

Equipment Decisions

In the "old days" equipment decisions were generally less complex and involved a smaller investment than they do today. Today the equipment under consideration is likely to span larger, integrated, linked systems rather than single machines. One tape-controlled milling-drilling-tapping combination costs $250,000 or more in contrast to a milling machine at $25,000. The purchase of one of these new systems typically has a substantial effect on the whole factory—on product design, quality, maintenance requirements, materials handling, plant layout, wage systems, employee morale, production scheduling, and work-in-process inventories.

With rapidly changing technology, a high degree of uncertainty over the reliability, feasiblity, and economic life of new equipment is common. How well will it work? When will something better be coming along? Would it be better to invest now or wait for the next generation of technological improvements?

Engineering Changes

The factory is being transformed by the need to introduce new products more quickly and to handle a flood of engineering changes brought about by market pressures and expanded research and engineering efforts.

Under "mass production," when a product's design was accomplished, one complete stack of blueprints and specifications was "released" to the production department. Typically, the production department had a methods-engineering group that proceeded to design the necessary tooling and to detail the exact process by which the product was to be made. This was communicated to the foremen on "process sheets," and when the various jigs and fixtures were ready and material was available, production started.

In contrast, the new product in today's plant often is released in bits and pieces as each part is designed. In the case of one computer manufacturer, the commercial model followed the first prototype down the assembly line only two days later—an experience that is not unusual. Equally common is the fact that, in an effort to save time and improve the product, the company was making engineering changes on the product at a rate of 100 per day! The defense industry is famous for this kind of pressure for delivery of new products, but no longer are crash programs confined to defense production. Manufacturing managers in most industries are forced to produce a product while it is still being designed.

Materials and Processes

Another source of problems for today's production manager rises from challenges and opportunities brought about by a flood of new developments in materials and processes. The vast outpouring of research and development laboratories and engineering groups is deluging production with decisions to be made on a scale never before seen.

New materials and new processes are coming along at a rate old-timers consider fantastic. Each must be considered and accepted, or rejected or ignored. The diverse properties and higher strengths of these materials often require new processes and equipment. New manning, maintenance, and control approaches generally follow.

CAUSES FOR CONCERN

These trends and pressures contribute substantially to the spotty performance of manufacturing. They have serious implications. They are causal forces behind the evolution that makes mass production concepts outmoded.

The combination of shrinking factory profit margins, more pressure from the marketing side of the business, and the accelerating pace of technology have made the production manager's job more exacting. Present tensions are due to new and more stringent demands coupled with inadequate improvements in the means of handling them.

Outmoded Tools

Production managers are still attempting to function with generally outmoded tools. Management concepts and techniques being used in manufacturing are frequently inadequate for today's problems. Some available techniques, both old and new, are ignored by firms that would find them helpful. And new circumstances and conditions also require brand new management tools.

In the past the techniques of Taylor, Gilbreth, and other industrial engineering pioneers were generally sufficient for planning and control. These techniques were based on analyzing a job, breaking it down into its parts, improving each part, and setting standards. The techniques of time and motion study, work analysis, job evaluation, job standards, piece-rate wages, quality sampling. Gantt charts, simple payback calculations, and computation of economic order quantity for lot-size calculations were adequate for cost control, equipment planning, and production scheduling.

But these tools alone are not adequate today. Indirect labor is less susceptible to time and motion study and standards, and mechanization has changed the nature of so many direct labor jobs that present job-evaluation bases are often inappropriate. Planning for expensive, integrated yet flexible systems can seldom be accomplished with Gantt charts. The introduction of complex new products that are still in the design stage cannot be handled with a simple release system.

Given the complexity of today's demands, production managers have to think more comprehensively than heretofore. Systems are more inter-related. From the start of a project, they must be able to plan and co-ordinate the technological functions, the work of people, and informational procedures. With more continuous processes, mechanization, linked or integrated flows, specialized equipment, highly paid indirect workers, and fewer discretely separable pieces of equipment, materials-handling and communications systems must be built into the production system.

New management tools that help managers to cope with some of these problems are being used in many companies. But my observations indicate that in industry generally progress in introducing the new tools and techniques is slow. In fact, it is surprising and even alarming to note that many companies are just now learning the "old" tools and techniques developed in the early days of industrial engineering. For instance, I visited a well-known company that had just discovered the enormous potential of savings in economic-order-quantity formulas. Executives' excitement was almost boastful as they discussed reductions in costs of setup labor and improved equipment utilization using a technique that had been available fully 50 years before they discovered it!

Actually, some approaches with which companies have not caught up do not require specialized knowledge at all. Consider "work simplification"—a rudimentary application of common sense applied in an orderly process to almost any job. Ignoring its simplicity and potential, our plants are full of wasteful methods and systems. Go into any plant or office and analyze an operation picked at random. In my experience the chances are 9 out of 10 that one can develop an improvement within 30 minutes that will save 10% or more worker time. We are surrounded by inefficiency.

Useful New Methods

Many relatively new tools are available to managers. They include techniques such as work sampling, linear programming, heuristic algorithms, PERT, statistical quality control, computer process control, learning curve theory, queuing theory, simulation, inventory models, investment policy models, and others. However, these tools are complex and take training to understand and put into practice. So their use developed slowly. The potential benefits in better decisions and better design of production systems are tremendous, however, because these concepts are designed to handle more complex problems. One characteristic of the new family of management techniques is that they are designed to integrate, to consider systems as a whole, rather than to take jobs apart and analyze the parts—the approach that was the basis of mass production industrial and engineering techniques.

While complexity alone might explain why the new tools are spreading so slowly, there are usually severe problems in their application. Mathematical models that include enough variables to be realistic can become fantastically difficult to formulate and program. And oversimplified models, eliminating vital factors, are inaccurate and misleading. Research in new techniques and theoretical concepts still outruns the investment needed for developing practical applications.

THE TALENT SHORTAGE

If it is clear that industry is losing ground, that transitions to automation and the computer are unnecessarily expensive and painful, that quality is often unsatisfactory, and that many production managers possess inadequate tools for coping with their mounting problems, what can be done?

Underlying the problem is the fact that the job of production management in most industries is greatly different today from what it was a few years ago. With the mechanization of part of direct labor and much of management's paperwork and short-term scheduling decisions, managers may now spend more of their time on tomorrow's equipment and systems and less on today's personnel assignments and grievances, parts shortages, and one-at-a-time machine choices. Here is an opportunity, but it comes at a price. To take advantage of it, more planning and system-designing skills are needed. There is an increasing requirement for specialists, and the production manager must be able to direct these experts and not be overwhelmed by them.

This is a tall order, and there seem to be too few people in industry who can fill it. As a result, the production group in many companies is constantly on the defensive—criticized for late deliveries, high inventories, shoddy quality, automation and computer fiascoes, crippling strikes, and low profit margins. These companies have to compete without the benefit of a crack manufacturing function. Their poor manufacturing performance becomes a corporate millstone.

We are not receiving enough of the kind of people needed in manufacturing, either from the lower ranks of industry or from the graduate schools of business. A generation ago those with ability but without the means for college became skilled mechanics and craftsmen; many moved up to become foremen and managers. Now there are far too few who train themselves for manufacturing management.

The manufacturing life typically has had little appeal for college graduates. Factories represent grease and sweat and unimportant trivia, the minutiae of a multitude of small details, and the confrontation with rough, uneducated people and a militant union. A factory career is often expected to begin at the bottom and proceed at a slow and boring pace, dealing with small decisions and uncooperative masses, and learning to work under "bull of the woods" kinds of superintendents. Presumably missing is the glamour and breadth of exposure in marketing, the big dollar deals in finance, and the precision and sense of the overall business felt in the field of control. "Factories are for engineers" is the theme of most business school graduates.

But too few engineers see it that way. Manufacturing engineers are accurately perceived by the engineering graduate as being comparatively low in prestige and pay, while research and development is seen as offering more freedom and enlarged opportunity for individual, creative work. Besides, engineering training by itself is not enough for the production manager today. Managerial education and broad training in new concepts and techniques are becoming more vital, while strictly technical training is probably less essential than it used to be.

QUESTIONS AND GUIDELINES

Although pressures of competition and economic survival have already begun to bring about changes needed on the production scene, they are coming too slowly. Many companies, industries, and people are being hurt in the process. Beyond the mere recognition of these mounting pressures, problems, and trends, top management, production managers, and educators have many alternatives for improving production performance.

Corporate Policy

Many top managements groups are unaware of the potential power of a top-flight production organization as a competitive weapon. Companies dominated by any one functional point of view are liable to find themselves in trouble, and too often production is perceived as less critical to corporate survival and growth than is marketing, finance, or engineering. When this happens, manufacturing people play subordinate roles in strategic planning, and the agressive quality of performance usually deteriorates.

Top management can ask itself whether production is being developed and deployed to competitive advantage, while appraising the management approaches employed, for example:

- The use of well-established industrial engineering tools.
- The use of new concepts and techniques of operations mangement.
- The source and quality of production management people.
- The evaluation, compensation, and promotional policies used for production managers.

A vital question is whether the company recognizes the need and is developing a contemporary breed of managers in manufacturing.

Production Management

How can production people take the offensive and get away from a defensive posture? A critical self-appraisal of results and the establishment of new objectives can help. Key performance standards may be measured in terms of delivery responses, inventories, cycle time, costs, and quality. Top management can be asked: What improvements in these standards would give us a significant competitive advantage? The detailed appraisal involved in initiating revision of standards of performance generally leads to searching reexamination of basic systems, procedures, and processes and challenges fundamental assumptions that have been accepted for years without question.

But production management people must go even further in self-appraisal today, inquiring into two key areas: (1) new kinds of managers, and (2) new analytical and planning techniques.

Executives might ask themselves whether they are employing and developing people who have a broad, integrative point of view, who can perceive the production system as a whole, take a company rather than a department point of view, and supervise the new breed of specialists. And does the company have or have access to the specialists—the highly trained people who can put the new, improved quantitative techniques to work? Do factory promotional and personnel policies encourage or discourage such people? Do the manufacturing engineers compare favorably in ability, potential, and pay to the company's research engineers?

Do we understand the potential of new computer-based analytical and production techniques, and are we taking advantage of their existence? The new techniques such as CAD and CAM[1] are fast being developed, and needed refinements and practical improvements are coming; but a company cannot afford to wait until new tools are "perfected." It will take a company many years to acquire, absorb, and practice pertinent new concepts and tecniques. Lead times are long, and the crash programs sometimes attempted are liable to be dangerous and ineffectual. Leading firms are getting started in patterns appropriate to their means and needs. Excellent companies regard self-education and renewal as a continuing process.

Business Education

As a teacher in a graduate school of business I am both proud and self-critical. I am proud of the progress being made in many schools in developing the new techniques that can help hard-pressed production managers to cope with their more demanding environment. However, I am critical of U.S. business schools on three counts:

1. We have done much more to develop new techniques than to help business bridge the gap between theory and application.
2. In the intellectual excitement of developing quantitative concepts, business education tends to ignore the development of the generalist—the executive whose chief skill is broad judgment and leadership—in favor of educating the quantitative specialist.
3. We educators have failed to communicate effectively to students that life in the factory is changing, and that the needs and opportunities for creative and skilled production managers are increasing dramatically now; that the production management decisions will not be big ones; that promotion to positions of responsibility will not be weighted solely in favor of operating or line experience; and that the old excitement of managing a complex mix of people, machines, and materials is now being supplemented with a major new challenge, that of systems plan-

[1]Computer-Aided Design and Computer-Aided Manufacturing

ning and control. When we begin to communicate this better, we can start to attract more good people into manufacturing life, people whom industry badly needs.

CONCLUSION

Technology, competition, and social change have brought serious problems for manufacturing. Further technological and social changes will take place and, in combination with the natural competitive processes, will continue to force an accelerating evolution in the factory. Mass production as we have known it is an outmoded concept. Changes in production management thinking and skills are essential. The corporations and managers that are taking the lead in bringing about changes in manufacturing management are gaining important competitive advantages.

It is the thesis of this book that manufacturing management needs to change in five respects. First, manufacturing because it involves long lead times for changes in "brick and mortar" and equipment-and-process technology demands a longer time horizon and longer-term thinking. Instead, its management is more typically preoccupied with short-term schedule and cost issues and a predominately operational point of view.

Second, manufacturing tends to focus on productivity and efficiency as its chief performance yardsticks. These criteria need to be expanded to include, selectively, quality, service, delivery, investment, and flexibility for change.

Third, manufacturing in its short-term operational focus on productivity often drifts into highly important structural decisions instead of its top management concentrating on structural issues, that is, number, size, and location of plants, choices of technology and equipment, and basic systems for controlling operations.

Fourth, a strategic point of view is frequently lacking. What is needed is a manufacturing strategy that links manufacturing to the corporate strategy.

The final set of changes which today's industrial malaise calls for is the development of a "new breed" of manufacturing manager better able to think in overall corporate strategic terms and provide technological leadership in these times of rapid technological innovation.

The book takes up these various concerns. The next three chapters focus on concepts of manufacturing strategy, beginning with "The Anachronistic Factory," which makes the point that the assumptions on which manufacturing is conventionally managed are out of date, as to both the values and expectations of employees and the processes of thinking in which problems are addressed one at a time, in the order in which they occur.

CONCEPTS OF MANUFACTURING STRATEGY

The next three chapters offer a new approach to manufacturing management that may help to meet some of the increasing challenges of these times. The concepts suggested are based on a top-down approach that ends the isolation of manufacturing managers from the corporate strategy and top management so typical in manufacturing. Their objective is to form manufacturing into a competitive weapon.

Chapter 3 focuses on how old, conventional management practices have allowed factories to become obsolete. Chapter 4 deals with the long-term, often implicit changes that, if not recognized make "white elephants" out of formerly excellent facilities. Chapter 5 sets forth the key concepts of manufacturing strategy.

The
Anachronistic
Factory

The conventional factory has become an anachronism. Many of the values and assumptions on which its productivity has depended are now running head-on into changing beliefs and expectations in our society. The effect of this collision is worker dissatisfaction and repugnance toward the factory as a place to work. Conventional methods of managing and making decisions in manufacturing are equally out of touch with the times. In many instances the result is low utilization and efficiency of expensive equipment and inadequate quality. As a final measure of industrial ineffectiveness, total productivity is frequently inadequate for meeting the facts of worldwide competition.

Some call the problem one of "productivity." Others label it as "blue-collar blues." Or it elicits the question, "Can the United States stay competitive?" The fact is that U.S. industry is in trouble on all three counts.

Combining to produce a powerful impact on industry are three environmental factors: (1) accelerating foreign competition; (2) technological changes in production and information-handling equipment; and (3) social changes in the work force. The massive effect of these rapidly moving, simultaneous changes is rendering the typical factory an obsolete institution. Changes in our conventional management methods of accomplishing improved manufacturing plant performance have become mandatory for industrial success.

In this chapter I report on the anachronistic status of the factory system by first arguing that changes are essential in the factory infrastructure. I show that the normal approach of attempting to improve factory results by pecking away at the various elements of the plant complex—that is, making modifications one by one—can no longer be tolerated by owners, employees, and society at large. Then in the balance of the chapter I offer my recommendations on the changes needed in conventional concepts of managing manufacturing and meeting human needs in manufacturing careers.

PRESSURE FOR CHANGE

An indisputable fact is that as worldwide competition spreads, U.S. companies in a steadily increasing number of industries are finding the going rough, with high wages placing producers at a comparative disadvantage. American industry is also wrestling with some puzzling and stubborn internal problems, such as assimilating new technology, the will to work, and shortages of highly skilled workers—all key elements in achieving better productivity.

As a result, we are being forced to challenge from the ground up all pieces of conventional wisdom concerning every facet of industrial management from individual job definitions, work-force management, the foreman's job, and equipment and process design to scheduling and inventory control.

In sum, innovative, even radical, changes in the factory as a total social and technological institution are already necessary because rapid obsolescence of the factory as an institution has already set in. And wholesale, broad, sweeping changes are in order because whatever is done must be internally consistent.

Piecemeal Syndrome

Industrial leadership and competitive productivity in the United States eroded so quickly that manufacturing executives in many industries can no longer permit themselves the luxury of a piecemeal approach to improving production performance.

The XXX Company, concerned over low profit, set out to modernize its plant. Over a two-year period new automated, highly mechanized machines were analyzed, justified, and purchased one by one. But productivity improved very little. Since low utilization of equipment was one obvious culprit, a computer-based information, planning, and scheduling system was installed. This system clearly revealed that changes in plant layout and materials handling were needed.

All this took several more years, and profit margins improved somewhat. But absences, workmanship, effort, and morale were being adversely affected by the prior changes in physical facilities and the information system.

Further analysis suggested that the pay system was apparently inappropriate to the new production and scheduling methods and that an inconsistent span of individual jobs was contributing to poor morale. Supervisory assumptions and practices were challenged, along with employment procedures. These changes spanned another year and a half.

About that time, the company's strategic approaches to competing in worldwide markets were revised, placing an emphasis on fewer standard items and on more customer specials and model changes. Management realized that not only would the scheduling and information system need changes but much of the basic production equipment as well, if the plant was to fulfill the revised manufacturing task imposed by the new corporate strategy.

The entire period of time represented six and a half years of frustration, inadequacy, and the constant pressure of making changes. In the end the system needed as much revision as in the beginning. During no single year were results even marginally satisfactory. Stockholders, managers, employees, and engineers shared one mutual sentiment—that of unrelenting dissatisfaction.

This example represents a reasonably accurate model of how many factories are being managed. To manage manufacturing differently is a difficult undertaking because of the obvious problems in developing planned and coordinated systems that require long lead times and heavy capital investments and involve little-understood sociological phenomena. And it will also be difficult because of the problem of keeping production going while changing it.

These are not impossible tasks. They are entirely "doable" once a manager knows what to do. First, however, manufacturing executives must begin to develop—at some personal and corporate risk—new concepts in organizing and managing factories as complete social and technical institutions.

But what is to be done to update our industrial system and to improve our productivity? One possibility has been that of more automation. It is puzzling to many people that increased mechanization, automation, and computerization in industry have not been more effective in boosting industrial productivity. The temptation of seizing on new technology as the answer to our industrial dilemmas is appealing. For surely one way out of the growing difficulties in remaining competitive lies in the possibilities of increased mechanization and automation. As James Bright wrote several years ago, our problem is not that we are mechanizing too fast but that we are mechanizing too slowly.[1]

Thus, if mechanization, automation, and computerization can do any good at all in the factory, they should help to reduce costs and improve quality. They should also help to reduce boredom from dull jobs, and by their very complexity to attract, as the factory formerly did, bright and able young people into new knowledge and skill-oriented jobs in industry.

This sounds promising—and it is—but the gap between promise and payoff is proving to be very wide. Increased mechanization is coming about neither smoothly nor quickly enough to meet the cost and productivity improvements that are apparently needed. Automation is not a consistent success, nor does it lack confusing and paradoxical elements. Consider:

- In the face of a pressing need to change the factory, increasing both its mechanization and its humanization, we are apparently making slow progress.
- In the face of an increasing rate of technological change and potential for automation, actual applications are surprisingly cautious.
- In the face of expanding uses for the computer, its effects in reducing lead times and costs and in improving quality of output are disappointing.
- In the face of what appear to be enormous opportunities for retooling with modern computer-controlled gear, we see slow progress.

In the meantime, a combination of growing competition and changing social expectations is obsoleting many plants and many industries. One effect is on the appeal of factory life to able men and women. The problem of attracting better employees to the factory will multiply unless industrial managers are able to perform several orders of magnitude better in introducing computer-based systems and automated industrial equipment. They must also somehow change the time-hardened image of the factory as an undesirable workplace for intelligent, independent, and resourceful people. But changing over the American factory is proving to be a sticky and sluggish problem, fraught with stubborn internal resistances that block progress.

What is going wrong? Why is progress so slow and painful? Why is it so difficult to meet the problems, to change over and renovate the factory, and to employ without nightmare the fruits of amazing technologies?

[1]"Are We Falling Behind in Mechanization?" *Harvard Business Review* (November–December 1960).

RESEARCH FINDINGS

I have analyzed many situations that involve the introduction of numerically controlled machine tools and other complex automated equipment and the use of the computer in the factory. Some tentative findings are beginning to emerge from this research.

First, the complexities involved in achieving successful, large-scale increases in mechanization and computerization are simply enormous— in number as well as in potentially devastating effects—and they are typically much greater than anticipated. This finding may hardly be news to industrialists, but its significance is not inconsequential.

The warning is clear: Automation and computer-aided production must not be undertaken without extensive and exhaustive planning. Even then, start-up problems and side-effect falldowns will occur. More is involved than mere technology. Side effects are often more important (for better or worse) than the primary goals contemplated for the technological change.

Interesting Patterns

My study of the anatomy of automation/mechanization/computerization experiences is turning up some interesting patterns. To illustrate:

A typical problem is the case of a company in which expensive new automated equipment took a year and a half to become fully operational, and even then its utilization was about half of that on which acceptable paybacks had been based. Why? The reason was a complex myriad of cause-and-effect relationships: inadequate operator and programming skills, unrealistic demands for precision, and difficulties in matching market demands with shop scheduling.

In another company a computer-aided, automated line of process equipment proved unable to handle the process it was designed to control. The problem was finally traced to the operators, who prior to mechanization had been handling certain material and process-introduced variables with a kind of experience-developed intuition that was too complex for the computer and sensors to handle.

In still another company, a new multimillion-dollar plant performed according to specifications, but it was ruining the company's ability to compete. The problem was a lack of flexibility in the process, which resulted in lead times for new products and special product variations that were significantly longer than those offered by the competition.

Case examples such as these prove a kind of Murphy's Law—if something can go wrong, it will. An inconsistency or lack of congruence in any one of dozens of ingredients in the system will often ruin the performance and utility of the whole. These are not just technical or engineering problems, but also problems of marketing, scheduling, engineering, inventory, changeover, cost control, accounting, volume sensitivity, worker acceptance, training, supervision, safety, wage system, motivation, union contract, utilities, maintenance, pollution/effluents, community relations, vendor requirements, plant organization structure, executive performance evaluation, and communications and information flows.

In short, everything counts. One subtle flaw may immobilize or neutralize the benefits of an otherwise marvelously planned and conceived project. This interconnectedness signals the need for a "total systems" approach, which will surprise few. But the massive inertia and complexities attendant to bringing about change also say something about the kind of system the factory is: a complex network of social and technological factors with both economic and strategic payoffs.

Infrastructure Problem

My analysis of companies that have invested in new technology as a means of overcoming competitive disadvantage suggests that the potentially positive results of automation and computer technology are being largely neutralized by failings or inconsistencies in other elements of the factory institution. By this I mean the internal systems through which work is carried on—what I call the "infrastructure" of the factory. The infrastructure includes elements such as organizational levels, work-force management, supervisory practices, production control and scheduling approaches, and job design and methods concepts.

By analogy, we are learning that a new engine does not make an old automobile new. Any one part—such as the transmission, body, suspension, or electrical system—dates the vehicle's performance and can render it inadequate. To carry on this analogy, the new engine may in fact bring out new problems that make total performance worse than before the old engine was replaced.

The entire factory must be planned and renovated as a unit lest any one element undermine the entire structure. To introduce advanced mechanization successfully and to achieve full productivity the entire makeup of the factory in all its interconnected intricacies must be retooled to make it internally consistent with the new process.

Without substantial changes in equipment and technology we will not be able to withstand foreign competition; but without changes in methods of work, concepts of supervision, control and direction, and promotion and salary practices, it is doubtful that the factory can have the appeal it

Exhibit 3.1 How Pressures Impinge on the Factory System

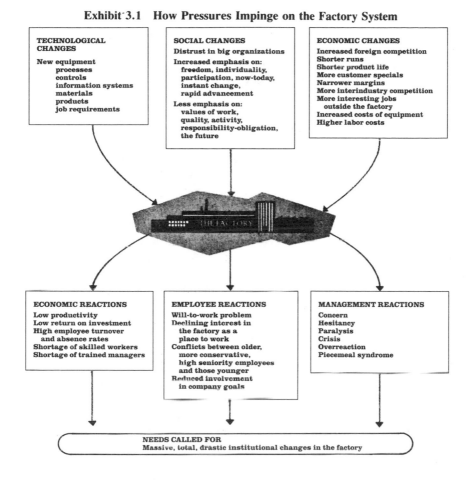

TECHNOLOGICAL CHANGES

New equipment
  processes
  controls
  information systems
  materials
  products
  job requirements

SOCIAL CHANGES
Distrust in big organizations
Increased emphasis on:
  freedom, individuality,
  participation, now-today,
  instant change,
  rapid advancement
Less emphasis on:
  values of work,
  quality, activity,
  responsibility-obligation,
  the future

ECONOMIC CHANGES
Increased foreign competition
Shorter runs
Shorter product life
More customer specials
Narrower margins
More interindustry competition
More interesting jobs
  outside the factory
Increased costs of equipment
Higher labor costs

THE FACTORY

ECONOMIC REACTIONS
Low productivity
Low return on investment
High employee turnover
  and absence rates
Shortage of skilled workers
Shortage of trained managers

EMPLOYEE REACTIONS
Will-to-work problem
Declining interest in
  the factory as a
  place to work
Conflicts between older,
  more conservative,
  high seniority employees
  and those younger
Reduced involvement
  in company goals

MANAGEMENT REACTIONS
Concern
Hesitancy
Paralysis
Crisis
Overreaction
Piecemeal syndrome

NEEDS CALLED FOR
Massive, total, drastic institutional changes in the factory

needs to attract sufficient numbers of outstanding people. In a nutshell, our methods of decision making, communicating, scheduling, and supervising make up the infrastructure of our plants; and these internal elements are proving more resistant to change than the purely technological ingredients on which factory managers and engineers tend to focus.

One way of looking at the present situation is shown in *Exhibit 3.1.* Changes in technology, society, and the economic situation are impinging on the factory system—all at the same time.

By no means is it surprising that production executives with orders to fill, schedules to meet, budgets to hold, and unions to negotiate with are hesitant to risk wholesale change. The stability of evolutionary change is demanded by the practical person, and this is eminently reasonable. But my view of the scene today is that there has been and is yet a great deal of paralysis and hesitancy, a real sense of crisis and floundering in many industries, and frequently a sluggishness and failure of nerve among top managements. All of this is ominous for the overhauling of our factory institutions and the raising of productivity levels.

RECOMMENDED CHANGES

How might top managers of manufacturing go about making basic changes in the stubborn infrastructure of the conventional factory to make it less anachronistic, more productive, and more relevant to today's social and economic facts of life?

There is a great deal that managers responsible for manufacturing can do to make their factories more productive and less anachronistic. My recommendations fall into two groups:

1. Changes in *conventional concepts* of managing manufacturing.
2. Changes in *meeting human needs* in manufacturing careers.

Conventional Concepts

Manufacturing management was derived in a conceptual sense from engineering and technologically oriented variables. Because manufacturing requires specialized expertise and constant improvement of often complex equipment and processes, as a sector of management its focus has been on technology, efficiency, and equipment. As a result of this legacy, manufacturing executives have typically been more expert in those areas of their work than in other parts.

Indeed, the potential of manufacturing as a competitive weapon and the concept of using manufacturing as a strategic asset have been almost always overlooked in management's single-minded attention to efficiency, costs, and engineering.

Manufacturing can be managed quite differently from the way most companies manage it. What is required are two fundamental changes to bring about (1) recognizing and discarding a number of fallacious myths and assumptions about manufacturing, and (2) the acceptance of a concept of manufacturing as an institution, with an extensive and influential infrastructure of internally consistent technological and sociological elements.

Let me take each of these conceptual changes in manufacturing management in turn.

Myths and Assumptions

Myths and assumptions have seriously hurt our progress by having led us into planning and managing plants in ways that result in disappointments and away from more fruitful approaches.

The main criterion for evaluating factory performance is efficiency and cost.

This statement is wrong. Manufacturing can also be a competitive weapon when it is less "efficient" but more flexible in terms of product change, in managing inevitable ups and downs in volume, in getting new products into production quickly, in providing for and consistently meeting short-delivery promises, and in producing with a minimum investment in inventory and fixed assets.

Criteria for judging a factory should not be limited to efficiency and cost, for these criteria ignore the fact that in the context of a particular company's competitive strategy, other criteria may be vastly more important.

A good factory can simultaneously accomplish low costs, high quality, minimum investment, short-cycle times, high flexibility, and rapid introduction of new products.

Wrong again. A factory system—like an airplane or a building—can be designed to do only certain things well. The failure to identify design objectives clearly or to compromise among many criteria results in manufacturing systems that do not perform well by any criteria.

The management of factories is essentially a task for engineers.

This assumption is a grievous mistake—blindly employed since the turn of the century and now made even more seductive by advancing technology—that has generally entrusted the direction of manufacturing to people conditioned with a technical point of view. The technical dimension is important, but time is proving that social and strategic dimensions are equally or more important. Moreover, the technical obsession often delegates the production function to those who are inadequately trained and oriented toward human and social factors, financial problems, and the strategy and markets of the entire firm.

Increasing mechanization is a job for industrial engineers and operations researchers.

Another wrong assumption. Tackling complex multidimensional problems with the limited array of disciplines offered by even those broadly intentioned professionals is simplistic.

A systems approach and a high level of conceptualization are a substitute for experience and substantive knowledge and strong, hands-on management.

This fallacy is implicit in theoretical and conceptual planning exercises, which have caused a multitude of errors in judgment and swarms of "bugs" in automated factories.

The ultimate objective of automation is to reduce the numbers of people required; problems with and costs of people can be avoided and overcome with automation and mechanization; people problems can be bypassed with good equipment.

These three interrelated misconceptions should have been demolished by the experiences of the past 10 years.

Nearly every worker can be replaced by machinery.

This is a myth because the fantastic abilities of people to plan, remember, and use judgment, wisdom, and intelligence extend far beyond the capabilities of computers and mechanization. To try to make such facilities substitute for people has repeatedly proved expensive, especially when reliable back-ups are built in to achieve a hands-off operation. When a skilled person is to be replaced by a machine, the cost of the equipment replacing the person may run into hundreds of thousands of dollars. Therefore, economics often favors the use of people.

In total, these myths and assumptions about plants and people have led us into an excessively technically oriented point of view of the factory. They have allowed us to overlook key dimensions in industrial change and to attempt to introduce machines and equipment without changing organizations, responsibilities, job contents, information systems, promotion and pay systems, and control and motivational approaches—in short, the stubborn total infrastructure of the factory as an institution.

The simplistic view of the factory as measured largely by efficiency not only drives away good men and women, but fails to use the factory as a competitive weapon to meet specific manufacturing tasks demanded by corporate strategy. Delegation of their own responsibility by top managers allows too many plants to be managed by technologists who do not have a general management point of view.

Wise managers recognize the multidimensional complexity of the problems with which they deal. To bring about change in the infrastructure of manufacturing involves a great deal more than new technology and technological innovation. Production managers are asking for heartache, frustration, and frequent defeat when they attempt to go it alone.

We walk innocently into an ambush when we attempt to develop new production systems without looking at their strategic and social implications as well as their technological aspects. Present know-how and skills will be multiplied enormously, and failures and delays will be prevented when we recognize that factory problems are just as complex and demanding as all the other problems involved in renewing major social institutions. They require a multidimensional team approach.

Concept of Manufacturing

Seen as a major institution, manufacturing at once takes on new dimensions that have existed often unrecognized all along. Certain conclusions then follow:

- Elements of the infrastructure must be mutually and internally consistent.
- Everything counts, since one overlooked element may ruin the total.
- Manufacturing decisions must span the infrastructure; changes can no longer be made piecemeal if they are to be successful.
- The span of changes must be broader and take in more elements.

The interaction between the various elements of the infrastructure is complex and often not easily understood; but their resulting effects warrant attention and improved expertise.

Meeting Human Needs

A different kind of recommendation from those representing conceptual changes involves the organization and operation of production systems in terms of societal and personal values. If an institution is to be productive in the short run and viable over the long run, it must (1) meet or change the felt needs and expectations of employees so as to be generally satisfying, and (2) develop an image that attracts sufficient numbers and varieties of people to allow for the selection of an able total cadre of employees and managers.

As stated earlier, we have much evidence that the factory as a social institution is outdated. Who, after all, wants to work in a factory these days? And what does the common answer, "Not very many," mean? It suggests that the values and demands that today's factory institution imposes on its members are beginning to conflict with the values and expectations of an increasing fraction of modern Americans.

Specifically, *Exhibit 3.2* suggests a number of these conflicts and growing incongruencies and anachronisms.

What can be done with this vital "people segment" of the factory infrastructure? While it is probably the most difficult element with which to cope, I suggest, albeit cautiously, that the people area is not so impossible to deal with as is often assumed. It can be resolved more satisfactorily, but it will take some daring and innovative management nerve, for changes in people policies can be explosive; and this means that top management must take responsibility and be involved.

But the picture is not all negative, for the factory can offer a great deal that employees want and need. Employees, particularly in metropolitan, big-city environments, are often lonely in the crowd; do feel needs for group memberships and cooperative, nonaggressive, nondefensive, fulfilling experiences; wish to identify with a successful organization and quality products; and seek outlets for their ideas and opinions.

Seen in this sense, the factory can be attractive if it meets some of these needs. Some factories are already doing a superb job in certain facets. In fact, it appears to me that the factory is in an ideal position to meet many of today's unfulfilled social needs and expectations.

But to do so, what must be changed? Consider these anachronistic elements of many conventional factories:

- Pay systems based on hours worked.
- Physical arrangements that treat employees with disrespect and supervisory assumptions that fail to treat them as individuals.
- Decision-making processes that leave out the opinions and ideas of involved employees.
- Promotion and job security policies that emphasize only experience and seniority.
- Communications practices that withhold information or present only one point of view.
- Job designs and work content that focus solely on motor-mechanism/physiological aspects of an employee's capacities and leave out the emotional and spiritual dimensions.

Exhibit 3.2 Conflicts Between Current Factory and Societal Viewpoints

Factory Expectations and Values	Common Social Expectations and Values
Employees are to perform jobs designed by management.	Employees know better than their boss how to do their own work.
Advancement is to be by seniority and long-proven performance.	Employees want continued and steady advancement.
Experience is important.	Experience is overemphasized.
Time is important.	Time is pressure.
Work, activity, achievement on one's job are to come first.	Family, leisure, and balanced life are most important.
Decisions are to be made quickly and efficiently.	Employees don't want anyone to decide anything that concerns them as individuals without first getting their opinions.
Employees are to adjust to the demands of expensive machinery.	Employees don't want to be treated like machines.
Following orders is essential.	Freedom is essential.
The individual is to be paid what he or she is worth.	Employees are entitled to a decent standard of living.
Productivity is essential to economic well-being.	Friends, conversation, and social interaction are essential to human well-being.
Employees are to perform well (even under adverse physical conditions).	Employees don't want to work under adverse physical conditions.
Seniority entitles employees to job protection and privileges.	Each person has one vote.
Loyalty to the company is owed by employees.	Loyalty to one's beliefs is more important than loyalty to the corporation.
The corporation cares for its people.	The corporation cares little about its employees.
Employees are to perform work per schedules, quotas, and budgets.	Schedules, quotas, and budgets are mechanisms to exert control over people.

- Union contracts and governance systems that restrict change and stifle initiative.

Innovative Examples

Lest the foregoing discussion strike the reader as excessively idealistic let me cite several real-life examples of changes going on now in manufacturing management. These are typical of what several innovative companies are doing in the light of the kinds of problems I have been discussing here.

Company A is a $50 million annual sales manufacturer of capital equipment whose manufacturing vice-president and president became concerned enough about late deliveries, high costs, shortages of skilled technicians, and rising labor problems to decide that total organization—rather than piecemeal—changes were in order. Their factory is now being overhauled from top to bottom.

The changeover process started with a determination of what manufacturing had to do to help marketing, which the executives identified as offering short lead times on an ever-increasing number and variety of products with a trend toward shorter runs of more customer specials. Subsequently, they tackled each element of the factory infrastructure, such as analyzing scheduling and information systems, supervisory and wage policies, equipment, and layout.

All of this factory's operations were reexamined and rethought so as (1) to be mutually consistent, (2) to provide short lead times on new product development and delivery, and (3) to cope with today's social and economic environments.

Company B is one of many firms experimenting with new work-force management practice. At one decentralized division where labor productivity has been marginal at best, a totally new approach to supervision and work-force management has been installed on a pilot basis. The approach features a "self-determining work group," consisting of about 30 workers in a general purpose, job shop, machine area who are permitted to govern themselves. The group members set their own rules and regulations within the framework of only the general and functional company objective of making parts as needed, per blueprint, and on schedule. Quality controls, scheduling of machines, discipline and work rules, and productivity are all under the control and direction of the group itself with the help of a "trainer," who functions as a nondirective, consultative coordinator.

Companies C and D are pursuing a less drastic approach to a new kind of supervision and work-force management. Entirely independent of each other—they are located 1200 miles apart and are in different industries—both have restructured traditional foremen jobs.

Concluding that the typical foreman's job is "impossible," Company C took four sections of 30 men each under four foremen and set up an enlarged section of 120 men with a team of the four former foremen in charge. One member of the team was asked to focus on quality, the second on training, the third on technical problems, and the fourth on scheduling, planning, and reporting.

In Company D the same kind of change took place, but with a three-man team in which the role of the quality specialist was omitted.

In each of these four companies positive responses to its innovative approaches and changes are taking place. Perhaps a kind of "Hawthorne effect" in which experiment and change always seem to produce beneficiary results regardless of the particular change is at work. Then again, perhaps the experiments are sound in themselves and will become models for other companies.

In any event, the climate for innovation and experimentation in manufacturing management has never been better. The recommendations in this article are derived from actual cases. Real progress is taking place among a relatively small number of companies whose managers are recognizing the seriousness of problems in industry and courageously taking the risks of bringing about substantial change.

CONCLUSION

The factory system is anachronistic on two counts:

1. Its management concepts are outdated, focusing on cost and efficiency instead of strategy, and on making piecemeal changes instead of changes that span and link the entire system.
2. Its infrastructure contains such conflict and paradox that the expectations and desires of its people are too often incongruent with the imperatives of its technology, the demands of its markets, and the strategies of its managers.

The internal inconsistency marks a failure to adapt to environmental change in a key functional area of business—the production function.

How ironic it is that in production, where scientific management techniques began, these conventional approaches now seem out of date and out of tune with the social and economic facts of the times. Production management is perhaps bringing to an end a long cycle that began with innovation and new concepts for accomplishing productivity, developed in maturity of ideas, subsequently grew into a "conventional wisdom," and finally arrived at the point where we now see massive obsolescence.

Looking ahead, the changes in economics, technology, and society that now affect the factory will lead us to new kinds of production infrastructures that can absorb and harness new technology and new social values. With creative and substantial change, led by the more intrepid, the factory institution may begin to achieve the productivity breakthrough our economy so sorely needs.

The next chapter demonstrates how these dated, conventional approaches, which have become so anachronistic, are actually causing once successful plants to now perform badly. Conversely, what brings about a turnaround in performance is the development of a successful manufacturing strategy, which provides an internally consistent focus for the plant directed toward the key results that it must obtain to become a competitive resource.

CHAPTER 4

The Decline, Fall, and Renewal of Manufacturing Plants

A successful manufacturing plant seldom stays successful for long. Somehow, competitive, efficient operations decline, to become corporate liabilities. One day its owners discover that it is no longer performing successfully. It has become a target of criticism for high costs, poor quality, and unreliable deliveries and is no longer a competitive asset.

Why should a modern and fully maintained manufacturing system, staffed with bright, energetic, and alert managers, be prone to such decay? For a number of years the plant seems to serve the corporation well and then, sometimes overnight, becomes a problem child. Why is it that a plant, set up and tooled, staffed, and organized for efficiency and effective competition seems to deteriorate somehow over a period of time?

What happens? It does not seem to be a matter of obsolescent equipment or the running down of physical facilities. It does seem to have something to do with the way in which the facility is managed.

CAUSES OF DECLINE

While there are many ways in which companies get into trouble in manufacturing, they may be grouped into four principal categories:

1. Mismatch of manufacturing structure and manufacturing task.
2. Multi-product, do-all general purpose plant.
3. Simplistic performance evaluation.
4. Inconsistent elements in the manufacturing structure.

Mismatch of Structure and Task

Manufacturing structure—like the structure of a building—consists of features that frame its operation. Manufacturing is structured by the following decisions:

- Location of a plant.
- What to make and what to buy.
- Size of a plant.
- The plant's capacity.
- Equipment and processes.
- Manufacturing organization.
- The key central approaches to production control, quality control, and inventory management.
- The key central approaches to the management of the work force, including the basic approach to job design and job content, wage system, and the amount and kind of supervision.

The *manufacturing task* may be defined as the unique manufacturing competence demanded by the combination of the firm's corporate strategy, its marketing policies, and any constraints imposed by the technology and financial resources.

The manufacturing task is normally clear at the start-up. Usually, it consists of making particular products with specific technology and marketing requirements. The plant equipment, policies, and procedures are designed to meet this particular set of demands.

When the plant began production, the management, plant policies, and personnel were apt to be inexperienced relative to the operation. Bugs had to be worked out. Production control and work-force management approaches were developed and improved to help the operation to perform its mission. Gradually the whole operation worked out its problems and became proficient.

Evolutionary Development

However difficult the start-up, given sufficient time, any reasonably diligent group of people develops experience and competence in performing the task. They work through many problems and crises and tend to get better at what they are doing. They have had team experiences that they share and discuss. Their ability to perform improves. Such experience breeds a high degree of competence over time. The subtle and intuitive reasoning that goes on, anticipating problems, predicting previously unexpected variations in the product, the market, the technology, and in operating the equipment and processes, dealing with particular workers—all of these subtle, basic elements become built into the total competence of a manufacturing management group over a period of time.

As these people become more experienced through successfully solving countless problems, they learn to anticipate and meet their problems with an even higher degree of intuitive intelligence. They tend to develop their own sense of what is "good manufacturing practice" in their business. They develop a body of "conventional wisdom" as to what works and what does not work. They say to themselves and to outsiders, "In our company we have developed an effective philosophy of manufacturing. We know the kinds of problems and difficulties that you can easily get into in this business and we have grown to be good at avoiding them."

What happens next in many instances is that the manufacturing task subtly changes. Market conditions change, and to be successful, a company may have to compete in quite different ways than in the past. It may be that the emphasis in the past had to be on quality and on-time delivery. Now, as the market changes, the emphasis may have to be on lower costs or getting new products into production quickly. The corporation's position in the industry may have changed from being a number one to a number two, or the company has become an innovator instead of a high-volume, low-cost producer. Or there may be changes in the technology that require new pieces of equipment, or considerable changes in the product design. Or finally, perhaps there have been considerable changes in the volume levels of production and a gradual shifting in the product mix.

How are these changes perceived by a strong, experienced, competent manufacturing team? Unfortunately, but not surprisingly, these changes are not always seen or their significance fully perceived. After all, such changes seldom take place dramatically. They take place gradually over a period of time. After a year or two, the task at which the plant must now excel may no longer be what it was. Most management groups naturally tend to continue to apply the successful "philosophy" and practices of manufacturing they have learned and proven over the past. The structure of the manufacturing operation tends to continue, with a kind of momentum of comfortable and satisfying familiarity with only relatively minor variations.

Limited Flexibility

To accomplish a new task would require changes in the manufacturing structure. But the elements of this are difficult, expensive, and time consuming to change. Once established, a given manufacturing structure limits the ability of a manufacturing system to be competent in other than a limited task pertaining to a limited product mix. A machine tool plant highly capable of turning out large volumes of standard milling machines at a relatively low cost would be incompetent to produce a wide variety and limited quantity each of centerless grinding machines unless its structure were rebuilt.

A manufacturing structure not only limits the degree of product flexibility of a plant but also limits its flexibility to handle major changes in volume. A plant of a certain size and setup, with a certain type of equipment, may be economic at its planned operating level but quite uneconomic and inefficient at a 30% lower level of output. A given production team and its facility may be highly competent at producing a limited product mix but entirely incompetent to produce much shorter runs of a more complex product mix due to the problems of setups and changeovers on its equipment. Furthermore, a given plant and its structure may be capable at producing with two-months' lead time, but if the market changes to allow only six-weeks' lead time, considerable changes in equipment and process technology as well as production control and inventory policies may be necessary. Finally, a given work force with certain skills, habits, attitudes, and concepts of what is "quality production" may be unable to change its mentality quickly and produce economically and efficiently at much different quality levels, either higher or lower.

The most important element of manufacturing structure is its equipment and process technology. The element of structure is usually the most difficult and the most expensive and requires the most time to change: hence, the importance of having "the right" equipment and process technology and hence, too, the difficulty of keeping the "right" equipment and process technology as products, markets, technology, and corporate strategy change.

Multi-Product, Do-All General Purpose Plant

A second typical process by which companies grow weak in manufacturing is the tendency to keep on adding additional products into one existing plant. The adding of products often makes it necessary to handle new technologies. It simultaneously adds a necessity for dealing with new and different market requirements.

In product A the emphasis may have to be on quality, in product B it may be on very short deliveries, and in product C it may be on very low costs. All three products are made in the same plant, with the same facilities, the same work-force management policies, the same production planning and control policies, the same cost-control system, the same accounting system, the same inventory management system, all typically under one manufacturing organization structure. The tendency is for the production control system to be well designed for product B, the wage and work-force management system to be well set up for product C, while the equipment and processes are designed for product A. The result of adding products in the same plant is that manufacturing is unable to perform effectively for any single product group.

The consequences are even more serious. The manufacturing personnel must be able to deal with an increasing variety of market requirements, presumably different strategic approaches for success in each product, and a different equipment and process technology as well. Since experience breeds competence, competence is diluted and delayed because of the necessity for spreading a given amount of experience over a wider variety of products.

Substantive Differences

Let me emphasize that I am not considering modest product changes or additions in the product mix, which do not involve products with different strategic or marketing requirements or considerably different equipment and process technologies. My reference is to products with substantially different requirements in terms of strategies, markets, volumes, and technologies.

A good example is a plant where an electronic fuel gauge and an electronic auto pilot were made together. The company was unable to make money on the electronic aircraft fuel gauge and after many years of experimentation and improvement finally decided to go out of the business. At the last moment the plant manager proposed building a wall around the fuel gauge operation. From that time forth no employees worked on both the fuel gauge and the auto pilot products. There was a separate production control system, somewhat separate work-force management policies and supervisory approaches, separate cost controls, separate equipment and process technology, a separate layout, a separate inventory and scheduling system. The fuel gauge business became profitable within approximately four months.

When high quality levels, high precision, tight specification products are mixed with those of less stringent requirements, the effects on both products are usually adverse. The high quality product is usually made with less quality than it needs and the low quality product is usually made more expensively. In the fuel gauge example the auto pilot gyroscope parts were nearly always carried around in special lined and padded boxes and the tendency was for the fuel gauge parts to be handled in the same way, adding totally unnecessary costs.

The mixing of quality levels within one plant is much more easily understood than other more subtle combinations, which are forced together by adding to the product mix. For example, a production control system may be excellent for products that require short delivery time but would be inadequate for products in which market the company had a low profit but needed a good return on investment and therefore was required to keep inventories at an absolute minimum. In each of these two product sets the successful "name of the game" would be quite different.

White Elephants

Why do companies tend to continue to add a more complex mixture of products into an existing plant? What typically happens is that the plant is designed for a limited range of products. Over a period of years some of those products approach the end of their normal life-cycle and other products take their place. A trend in many industries is to offer more specialized products in an effort to compete, resulting in shorter runs and a more complex product mix. Hence, as these products are added to an existing plant, the result is to force the plant management to attempt to mix a variety of technology and market requirements.

This problem is difficult to prevent. When a plant has built a trained labor force and a proven set of processes and equipment, there are strong economic reasons for using these facilties and not shutting them down simply because the products for which they were set up are no longer selling well. Nevertheless, there are better ways of handling these kinds of problems than simply lumping more products into the same factory, which will eventually turn that factory into a "white elephant."

Over the last several years I have had a number of opportunities to study plants that had become white elephants. In most cases the plant was unusually big and complex and handled an enormous variety of products. The products had been added into an existing mix one by one. In most cases costs were high. Delivery performance was low. Inventories were large; lead times were long. In total, the plant was satisfying no one market or executive either in production or in the various product or sales groups handling the mixture of products.

Most companies attempt to overcome these problems by adding people and staff groups. Clearly, it takes planning, more control, and more people to try to handle a wide, rich variety of products in one plant. It takes more effort in terms of inventory control, more personnel, labor specialists, more accountants and cost controllers and a great deal more paperwork to manage the large and complex multiproduct, multimarket plant.

The temptation seldom denied is to add on to the existing facility and assign the new product to the existing organization. The theory is that by adding the additional volume onto the same plant structure the net result will be "savings in overheads."

The fact that this is seldom true may at first seem paradoxical. What happens is that the increasing complexity ultimately requires overhead out of proportion to the additional volume, making the overhead and cost control problem even worse. As the organization deals with more products and technologies, it becomes more complex in its purposes and faces more varied marketing and competitive pressures. The usual response is to try to surround the problem with more staff, more expeditors, more analysts, and more people to plan, schedule, and control. The net result is additional confusion, which compounds the situation. In contrast, as a general rule, plants that have the best competitive market performance nearly always have a restricted and manageable scope of products, equipment, technologies, and marketing tasks.

A final reason for the general tendency to keep adding new products is the pressure to minimize capital expenditures for buildings and equipment. But it is often a false economy and a misguided philosophy to attempt to minimize capital expenditures while forcing manufacturing management to attempt to load more products with conflicting strategic and technical requirements into one plant. The frequent result of frugality in investment policy is an effort to make one plant and its equipment and process technology serve too many masters.

Simplistic Performance Evaluation

A third major cause of companies getting into trouble in manufacturing is the tendency for many managements to accept simplistic notions in evaluating the performance of their manufacturing facilities. By this I am referring to the general tendency in most companies to evaluate manufacturing primarily on the basis of cost and efficiency. There are many more criteria by which to judge performance than cost and efficiency. For example:

- Quality.
- Customer lead times.
- Reliability of promise dates given.
- Return on investment.
- Flexibility to introduce new products.
- Flexibility to handle substantial volume changes.
- Appropriate social criteria.

Companies get into trouble because of simplistic concepts for measuring performance by attempting to focus results on maintaining or improving cost and efficiency when other criteria are in fact more critical. In accepting the usual norms of achieving maximum productivity, management effort is typically focused first on minimizing direct labor costs and, second, other costs.

Sometimes, however, it may be much more important for a company to spend more on a product and improve its quality. Or it may be important to run a product in a smaller lot size, which might increase its cost, but could improve its flexibility for meeting customer demands. Similarly, if the emphasis is on low cost, very high investment in inventories may be required in order to result in maximum machine utilization and minimum direct labor through longer runs. Thus other potential critical performance criteria suffer, usually inadvertently, when cost and efficiency are given top attention.

Simplistic criteria cause further the problems when a set of criteria, which has been valid for judging plant performance for several years, becomes invalid under new conditions of technology, market, or corporate strategy. Executives of companies that appear to make these kinds of mistakes usually do not appear to understand the inexorable trade-offs that take place in choosing one criterion over another. It is seldom possible to maximize the plant's performance in accomplishing more than one or two of these criteria at the same time. Something else must give. Superb execution and discipline such as generally credited to Japanese managers and workers minimizes the trade-off penalties. Similarly, better management techniques or new technologies may produce better results in quality or service with attendant cost performance even improved on an absolute basis. But relatively the trade-offs still exist.

Inconsistent Elements

A fourth common cause of companies slipping into trouble in manufacturing is the frequent gradual growth of incongruent infrastructures within the plant. I use the word *incongruent* to indicate that the focus and objective of each of the elements of infrastructure should be directed toward the same goal. If they are not, they are incongruent.

Let me illustrate an incongruent infrastructure:

A large machinery and equipment manufacturer, Company C, found its sales of new machines dropping steadily while its sales of spare parts and replacement items gradually climbed. An analysis of C's basic elements of manufacturing policy indicated that the work-force management policies and production, planning, and control systems were designed for the requirements of the original equipment business. In the original equipment business quality and reliable delivery promises were particularly important, much more so than cost. The company seldom had any complaints over the performance of equipment, and it had not missed a delivery date of a new machine for over 10 years.

The replacement parts business, however, was entirely different. In the spare parts business the element of handling an extremely complex mix of parts with very short lead time became vital for corporate success because the company's service reputation was dependent on its keeping old machines in the industry running. When a machine broke down, early delivery of that replacement part was absolutely critical. In addition, handling an ever-increasing complexity of parts over the years became a major cost problem as machine models proliferated and more and more part numbers were active. Yet the production control system was set up to handle long runs of original new products rather than a fierce variety of short runs of special replacement parts.

Similar conflicts on internal systems occurred throughout the plant. The cost control system was not adequate for controlling costs of the large number of short run replacement parts. The production control system proved inadequate for handling the large numbers of short runs. The workforce management approach featured incentive wages that rewarded the workers with long runs of parts of the new pieces of equipment and penalized those who were making short runs of replacement parts. In fact, quite different skills were needed, and an examination of the equipment and process technology indicated that the machines that were capable of general purpose work on short runs were needed in higher proportion relative to the special purpose, long-run machine tools that had been used when the business was primarily one of producing original equipment. Thus the wage system, the recruiting approaches, and the allocation of job content to different workers were quite different for the two forms of business, and resulting head-on confrontations hurt performance on both ends of the business.

These incongruencies in internal manufacturing policy are not unusual. They are caused by adding more products into a given plant and simplistic criteria for judging performance.

MANUFACTURING AUDIT

A regular audit of manufacturing policies, manufacturing tasks, and manufacturing structure can prevent such gradual but costly declines. It is seldom realized that when there is a change in a company's strategy of technology, the company's manufacturing setup also needs an entirely different approach. These external changes are occurring ever more rapidly. Product life-cycles are shorter; we are being bombarded with more and more technology changes; there are more choices of new tools and equipment and processes and products than ever before; competition seems to move on and off the scene with ever more determination. All of this means that manufacturing policies and manufacturing structures must be examined more frequently.

A manufacturing audit can follow the form of asking and carefully answering questions from the president to the manufacturing vice-president *and* vice versa.

Questions the president should regularly be asking the manufacturing vice president are as follows:

1. What is your understanding of our manufacturing task?
2. What is *our* manufacturing setup especially *good* at?
3. How is manufacturing a competitive weapon for our company?
4. How often do we reexamine our manufacturing task?
5. What positions have we taken on key trade-offs in structuring our manufacturing?
6. What criteria do you use to evaluate manufacturing performance?
7. What alternate equipment and process technology (EPT) are available?
8. How does our EPT serve our manufacturing task?
9. Our work-force policies?
10. Our production control policies?
11. Our control procedures?
12. Your use of your time?
13. Are you "boxed in" by our present manufacturing structures? What do you need? What would it cost? What would it do for us? At what risks?
14. What changes are occurring that may make our manufacturing task and structure obsolete?

Questions the manufacturing vice-president should ask the president:

1. What is our competitive strategy?
2. How is (or is not) manufacturing now a competitive weapon?
3. What is your understanding of our manufacturing task?
4. What criteria will manufacturing be evaluated on over the next 12 to 18 months?
5. Do you concur with my general pattern for my use of my time?
6. Do you fully understand the positions we have taken on the various

trade-offs in structuring our manufacturing? Do you understand and concur in what are we giving up in order to make certain other gains?

Wrestling with these kinds of questions on a regular basis can be the beginning of building a new approach toward manufacturing management. This is a top-down manufacturing approach. It originates in a company's strategy and marketing problems. It focuses at the manufacturing policy level and does not get involved with operational details.

But what exactly is this top-down approach? Thus far, we have talked "manufacturing strategy" only in very general terms. We need to turn now to a more precise discussion of these questions leading to a step-by-step understanding of how a manufacturing management team can develop an effective overall strategy. The next chapter deals with these questions, describing how the concept of the design of a manufacturing structure is based on the technological constraints inherent in the equipment and process, and, subsequently, how a manufacturing strategy can be developed.

CHAPTER 5

Manufacturing: Missing Link in Corporate Strategy

A company's manufacturing function typically is either a competitive weapon or a corporate millstone. It is seldom neutral. The connection between manufacturing and corporate success is rarely seen as more than the achievement of high efficiency and low costs. In fact, the connection is much more critical and much more sensitive. Few top managers are aware that what appear to be routine manufacturing decisions frequently limit the corporation's strategic options, binding it with facilities, equipment, personnel, and basic controls and policies to a noncompetitive posture that may take years to turn around.

Top management unknowingly delegates a surprisingly large portion of basic policy decisions to lower levels in the manufacturing area. Generally, this abdication of responsibility results more through a lack of concern than by intention. And it is partly the reason that many manufacturing policies and procedures developed at lower levels reflect assumptions about corporate strategy that are incorrect or misconstrued.

MILLSTONE EFFECT

When companies fail to recognize the relationship between manufacturing decisions and corporate strategy, they may become saddled with seriously noncompetitive production systems that are expensive and time-consuming to change. Here are several examples:

Company A entered the combination washer-dryer field after several competitors had failed to achieve successful entries into the field. Company A's executives believed their model would overcome the technical drawbacks that had hurt their competitors and held back the development of any substantial market. The manufacturing managers tooled the new unit on the usual conveyorized assembly line and giant stamping presses used for all company products.

When the washer-dryer failed in the market, the losses amounted to millions of dollars. The plant had been "efficient" in the sense that costs were low, but the tooling and production processes did not meet the demands of the marketplace.

Company B produced five kinds of electronic gear for five different groups of customers; the gear ranged from satellite controls to industrial controls and electronic components. In each market a different task was required of the production function. For instance, in the first market extremely high reliability was demanded; in the second market rapid introduction of a stream of new products was demanded; in the third market low costs were of critical importance for competitive survival.

In spite of these highly diverse and contrasting tasks, production management elected to centralize manufacturing facilities in one plant in order to achieve "economies of scale." The result was a failure to achieve high reliability, economies of scale, or an ability to introduce new products quickly. What happened, in short, was that the demands placed on manufacturing by a competitive strategy were ignored by the production group in order to economize on equipment. This production group was obsessed with developing "a total system, fully computerized." The manufacturing program satisfied no single division, and the serious marketing problems that resulted choked company progress.

Company C produced plastic molding resins. A new plant under construction was to come on-stream in eight months, doubling production. In the meantime the company had a much higher volume of orders than it could meet.

In a strategic sense, manufacturing's task was to maximize output to satisfy large, key customers. Yet the plant's production control system was set up—as it had been for years—to minimize costs. As a result, long runs were emphasized. Although costs were low, many customers had to wait, and many key buyers were lost. Consequently, when the new plant came on-stream, it was forced to operate at a low volume.

The mistake of considering low costs and high efficiencies as the key manufacturing objective in each of these examples is typical of the oversimplified concept of "a good manufacturing operation." Such criteria frequently get companies into trouble, or at least do not aid in the development of manufacturing into a competitive weapon. Manufacturing affects corporate strategy, and corporate strategy affects manufacturing. Even in an apparently routine operating area, such as a production scheduling system, strategic considerations far outweigh technical and conventional industrial engineering factors invoked in the name of "productivity."

Shortsighted Views

Manufacturing is seen by most top managers as requiring involved technical skills and a morass of petty daily decisions and details. It is seen by many young managers as the gateway to grubby routine, where days are filled with high pressure, packed with details, and limited to low-level decision making—all of which is out of the sight and minds of top-level executives. It is generally taught in graduate schools of business administration as a combination of industrial engineering (time study, plant layout, inventory theory, etc.) and quantitative analysis (linear programming, simulation, queuing theory, etc.). In total, a manufacturing career has been perceived for many decades as an all-consuming, technically oriented, hectic life that minimizes one's chances of reaching the top and maximizes the chances of being buried in minutiae.

These perceptions are still not wholly inaccurate in many companies. The technically oriented concept of manufacturing is all too prevalent; and it is largely responsible for the typically limited contribution manufacturing makes to a corporation's arsenal of competitive weapons, for manufacturing's failure to attract the top talent it needs, and for its failure to attract more young managers with general management interests and broad abilities. Manufacturing is generally perceived in the wrong way at the top, managed in the wrong way at the plant level, and taught in the wrong way in the business schools.

These are strong words, but change is needed, and I believe that only a more relevant concept of manufacturing can bring change. I see no sign whatsoever that we have found the means of solving the problems mentioned. The new, computer-based "total systems" approaches to production management offer the promise of new and valuable concepts and techniques, but these approaches have not overcome the tendency of top management to remove itself from manufacturing. Years of development of "the factory of the future" have left us each year with the promise of a great new age in production management that lies just ahead. The promise never seems to be realized. Stories of computer-integrated manufacturing (CIM) and new automated equipment disasters are legion; these failures are always expensive, and in almost every case management has delegated the work to experts.

I do not want to demean the promise—and indeed some present contributions—of the "factory of the future" and, indeed, will discuss these developments in subsequent chapters. Nevertheless, close observation of the problems in industry has convinced me that the "answers" promised are inadequate. New technology and information systems cannot overcome U.S. industry's competitive problems until top management does a far better job of linking manufacturing and corporate strategy. What is needed is changes in thinking, not changes in technology.

PATTERN OF FAILURE

An examination of top management perceptions of manufacturing has led me to some notions about basic causes of many production problems. In every industry I have studied, I have found top executives delegating excessive amounts of manufacturing policy to subordinates, avoiding involvement in most production matters, anad failing to ask the right questions until their companies are in obvious trouble. This pattern seems to be due to a combination of two factors:

1. A lack of awareness among top executives that a production system inevitably involves trade-offs and compromises and so must be designed to perform a limited task well, with that task defined by corporate strategic objectives.
2. A sense of personal inadequacy on the part of top executives in managing production. (Often the feeling evolves from a tendency to regard the area as a technical or engineering specialty or a mundane "nuts-and-bolts" segment of management.)

The second factor is, of course, dependent in part on the first, for the sense of inadequacy would not be felt if the strategic role of production were clearer. The first factor is the one we concentrate on in the remainder of this chapter.

Like a building, a vehicle, or a boat, or any technology-based operation, a production system can be designed to do some things well, but always at the expense of other abilities. It appears to be the lack of recognition of these trade-offs and their effects on a corporation's abililty to compete that leads top management to delegate often-critical decisions to lower, technically oriented staff levels and to allow policy to be made through apparently unimportant operating decisions.

The balance of this chapter will do as follows:

- Sketch out the relationships between production operations and corporate strategy.

- Call attention to the existence of specific trade-offs in production system design.
- Comment on the inadequacy of many manufacturing experts and information system specialists to deal with these trade-offs.
- Suggest a new way of looking at manufacturing, which enables top management to understand and manage the manufacturing area so as to make it a competitive resource.

STRATEGIC IMPLICATIONS

Frequently the interrelationship between production operations and corporate strategy is not easily grasped. The notion is simple enough—namely, that *a company's competitive strategy at a given time places particular demands on its manufacturing function, and conversely, that the company's manufacturing policies and operations should be specifically designed to fulfill the task demanded by strategic plans*. What is more elusive is the set of cause-and-effect factors that determine the linkage between strategy and production operations.

Strategy is a set of plans and policies by which a company tries to gain advantages over its competitors. Generally, a strategy includes plans for products and the marketing of the products to a particular set of customers. Marketing plans usually include specific approaches and steps to be followed in identifying potential customers; determining why, where, and when they buy; and learning how they can best be reached and convinced to purchase. The company must have an advantage, a particular appeal, and special push or pull created by its products, channels of distribution, advertising, price, packaging, availability, warranties, or other factors.

Strategic Demands on Manufacturing

What is not always realized is that different marketing strategies and approaches to gaining a competitive advantage place different demands on the manufacturing arm of the company. For example, a furniture manufacturer's strategy for broad distribution of a limited, low-price line with wide consumer advertising might generally require the following:

- Decentralized finished-goods storage.
- Readily available merchandise.
- Rock-bottom costs.

The foregoing demands might in turn require the following:

- Relatively large lot sizes.
- Specialized facilities for woodworking and finishing.
- A large proportion of low- and medium-skilled workers in the work force.
- Concentration of manufacturing in a limited number of large-scale plants.

In contrast, a manufacturer of high-price, high-style furniture with more exclusive distribution would require an entirely different set of manufacturing policies. While higher prices and longer lead times would allow more leeway in the plant, this company would have to contend with the problems implicit in delivering high-quality furniture made of wood (which is a soft, dimensionally unstable material whose surface is expensive to finish and easy to damage), a high setup cost relative to running times in most wood-machining operations, and the need to make a large number of nonstandardized parts. While the first company must work with these problems too, they are more serious to the second company because its marketing strategy forces it to confront the problems head on. The latter's manufacturing policies will probably require the following:

- Many model and style changes.
- Production to order.
- Extremely reliable high quality.

These demands may in turn require the following:

- An organization that can get new models into production quickly.
- A production control group that can coordinate all activities to reduce lead times.
- Technically trained supervisors and technicians.

Consequently, the second company ought to have a strong manufacturing-methods engineering staff; simple, flexible tooling; and a well-trained, experienced work force.

In summary, the two manufacturers would need to develop very different manufacturing policies, personnel, and operations if they were to be equally successful in carrying out their corporate strategies.

Important Choices

In the example described, there are marked contrasts in the two companies. In fact, however, even small and subtle differences in corporate strategies should be reflected in manufacturing policies. Nevertheless, my observation is that few companies carefully and explicitly tailor their production systems to perform well those tasks that are vital to corporate success.

Instead of focusing first on strategy, then moving to define the manufacturing task, and next turning to systems design in manufacturing policy, most top executives and production managers simply look at their production systems with the notion of "total productivity" or the equivalent, "efficiency." They seek a kind of blending of low costs, high quality, and acceptable customer service. The view prevails that a plant with reasonably modern equipment, up-to-date methods and procedures, a cooperative work force, a computerized information system, and an enlightened management will be a good plant and will perform efficiently.

But what is "a good plant"? What is "efficient performance"? And what should the computer be programmed to do? Should the computer minimize direct labor or indirect labor? The company cannot do both. Should investment in equipment be minimized—or should outside purchasing be held to a minimum? There are many such choices.

The reader may reply: "What management wants is a combination of both ingredients that results in the lowest *total* cost." But that answer, too, is insufficient. The "lowest total cost" answer leaves out the dimensions of time and customer satisfaction, which must usually be considered. Because cost *and* time *and* customers are all involved, we have to conclude that what is a "good" plant for Company A may be a poor or mediocre plant for its competitor, Company B, in the same industry but pursues a different strategy.

The purpose of manufacturing is to serve the company—to meet its needs for survival, profit, and growth. Manufacturing is part of the strategic concept that relates a company's strengths and resources to opportunities in the market. Each strategy creates a unique manufacturing task. Manufacturing management's ability to meet the task is the ultimate measure of its success.

TRADE-OFFS IN DESIGN

Few executives realize the existence of trade-offs in designing and operating a production system. Yet most managers will readily admit that there are compromises or trade-offs to be made in designing an airplane or a truck. In the case of an airplane, trade-offs would involve matters such as cruising speed, takeoff and landing distances, initial cost, maintenance, fuel consumption, passenger comfort, and cargo or passenger capacity. A given stage of technology defines the limits of what can be accomplished in these respects. For instance, no one today can design a 500-passenger plane that can land on a carrier and also break the sonic barrier.

Much the same thing is true of manufacturing. The variables of cost, time, quality, technological constraints, and customer satisfaction place limits on what management can do, force compromises, and demand an explicit recognition of a multitude of trade-offs and choices. Yet everywhere I find plants that have inadvertently emphasized one yardstick at the expense of another, more important one. For example, an electronics manufacturer with dissatisfied customers hired a computer expert and placed manufacturing under a successful engineering design chief to make it a "total system." A year later its computer was spewing out an inch-thick volume of daily information. "We know the location of every part in the plant on any given day," boasted the production manager and his computer systems chief.

Nevertheless, the customers were more dissatisfied than ever. Product managers hotly complained that delivery promises were regularly missed—and in almost every case they first heard about failures from their customers. The problem centered on the fact that computer information runs were organized by part numbers and operations. They were designed to facilitate machine scheduling and to aid shop foremen; they were not organized around end products, which would have facilitated customer service.

This had come about largely because key managers had become absorbed in their own "system approach"; the fascination of mechanized data handling had become an end in itself. Top management had abdicated responsibility. Because the company's growth and success had been based on engineering and because top management was R&D-oriented, policy-making executives saw production as a routine function requiring a lower level of complexity and brainpower. Top management argued further that the company had production experts who were well paid and who should be able to do their jobs without bothering top-level people.

Recognizing Alternatives

To develop the notion of important trade-off decisions in manufacturing, let us consider *Exhibit 5.1*, which shows some examples.

In each decision area—plant and equipment, production planning and control, and so forth—top management needs to recognize the alternatives and become involved in the design of the production system. It needs to become involved to the extent that the alternative selected is appropriate to the manufacturing task determined by the corporate strategy.

Exhibit 5.1 Some Important Trade-Off Decisions in Manufacturing—or "You Can't Have It Both Ways"

Decision area	Decision	Alternatives
Plant and equipment	Span of process	Make or buy
	Plant size	One big plant or several smaller ones
	Plant location	Locate near markets or locate near materials
	Investment decisions	Invest mainly in buildings or equipment or inventories or research
	Choice of equipment	General-purpose or special-purpose equipment
	Kind of tooling	Temporary, minimum tooling or "production tooling"
Production planning and control	Frequency of inventory taking	Few or many breaks in production for buffer stocks
	Inventory size	High inventory or a lower inventory
	Degree of inventory control	Control in greater detail or in lesser detail
	What to control	Controls designed to minimize machine downtime, labor cost, time in process, or to maximize output of particular products or material usage
	Quality control	High reliability and quality or low direct costs
	Use of standards	Formal, informal, or none at all
Labor and staffing	Job specialization	Highly specialized or not highly specialized
	Supervision	Technically trained first-line supervisors or nontechnically trained supervisors
	Wage system	Many job grades or few job grades; incentive wages or hourly wages
	Supervision	Close supervision or loose supervision
	Industrial engineers	Many or few

Exhibit 5.1   (*continued*)

Decision area	Decision	Alternatives
Product design/ engineering	Size of product line	Many customer specials, few specials or none at all
	Design stability	Frozen design or many engineering change orders
	Technological risk	Use of new processes unproved by competitors or follow-the-leader policy
	Engineering	Complete packaged design or design-as-you-go approach
	Use of manufacturing engineering	Few or many manufacturing engineers
Organization and management	Kind of organization	Functional, or product, or geographical, or process focus
	Executive use of time	High involvement in investment, production planning, cost control, quality control, or other activities
	Degree of risk assumed	Decisions based on much or little information
	Use of staff	Large or small staff group
	Executive style	Much or little involvement in detail; authoritarian or nondirective style; much or little contact with organization

Making such choices is, of course, an ongoing rather than a once-a-year or once-a-decade task; decisions have to be made constantly in these trade-off areas. Indeed, the crux of the problem seems to be how to ensure that the continuing process of decision making is not isolated from competitive and strategic facts, when many of the trade-off decisions do not at first appear to bear on company strategy. As long as a narrow point of view dominates manufacturing decisions, a degree of isolation from the realities of competition is inevitable. Unfortunately, in industry today a provincial viewpoint is all too likely to prevail.

TACTICAL DOMINANCE

The similarity between today's emphasis on the technical experts—the computer specialist and the engineering-oriented production technician—and yesterday's emphasis on the efficiency expert—time-study expert and industrial engineer—is impossible to escape. For 50 years management relied on efficiency experts trained in the techniques of Frederick W. Taylor. Industrial engineers were kings of the factory. Their early approaches and attitudes were often conducive to industrial warfare, strikes, sabotage, and militant unions, but that was not realized then. Also not realized was that their tactical emphasis often produced an inward orientation toward cost that ignored the customer, and an engineering point of view that gloried in tools, equipment, and gadgets rather than in markets and service. Most important, the culture of industrial engineering tended to make many top executives feel technically disqualified from involvement in manufacturing decisions.

Since the turn of the century this efficiency-centered orientation has dogged manufacturing. It has created that image of "nuts and bolts," of greasy, dirty, detail jobs in manufacturing. It has dominated "production" courses in most graduate schools of business administration. It has alienated young people with broad management educations from manufacturing careers. It has "buffaloed" lots of top managers.

A group of industrial engineers asked me to offer an opinion as to why so few industrial engineers were moving up to the top of their companies. My answer was that perhaps a technical point of view cut them off from top management, just as the jargon and hocus-pocus of manufacturing often kept top management from understanding the factory. In their isolation they could gain only a severely limited sense of market needs and of corporate competitive strategy.

The Computer Expert

Today the industrial engineer is declining in importance in many companies and is being overshadowed by a new technical expert, the information system specialist—an individual who specializes in computer systems design and programming.

It has been demonstrated that a factory is 75% information handling system and only 25% a materials transforming system. Thus information system specialists have a very important job to do. But such specialists usually have no more of a top management view than was held by their predecessors, the industrial engineers. In my experience the information

experts have been forced to master a complex and all-consuming technology, a fact that frequently makes them parochial rather than catholic
in their views. Because they are so preoccupied with the detail of a system,
someone in top management must give them objectives and policy guidance. In their choice of trade-offs and compromises for their computer-
based systems, they need to be instructed and not left to their own devices.
Or, stated differently, they need to see the entire corporation as a system,
and not just one corner of it—the manufacturing plant.

Too often this is not happening. The computer is a nightmare to many
top managers because they have let it get out of hand. They have let
tactical experts continue to dominate; so the failure of top management
truly to manage production goes on.

How *can* top management begin to manage manufacturing instead of
turning it over to technicians who, through no fault of their own, are
absorbed in their own arts and crafts? How can production management
be helped to cope with the rising pressures of new markets, more rapid
product changes, new technologies, larger and riskier equipment decisions, and the swarm of problems we face in industry today? Let's look
at some answers.

BETTER DECISION MAKING

The answers I suggest are not panaceas. But surely we can improve on
the notion that production systems need only be "productive and efficient." Top management can manage manufacturing if it will engage in
the making of manufacturing policy.

The place to start is with the acceptance of a theory of manufacturing,
which begins with the concept that in any system design there are significant trade-offs (as shown in *Exhibit 5.1*) that must be explicitly decided.

Determining Policy

Executives also find it helpful to think of manufacturing policy determination as an orderly process or sequence of steps. *Exhibit 5.2* is a sche-
matic portrayal of such a process. It shows that effective manufacturing
policy must stem from corporate strategy and that the process of determining this policy is the means by which top management can actually
manage production. Use of this process can end manufacturing isolation
and tie top management and manufacturing together. The sequence is
simple but vital:

It begins with an analysis of the competitive situation, of how rival

Exhibit 5.2 The Process of Manufacturing Policy Determination

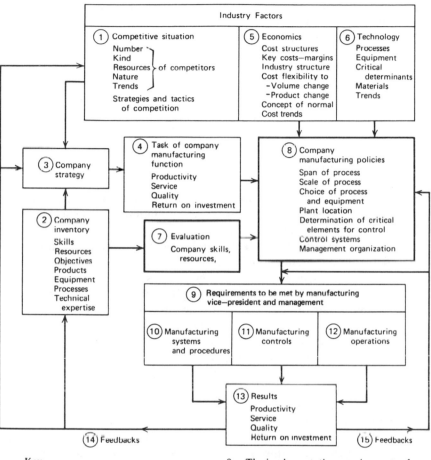

Key
1. What the others are doing
2. What we have or can get to compete with
3. How we can compete
4. What we must accomplish in manufacturing in order to compete
5. Economic constraints and opportunities common to the industry
6. Constraints and opportunities common to the technology
7. Our resources evaluated
8. How we should set ourselves up to match resources, economics, and technology to meet the tasks required by our competitive strategy

9. The implementation requirements of our manufacturing policies
10. Basic systems in manufacturing (e.g., production planning, use of inventories, use of standards, and wage systems)
11. Controls of cost, quality, flows, information, inventory, and time
12. Selection of operations or ingredients critical to success (e.g., labor skills, equipment utilization, and yields)
13. How we are performing
14. Changes in what we have, effects on competitive situation, and review of strategy
15. Analysis and review of manufacturing operations and policies

companies are competing in terms of product, markets, policies, and channels of distribution. Management examines the number and kind of competitors and the opportunities open to its company.

Next comes a critical appraisal of the company's skills and resources and of its present facilities and approaches.

The third step is the formulation of company strategy: How is the company to compete successfully, combine its strengths with market opportunities, and define niches in the markets where it can gain advantages?

The fourth step is the point where many top executives cut off their thinking. It is important for them to define the implications or "so-what" effects of company strategy in terms of specific manufacturing tasks. For example, they should ask: "If we are to compete with an X product of Y price for Z customers using certain distribution channels and forms of advertising, what will be demanded of manufacturing in terms of costs, deliveries, lead times, quality levels, and reliability?" These demands should be precisely defined.

The fifth and sixth steps are to study the constraints or limitations imposed by the economics and the technology of the industry. These factors are generally common to all competitors. An explicit recognition of them is a prerequisite to a genuine understanding of the manufacturing problems and opportunities. These are facts that a nontechnical manager can develop, study, understand, and put to work. *Exhibit 5.3* contains sample lists of topics for the manager to use in doing his or her homework.

The seventh and eighth steps are the key ones for integrating and synthesizing all the prior ones into a broad manufacturing policy. The question for management is: "Given the facts of the economics and the technology of the industry, how do we set ourselves up to meet the specific manufacturing tasks posed by our particular competitive strategy?" Management must decide what it is going to make and what it will buy; how many plants to have, how big they should be, and where to place them; what processes and equipment to buy; what the key elements are that must be controlled and how they can be controlled; and what kind of management organization would be most appropriate.

Next come the steps of working out programs of implementation, controls, performance measures, and review procedures (Steps 9–15 in *Exhibit 5.2*).

CONCLUSION

The process just described is quite different from the usual process of manufacturing management. Conventionally, manufacturing has been

Exhibit 5.3   Illustrative Constraints or Limitations That Should Be Studied

A. Economics of the Industry

Labor, burden, material, depreciation costs
Flexibility of production to meet changes in volume
Return on investment, prices, margins
Number and location of plants
Critical control variables
Critical functions (e.g., maintenance, production control, personnel)
Typical financial structures
Typical costs and cost relationships
Typical operating problems
Barriers to entry
Pricing practices
"Maturity" of industry products, markets, production practices, life-cycle
   phenomena analysis of economies of scale
Importance of integrated capacities of corporations
Ideal balances of equipment capacities
Nature and type of production control
Government influences

B. Technology of the Industry

Rate of technological change
Scale of processes
Span of processes
Degree of mechanization
Technological sophistication
Time requirements for making changes

managed from the bottom up. The classical process of the age of mass production is to select an operation, break it down into its elements, analyze and improve each element, and put it back together. This approach was contributed years ago by Frederick W. Taylor and other industrial engineers who followed in his footsteps.

What I am suggesting is an entirely different approach, one adapted far better to the current era of more products, shorter runs, vastly accelerated technological and product changes, and increased marketing competition. I am suggesting a kind of "top-down" manufacturing. This approach starts with the company and its competitive strategy; its goal is to define manufacturing policy. Its presumption is that only when basic manufacturing policies are defined can the technical experts, industrial and manufacturing engineers, labor relations specialists, and computer experts have the necessary guidance to do their work.

With its focus on corporate strategy and the manufacturing task, the top-down approach can give top management both its entrée to manufacturing and the concepts it needs to take the initiative and truly manage this function. When this is done, executives previously unfamiliar with manufacturing are likely to find it an exciting activity. The company will have an important addition to its arsenal of competitive weapons.

We turn now to operationalizing these concepts. There are three steps, or stages, involved. Most companies find that the notion of "focus" is a good place to start. Focused factories shape and direct every element of manufacturing structure and infrastructure around a limited yet critically vital performance task. This is step one. Step two, defining that task in realistic detail, and step three, the element-by-element design of the production system, are described in the chapters that follow.

OPERATIONALIZING MANUFACTURING STRATEGY CONCEPTS

These three chapters deal with the "how to" of following the basic ideas of early chapters. Chapter 6 introduces the idea of "focus" for a factory, discusses its many advantages, and offers some ideas for accomplishing focus. Chapter 7, a "nuts-and-bolts" chapter, goes into depth on the difficult and demanding yet absolutely essential job of clearly defining the manufacturing task. Chapter 8 offers various elements of the production system.

CHAPTER 6

The Focused Factory

M any years of taking our industry health and leadership for granted abruptly ended in the 1970s when our declining position in world markets weakened the dollar and became a national issue.

In the popular press and at the policy level in government the issue is perceived as a "productivity crisis." The National Commission on Productivity was established in 1971. The concern with productivity has appealed to many managers who had firsthand experience with our problems of high costs and low efficiency. Until 1984, when economic recovery began to moderately strain capacity in some industries, the productivity index showed little growth. In spite of that recent turnaround, loss of market shares to international competition in dozens of industries refutes any optimistic view of U.S. industrial performance.

So pessimism also pervades the outlook of many managers and analysts of the American manufacturing scene. The recurring theme of this gloomy view is that (1) labor is too expensive, (2) productivity has been growing at a slower rate than that of most of our competitors, and therefore (3) many of our industries have sickened one by one as imports mushroomed and unemployment became chronic in our industrial population centers.

In this chapter, however, I offer a more optimistic view of the productivity dilemma, suggesting that we have the opportunity to effect basic changes in the management of manufacturing, which could shift the competitive balance in our favor in many industries in spite of our high labor costs and sluggish productivity growth. What are these basic changes? I can identify four:

1. Seeing the problem not as "How can we increase productivity?" but as "How can we compete?"
2. Seeing the problem as encompassing the efficiency of the *entire* manufacturing system, including suppliers and all overheads as well, not only the efficiency of the direct labor and the work force.

3. Learning to focus each plant on a limited, concise, manageable set of products, technologies, volumes, and markets.
4. Learning to structure basic manufacturing policies and supporting services so that they focus on one explicit manufacturing task instead of on many inconsistent, conflicting, implicit tasks.

A factory that focuses on a narrow product mix for a particular market niche will outperform the conventional plant, which attempts a broader mission. Because its equipment, supporting systems, and procedures can concentrate on a limited task for one set of customers, its costs and especially its overheads are likely to be lower than those of the conventional plant. But, more important, such a plant can become a competitive weapon because its entire apparatus is focused to accomplish the particular manufacturing task demanded by the company's overall strategy and marketing objective.

My research indicates that in spite of their advantages, focused manufacturing plants are surprisingly rare. Instead, the conventional factory produces many products for numerous customers in a variety of markets, thereby demanding the performance of a multiplicity of manufacturing tasks all at once from one set of assets and people. Its rationale is "economy of scale" and lower capital investment.

The result in the conventional factory is usually a hodgepodge of compromises, high overhead, and a manufacturing organization that is constantly criticized by top management, marketing management, the controller, and customers.

My purpose in this chapter is to set forth the advantages of focused manufacturing. I begin with the characteristics of the focused factory, then follow with an analysis of the productivity phenomenon that tends to prevent the adoption of the focused plant concept. Finally, I offer some specific steps for managing manufacturing to accomplish and take advantage of focus.

BASIC CHARACTERISTICS

Focused manufacturing is based on the concept that simplicity, repetition, experience, and homogeneity of tasks breed competence. Furthermore, each key functional area in manufacturing must have the same objective, derived from corporate strategy. Such congruence of tasks can produce a manufacturing system that does the important but limited things very well. Within the factory, managers can make the manufacturing function a competitive weapon by outstanding accomplishment of one or more of the yardsticks of manufacturing performance. But managers need to know: "What must we be *especially* good at? Cost, quality, lead times, reliability, changing schedules, new-product introduction, or low investment?"

Focused manufacturing must be derived from an explicitly defined corporate strategy that has its roots in a corporate marketing plan. Therefore, the choice of focus cannot be made independently by production people. It has to be a result of a comprehensive analysis of the company's resources, strengths and weaknesses, position in the industry, assessment of competitors' moves, and forecast of future customer motives and behavior.

Conversely, the choice of focus cannot be made without considering the existing factory, because a given set of facilities, systems, and people skills can do only certain things well within a given time period.

Five key characteristics of the focused factory are as follows:

1. *Process technologies.*   Typically, unproven and uncertain technologies are limited to one per factory. Proven, mature technologies are limited to what their managers can easily handle, typically two or three (e.g., a foundry, metalworking, and metal finishing).

2. *Market demands.*   These consist of a set of demands including quality, price, lead times, and reliability specifications. A given plant can usually only do a superb job on one or two demands at any given period of time.

3. *Product volumes.*   Generally, these are of comparable levels, such that tooling, order quantities, materials handling techniques, and job contents can be approached with a consistent philosophy. (But what about the inevitable short runs, customer specials, and one-of-a-kind orders that every factory must handle? The answer is usually to segregate them, which I discuss later).

4. *Quality levels.*   These employ a common attitude and set of approaches so as to neither overspecify nor overcontrol quality and specifications. One frame of mind and set of mental assumptions suffice for equipment, tooling, inspection, training, supervision, job content, and materials handling.

5. *Manufacturing tasks.*   These are limited to only one or two at the most at any given time. The task at which the plant must excel in order to be competitive focuses on one set of internally consistent, doable, noncompromised criteria for success.

Research evidence makes it clear that the focused factory will outproduce, undersell, and quickly gain competitive advantage over the complex factory. The focused factory does a better job because repetition and concentration in one area allow its work force and managers to become effective and experienced in the task required for success. The focused factory is manageable and controllable. Its problems are demanding, but they are limited in scope.

PRODUCTIVITY PHENOMENON

The conventional wisdom of manufacturing management continues to be that the measure of success is productivity. Now that American companies in many industries are getting beaten hands down by overseas competitors with lower unit costs, we mistakenly cling to the old notion that "a good plant is a low-cost plant." This is simply not so. A low-cost plant may be a disaster if the company has sacrificed too much in the way of quality, delivery, or flexibility to get its costs down.

Too many companies attempt to do too many things with one plant and one organization. In the name of low investment in facilities and spreading overheads, they add products, markets, technologies, processes, quality levels, and supporting services that conflict and compete with each other and compound expense. They then hire more staff to regulate and control the unmanageable mixture of problems. In desperation, many companies haphazardly strike out at anything to reduce the resulting high costs. But we can only regain competitive strength by stopping the process of increasing complexity and overstaffing.

This behavior is so illogical that the phenomenon needs further explanation. Our plants are generally managed by extremely able people; yet the failure to focus manufacturing on a limited objective is a common managerial blind spot. What happens to produce this blind spot in competent managers? Engineers know what can and cannot be designed into planes, bridges, boats, and buildings. They accept design objectives that will accomplish a specific set of tasks that are possible, although often difficult.

In contrast, many manufacturing managements attempt a complex, heterogeneous mixture of general and special-purpose equipment, long- and short-run operations, high and low tolerances, new and old products, off-the-shelf items and customer specials, stable and changing designs, markets with reliable forecasts and unpredictable ones, seasonal and nonseasonal sales, short and long lead times, and high and low skills.

Lack of Consistent Policies

That each of the contrasting features generally demands conflicting manufacturing tasks and hence different manufacturing policies is typically not well understood. But the particular mix of these features should determine the elements of manufacturing policy.

Instead of designing elements of manufacturing policy around one manufacturing task, what usually happens? Consider, for example, that the wage system is often designed to emphasize high productivity, production control to maximize short lead times, inventory to minimize stock levels, order quantities to minimize setup times, plant layout to minimize materials handling costs, and process design to maximize quality.

While each of these decisions looks sensible to professional specialists in his or her field, the resulting conventional factory ends up by consisting of six or more inconsistent elements of manufacturing structure, each of which is designed to achieve a *different* implicit objective. Such inconsistency usually results in high costs since one or another element is excessively staffed or operated inefficiently because its task is being exaggerated or misdirected. Or several functions may require excess staff in order to control or manage a plant that is unduly complex.

But often the result is even more serious. The chief negative effect is not on productivity but on ability to compete. The plant's manufacturing policies are not designed, tuned, and focused as a whole on that one key strategic manufacturing task essential to the company's success in its industry.

Reasons for Inconsistency

Noncongruent manufacturing structures appear to be common in industry. In fact, research reveals that a fully consistent set of manufacturing policies resulting in a congruent system is rare. Why does this situation occur so often? In the cases I studied, it seemed to come about essentially for one or more of the following reasons:

- Professionals in each field attempted to achieve goals that, although valid and traditional in their fields, were not congruent with goals of other areas.
- The manufacturing task for the plant subtly changed while most operating and service departments kept on the same course as before.
- The manufacturing task was never made explicit.
- The inconsistencies were never recognized.
- More and more products were piled into existing plants, resulting in an often futile attempt to meet the manufacturing tasks of a variety of markets, technologies, and competitive strategies.

Let me elaborate on several of these causes.

"Professionalism" in the Plant

Production system elements are typically set up or managed by professionals in their respective fields, such as quality control, personnel, labor relations, engineering, inventory management, materials handling, systems design, and so forth. These professionals, quite naturally, seek to maximize their contributions and justify their positions.

They have conventional views of success in each of their particular fields. Of course, these objectives are generally in conflict. I say "of course" not to be cynical, but these fields of specialty have come into existence for many different reasons—some to reduce costs, others to save time, others to minimize capital investments, still others to promote human cooperation and happiness, and so on. So it is perfectly normal for them to pull in different directions, which is exactly what happens in many plants.

This problem is not totally new. But it is changing because professionalism is increasing; we have more and more experts at work in different parts of the factory. So it is a growing problem.

Product Proliferation

The combination of increasing foreign and domestic competition plus an accelerating rate of technological innovation has resulted in product proliferation in many factories. Shorter product life, more new products, shorter runs, lower unit volumes, and more customer specials are becoming increasingly common. The same factory that five years ago produced 25 products may today be producing 50 to 100.

The inconsistent production system grows up, not simply because there are more products to make—which is of course likely to increase direct and indirect costs and add complexity and confusion—but also because new products often call for different manufacturing tasks. To succeed in some tasks may require superb technological competence and focus; others may demand extremely short delivery; and still others, extremely low costs. Yet almost always, new products are added into the existing mix in the same plant, even though some new equipment may be necessary. The rationale for this decision is usually that the plant is operating at less than full capacity. Thus the logic is, "If we put the new products into the present plant, we can save capital investment and avoid duplicating overheads."

The result is complexity, confusion, and worst of all a production organization, which, because it is spun out in all directions by a kind of centrifugal force, lacks focus and a doable manufacturing task. The factory is asked to perform a mission for product A which conflicts with that of product B. Thus the result is a hodgepodge of compromises.

When we may have, in fact, four tasks and four markets, we make the mistake of trying to force them into one plant, one set of equipment, one factory organization, and one set of manufacturing policies. We try to cram into one operating system the ability to compete in an impossible mix of demands. Each element of the system attempts to adjust to these demands with variation, special sections, complex procedures, more people, and added paperwork. This syndrome, starting with added market demands and ending with incongruent internal structures, accounts to a large extent for the human fustrations, high costs, and low competitive abilities we see so much in industry today.

Who gets the blame? Manufacturing executives, of course, get it from corporate headquarters for high costs, poor productivity, low quality and reliability, and missed deliveries. In turn they tend to blame the situation on anything that makes sense, such as poor market forecasts, subpar labor, declining work ethic, unconcern over quality, inept engineering designs, faulty equipment, and so forth.

Experience accomplishes wonders, but a diffused organization with conflicting structural elements and competing manufacturing tasks accumulates experience and specialized competence very slowly.

TOWARD MANUFACTURING FOCUS

A new management approach is needed in industries where diverse products and markets require companies to manufacture a broad mix of items, volumes, specifications, and customer demand patterns. Its emphasis must be on building competitive strength. One way to compete is to focus the entire manufacturing system on a limited task precisely defined by the company's competitive strategy and the realities of its technology and economics. A common objective produces synergistic effects rather than internal power struggles between professionalized departments. This approach can be assisted by these guiding rules:

- Centralize the factory's focus on relative competitive ability.
- Avoid the common tendency to add staff and overhead in order to save on direct labor and capital investment.
- Let each manufacturing unit work on a limited task instead of the usual complex mix of conflicting objectives, products, and technologies.

Manufacturing managers are generally astounded at the internal inconsistencies and compromises they discover once they put the concept of focused manufacturing to work in analyzing their own plants. Then, when they begin to discern what the company strategy and market situation are implicitly demanding and compare these implicit demands with what they have been trying to achieve, many submerged conflicts surface. When they then ask themselves what a certain element of the structure or of the manufacturing policy was designed to maximize, the built-in cross-purposes become apparent.

At the risk of seeming to take a cookbook approach to an inevitably complex set of issues, let me offer a four-step recipe for the focused factory based on an actual (but disguised) example of an industrial manufacturing company, a producer of mechanical equipment, which attempted to adapt its operations to this concept.

1. *Develop an explicit, brief statement of corporate objectives and strategy.* The statement should cover the next three to five years, and it should have the substantial involvement of top management, including marketing, finance, and control executives.

In its statement, the top management of the company agreed to the following:

Our corporate objective is directed toward increasing market share during the next five years via a strategy of (1) tailoring our product to individual customer needs, (2) offering advanced and special product features at a modest price increment, and (3) gaining competitive advantage via rapid product development and service orientation to customers of all sizes.

2. *Translate the objectives-and-strategy statement into what this means to manufacturing.* What must the factory do especially well in order to carry out and support this corporate strategy? What is going to be the most difficult task it will face? If the manufacturing function is not sharp and capable, where is the company most likely to fail? It may fail in any one of the elements of the production structure, but it will probably do so in a combination of some of them.

To carry on with the mechanical equipment company example, such a manufacturing task might be defined explicitly as follows:

Our manufacturing task for the next three years will be to introduce specialized, customer-tailored new products into production, with lead times that are substantially less than those of our competitors. Since the technology in our industry is changing rapidly, and since product reliability can be extremely serious for customers, our most difficult problems will be to control the new-product introduction process, so as to solve technical problems promptly and to maintain reliability amid rapid changes in the product itself.

3. *Make a careful examination of each element of the production system.* How is it now set up, organized, focused, and manned? What is it now especially good at? How must it be changed to implement the key manufacturing task?

4. *Reorganize the manufacturing structure to produce a congruent focus.* This reorganization focuses on the ability to do those limited things well that are of utmost importance to the accomplishment of the manufacturing task.

To complete the example of the mechanical equipment company, *Exhibit 6.1* lists each major element of the manufacturing system of the company, describes its present focus in terms of that task for which it was implicitly or inadvertently aimed, and lists a new approach designed to bring consistency, focus, and power to its manufacturing arm.

What stands out most in this exhibit is the number of substantial changes in manufacturing policies required to bring the production system into a total consistency. The exhibit also features the implicit conflicts between many manufacturing tasks in the present approach, which are the result of the failure to define one task for the whole plant.

The reader may perceive a disturbing implication of the focused plant concept—it seems to call for major investments in new plants, new equipment, and new tooling, in order to break down the present complexity. For example, if the company is currently involved in five different products, technologies, markets, or volumes, does it need five plants, five sets of equipment, five processes, five technologies, and five organizational structures? The answer is probably *yes.* But the practical solution need not involve selling the big multipurpose facility and decentralizing into five small facilities. In fact, companies that have adopted the focused plant concept have approached the solution quite differently. There is no need to build five plants, which would involve unnecessary investment and overhead expenses.

The more practical approach is the "plant within a plant" (PWP) notion in which the existing facility is divided both organizationally and physically into, in this case, five PWPs. Each PWP has its own facilities in which it can concentrate on its particular manufacturing task, using its own work-force management approaches, production control, organization structure, and so forth. Quality and volume levels are not mixed; worker training and incentives have a clear focus; and engineering of processes, equipment, and materials handling are specialized as needed.

Each PWP quickly gains experience by focusing and concentrating every element of its work on those limited essential objectives that constitute its manufacturing task. Since a manufacturing task is an offspring of a

Exhibit 6.1 Conflicting Manufacturing Tasks Implied Incongruent Elements of the Present Production System

Production System Elements	Present Approach (conventional factory)	Implicit Manufacturing Tasks of Present Approach	Changed Approach (focused factory)
Equipment and process policies	One large plant; special purpose equipment; high-volume tooling; balanced capacity with functional layout.	Low manufacturing costs on steady runs of a few large products with minimal investment.	Separate old, standardized products and new customized products into two plants within a plant (PWP). For each new PWP, provide general purpose equipment, temporary tooling, and modest excess capacity with product-oriented layout.
Work-force management policies	Specialized jobs with narrow job content; incentive wages; few supervisors; focus on volume of production per hour.	Low costs and efficiency.	Create fewer jobs with more versatility. Pay for breadth of skills and ability to perform a variety of jobs. Provide more foremen for solving technical problems at workplace.

Production scheduling and control	Detailed, frequent sales forecasts; produce for inventory economic lot sizes of finished goods; small. decentralized production scheduling group.	Short delivery lead times.	Produce to order special parts and stock of common parts based on semi-annual forecast. Staff production control to closely schedule and centralize parts movements.
Quality control	Control engineers and large inspection groups in each department.	Extremely reliable quality.	No change.
Organizational structure	Functional; production control under superintendents of each area; inspection reports to top.	Top performance of the objectives of each functional department (i.e., many tasks).	Organize each PWP by program and project in order to focus organizational effort on bringing new products into production smoothly and on time.

corporate strategy and marketing program, it is susceptible to either gradual or sweeping change. The PWP approach makes it easier to perform realignment of essential operations and system elements over time as the task changes.

CONCLUSION

While the economy has moved toward an era of more advanced technologies and shorter product lives, we have not readjusted our concepts of production to keep up with these changes. Instead, with the mistaken rationale that the keys to success are maximizing efficiency and productivity, limited investment, economies of scale, and full utilization of existing plant resources to achieve low costs, we keep adding new products to plants that were once focused, manageable, and competitive.

Reversing the process, however, is not impossible. In most of the cases I have studied, capital investment in facilities is not difficult to justify when payoffs that will result from organizational simplicity are taken into account. Resources for simplifying the focus of a manufacturing complex are not hard to acquire when the expected payoff is the ability to compete successfully, using manufacturing as a competitive weapon. Moreover, better customer service and competitive position typically support higher margins to cover capital investments. And when studied carefully, the economies of scale and the effects of less than full utilization of plant equipment are seldom found to be as critical to productivity and efficiency as classical economic approaches predict.

The problem of productivity in the United States is real indeed. But seeing the problem as one of "how to compete" can broaden management's horizon. The focused factory approach offers the opportunity to stop compromising each element of the production system in the typical general-purpose, do-all plant, which satisfies no strategy, no market, and no task.

Not only does focus provide punch and power; it also provides clear goals that can be readily understood and assimilated by members of an organization. It provides, too, a mechanism for reappraising what is needed for success, and for readjusting and shaking up old, tired manufacturing organizations with welcome change and a clear sense of direction.

In many sectors of American industry such change and such a new sense of direction are needed to shift the competitive balance in our favor. But experience in focusing factories demonstrates that results depend on how thoroughly and concretely the task around which to focus is thought through.

This is the subject of the next chapter: how to define the manufacturing task in a way that gets it down to specific reality. This requires not only determining what the plant must do particularly well but also what will be particularly difficult, and communicating the essence of the task to the organization.

CHAPTER 7

Defining the Manufacturing Task

When a manufacturing facility is focused on a limited task, top management can concentrate its attention on the accomplishment of that task and in that way acquire a point of view and a concept for managing manufacturing, preventing their being dominated by production management specialists.

My purpose in this chapter is to illustrate the importance of the process of defining the task by offering a set of specific "how to's," based on a high-technology company that makes chemical processing equipment. The concept of "task" relates manufacturing to the corporate strategy so as to form manufacturing into a competitive weapon. Without exception the process of defining the manufacturing task is always difficult. It is easy to define *a* manufacturing task but hard to define it in sufficient depth and understanding that it becomes a powerful, mobilizing force that produces a set of integrated and consistent structure and actions.

The manufacturing task statement begins with a clear and explicit concept of what the manufacturing function must accomplish. The manufacturing task statement is an exposition of manufacturing philosophy in the sense that "philosophy" relates ends and means and links them together conceptually with a total plan and its rationale.

In working with managers, and in attempting to learn the art myself, I have observed five impediments to the development of focused manufacturing policies.

1. The importance of the manufacturing task is not understood, and the process of defining it is therefore given short shrift. The result is an academic statement rather than an effective, pervasive philosophy of manufacturing.

2. Corporate strategy, marketing, industry technology, or industry economics are not fully studied, thought through, and incorporated into the thinking of the manufacturing team and the task statement.
3. The statement of manufacturing task fails to go beyond a mere ranking of the criteria (see Chapter 5) for judging manufacturing performance into a set of priorities. For example, "the highest priority is reduced lead times; second is costs; third is quality. . . ."
4. The manufacturing task is excessively general. It does not include specific objectives or standards, and it does not identify which of these are going to be most difficult to attain.
5. The manufacturing task does not clearly state its implications and its disclaimers (e.g., what we will *not* do).

If it does not include these elements, the manufacturing task has not been thought through nor will it be effective as an end product. And most important, the process itself will not have been as vital and effective as it must be. As the following case shows, the length and complexity of the process illustrates both the difficulty and the power of developing a manufacturing strategy. An important product is the impact the process has on the firm's manufacturing management team and its subsequent behavior.

MAINSTREAM TECHNOLOGY COMPANY

The "Mainstream Technology Company" (MTC) decided to define its manufacturing task. MTC is a company on the sophisticated, high-technology end of chemical processing equipment with a history of rapid growth. Its rapid growth was based on a technical breakthrough achieved in 1980, a breakthrough that gave the company a major competitive advantage that was expected to continue for at least the next five years. Sales were approximately $150 million.

THE ORIGINAL PROBLEMS

The vice-president of manufacturing felt that while manufacturing had been generally successful in coping with the challenges of rapid and massive growth, overhead costs and inventories had been rising to a level he now considered unsatisfactory. Furthermore, having made continual annual additions to production capacity resulting in a complex multiplant network, he was concerned about a possible lack of focusing, plant by plant, on a manageable span of products, market demand, technologies, and tasks.

OBJECTIVES

MTC decided to hold a set of meetings to clarify MTC's manufacturing task in order to examine and possibly restructure the company's manufacturing policies and structure. The goal for the manufacturing team was to develop a structure and rationale concerning which products should be produced where. Such a focus would assist MTC in articulating its manufacturing task and reducing overhead costs and inventory investment. Outside consultants were to stimulate, question, interpret, challenge, and ultimately summarize the thinking and conclusions of the manufacturing team.

ACCOMPLISHMENTS

The accomplishments of the six days of discussion may at first seem modest. The experiences and changes in understanding for each person could be reported only individually. However, the group as a whole made a great deal of concrete progress in defining the manufacturing task on which structural decision must hinge. The result was a product-process-plant matrix to be in place by 1985. This matrix structure not only differed from the company's 1980 set-up, but more important, it appeared to be promising for improving the focus on its manufacturing task ahead and reducing overhead costs and inventory. Significant progress was made toward three key conceptual goals:

1. *The assimilation of a a nonconventional approach to manufacturing management.* Instead of attempting to optimize along all the usual performance parameters (cost, quality, delivery, investment, etc.), which are inevitably in conflict and make manufacturing vulnerable to continual external criticism, the basic task of manufacturing was derived from corporate strategic and marketing factors in conjunction with the constraints of the technology and economics of the industry. Manufacturing policy then aligned the physical setup and organizational infrastructure to focus on a central manufacturing task. The MTC group wrestled and experimented with this concept enough to become capable of applying it to production management.

2. *The understanding that many (rather than few) alternatives exist.* This seems to be obvious. However, inevitably managers establish an experience-restricted span of the range of options open to them. This limits their sense of the range of available alternatives for choosing equipment and process technology; the number, size, and location of plants; groupings of products by plants; organization structure; work-force management; production planning and scheduling; and management controls. MTC made considerable progress toward the goal of opening up the range of structural choices available and thus exposing the present structure to challenge.

3. *An evolution in thinking about the manufacturing task.* The evolution that took place involved digging even more deeply into what the manufacturing really had to be when the whole strategic economic and technological facts were considered.

The struggles over what the manufacturing task means started with case discussions of how other companies had made decisions that involved a manufacturing task. There followed lengthy debates over MTC's task, a debate that went on for six days. The discussion went through four distinct phases (*Exhibit 7.1*), back and forth to be sure, but gradually evolving as follows:

Exhibit 7.1   Stages in the Development of a Statement of Manufacturing Task

Stage	Statement: "Our Manufacturing Task Is:"	Characteristic
1	Grow at 30% per year React to mix change of 30% to 40% React to volume changes of + 10% Improve asset utilization (ROA) from 7.5% to 15% Improve productivity (output per person) 50% Move toward product specific manufacturing Make a functional organization work Product reliability and process control improvement × 3	A collection of goals
2	First of all, to be flexible and grow. But we've got to do it with a doubling of ROA. This requires improvements in both productivity and inventory.	Goals with priorities
3	To try to meet corporate demand by tracking the market. But we could sink the company if we can't meet the commitments we make on deliveries, ROA, costs, and inventory levels. So our task is to	"Musts" with priorities related to the corporation's critical strategic needs for successfully competing in its industry and financing its growth

Exhibit 7.1 (*continued*)

Stage	Statement: "Our Manufacturing Task Is:"	Characteristic
	maximize growth while meeting marketing and financial commitments.	
4	First and foremost, we must be predictable. Manufacturing's role is to be a predictable known who makes clear commitments (cost, budgets, quality, schedule, ROA, etc.) and then meets them. When we are predictable, the rest of the company won't have to spend time or effort figuring out what we're up to or reacting to our surprises.	The "name of the game" is made explicit

Next our task is to grow—but only from a controlled base and only after we have met the minimum constraints below:

a. Cost. Maintain competitive product costs +5% of those of our best competitors.

b. Quality/reliability. Maintain quality at +5% of industry norms.

c. Delivery performance. 95% on time.

d. Asset utilization. We will construct budgets that meet our ROA goals. Company inventory turns will be at least 2.5%.

e. Employee relations. Maintain so that our employes judge us to be among the top quartile of companies to work for.

In summary, we must be predictable. We will sacrifice growth to perform no worse than any of the minimums above.

At stage 1 the task was seen as a set of objectives—for example, "We've got to grow at 30 to 40% and double our ROI, develop integratable products, deal with separated businesses, reduce cost on A items, and improve response time and flexibility on B and C items."

The problem with stage 1 was that this kind of definition was merely a collection of goals. It lacked ranking by priorities as a minimum conceptual step for answering the question: How do we *manage* manufacturing for the next four to five years?

As discussion proceeded, MTC arrived at a more advanced stage. Stage 2 was better than stage 1 because they recognized conflict and the need for priorities by deciding on ratings for the objectives. They began to develop a sense of strategy for being successful. Decision rules were developed to provide some consistency. But stage 2 still was not very useful because (1) they had not suggested a rationale for *how* manufacturing was to be successful, and (2) there was no explicit recognition, or even an inference, of what goals would be particularly difficult to achieve in the next few years.

At stage 3, the definition began to include some specific tasks that would be particularly difficult to undertake but if well handled would lead to success. The task at this stage was again a collection of "musts," but with some priorities and awareness of constraints imposed by financial resources, technology, and marketing strategy. It included tracking the market, meeting commitments made to the company but also keeping costs within 5% of industry costs, making deliveries reliable but with comparable lead times to those of competitors, and improving the sales-to-assets ratio.

Stage 3 was more specific and realistic than stage 2, but MTC still had not articulated a key task with a rationale that would pervade decision making and thereby ensure consistency. And the statement did not lead managers directly to action nor clearly infer what should be the essential decisions.

Stage 4 took these requirements into account. It included objectives, priorities, constraints, and it identified which of these would be most difficult. The definition now encompassed and dealt with the corporate financial and marketing tasks and strategy. Most important, perhaps, it inferred a "how to" and led to action in a way that was so simply understood that it carried with it its own cardinal imperative, a kind of "name of the game" for making consistent structural and operating decisions. It conveyed a real sense of manufacturing strategy. For instance, the message perceived by one manager is reproduced as *Exhibit 7.2*.

Its key inclusion of "being predictable," for example, derives from MTC's being a large corporation growing massively, which means that

Exhibit 7.2 The Message from Stage 4 Manufacturing Task

1. You *must* be in control. This means meeting all your goals (cost, schedule, quality, assets, and employee relations) against current budgets.
2. Different plants/operations have more or less ambitious goals for all five parameters (one focused on cost reduction, one on flexibility, etc.). But *all* plants/operations have *all* five goals that must *all* be met.
3. "Over success" on one goal that results in failure to meet another goal is unacceptable.
4. "Surprise" is unacceptable!

SOURCE: An MTC manager.

the financial demands of growth create a situation in which the risks of not growing or not producing the absolutely necessary cash flows, of misleading or failing top management would be disastrous.

Being predictable carries with it a clear lead into action that is an essential part of effective manufacturing at MTC, for being predictable in a time of massive growth both in physical volume and in new products means that *control* is the key management tool and the key state of mind. If control and predictability is paramount, it begins to say a lot about the 1980 product/process/plant matrix.

I emphasize this evolution because it was based on an essential development in thinking that took place only after six days of difficult wrestling with the issues. Because conventional approaches to manufacturing were "burned" into MTC managers in their formative years, they slide back into them repeatedly before reaching new ground.

After all that went into this definition, can we improve on it? To try to do so is probably as risky as making a modest touch-up to improve a Michelangelo. But brush in hand, here goes!

THE MANUFACTURING TASK—A STAGE 5 STATEMENT

The MTC team defined the manufacturing task with a variety of words, but since the words used in Exhibits 7.1 and 7.2 seem to capture the ideas on which the group concurred, I refer to those words in the following comments:

1. As a statement of manufacturing task, it is quite useful, especially because its acceptance carries with it a number of structural and operational implications. However, in the heat and time pressure of the group discussion, there was no final disciplined effort to tighten the statement so as to be easier and more foolproof to communicate.

2. It is less than perfect as it now stands because:
It doesn't say why the task is what it says it is.
It doesn't state explicitly what may be most difficult.
It contains some conflicting goals that have to be traded off against each other and therefore should be ranked.
It contains some possible internal inconsistencies.

The Manufacturing Task—A Revised Statement

MTC's competitive strategy is to gain a commanding, preemptive market share by aggressive engineering, product development, and marketing in an industry that is growing rapidly while beginning to mature with price competition and the shake-out of marginal competitors. MTC's critical top management task is reaching this preemptive market position while financing the massive growth it requires, for MTC risks insufficient funds in the event of missing sales targets.

Manufacturing's dilemma is how to handle the corporate imperative of sheer physical growth through rapid product and technology change while minimizing the funds it needs for assets and maximizing the funds provided by minimizing the cost of goods sold. The dilemma is how to avoid disastrous falldowns in delivery or cost performance (which would cripple the entire corporation and its finances and strategic position), without the equally unsatisfactory outcome of playing a lower risk game of promising and delivering less on growth, new product introduction, and return on assets.

The key job of manufacturing therefore is to promise and deliver vital, difficult improvement in sales and return on assets while keeping the risks of failure at an acceptable level. The manufacturing task, simply stated, is to be able to predict accurately and manage the accomplishment of acceptable but difficult goals. Basically, it is to manage the risk-commitment curve. Such a curve is shown on Exhibit 7.3. This is the "name of the game" for MTC manufacturing.

This task has at least four clear implications:

1. It requires high skills and judgment to relate commitments to risk (on Exhibit 7.3, to be able to draw this curve with specifics, relative to various demands and needs—sales levels, new product introduction, CGS %, assets employed, ROA).
2. It requires obtaining and clarifying from corporate management the boundaries of what is acceptable and unacceptable (i.e., the shaded area on Exhibit 7.3).
3. It requires uniquely competent managers and management systems— information, control, communication—so as to deliver on the difficult commitments it makes.

Exhibit 7.3   The Commitment Risk Curve

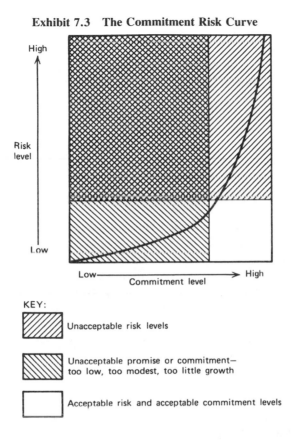

KEY:

Unacceptable risk levels

Unacceptable promise or commitment—
too low, too modest, too little growth

Acceptable risk and acceptable commitment levels

4. It requires, in all probability, systemwide improvements so as to be able to move the Exhibit 7.3 curves down and to the right.

It is often useful to try to paraphrase the manufacturing task into a book title or a picture. One picture that tells the story fairly well is that of Babe Ruth, with two strikes showing on the scoreboard, pointing to the right field stands just before he hit the famous home run. Difficult but predictable and achievable, an acceptable risk for an acceptable payoff.

CONCLUSION

This work with MTC executives demonstrates that developing a manufacturing strategy is a process and that the process itself is as important as the product. If the specifications for the product—the statement of the manufacturing task—are demanding, and the product is inspected against those specifications, a valuable experience can result.

In summary, these specifications for the manufacturing task are as follows:

1. It must be written in sentences and paragraphs, not merely outlined.
2. It must explicitly state the demands and constraints on manufacturing derived from:
   The corporate strategy for competing successfully.
   Marketing policy.
   Financial policy.
   The technology of the industry and the firm.
   The economics of the industry and the firm.
3. It must state what manufacturing must accomplish to be a competitive weapon and, conversely, how performance can be judged.
4. It must identify what will be especially difficult ("the name of the game"). Its difficulty is forced by economic, human, competitive, or technological problems generally common to the industry. Therefore when the difficult task is accomplished, this will differentiate our company and its manufacturing policies and performance from others. The differences will result in successfully competing via the creation in manufacturing of a unique competitive advantage.
5. It must explicitly state priorities, including what may have to suffer.
6. It must explicitly state the inferences or impact of requirements on the manufacturing infrastructure[1], i.e., to accomplish this task we are going to have to improve, for example, production control by such and such policies or procedures or changes.
7. The communication of the manufacturing task may be facilitated by "boiling down" the task statement to a book title, a picture, cartoon, or slogan. This may seem breezy or "corny" but it has the result of bringing to larger numbers of managers what is key for the next period ahead. It puts a capstone on the process by permeating the organization with a functioning understanding of the manufacturing task.

Once the focus and manufacturing task are clearly defined and communicated, the third step in operationalizing a manufacturing strategy is step-by-step design of the system. The basic notion is that each step in the design offers a spectrum of choices and that the particular choice should be such as to maximize performance toward achievement of the strategic-determined task. The "how-to's" of system design are the subject of the next chapter.

---

[1]By manufacturing infrastructure we mean the policies, procedures, and organization by which manufacturing accomplishes its work, specifically production and inventory control systems, cost and quality control systems, work-force management policies, and organizational structure.

CHAPTER 8

Designing the
Production System

Previous chapters have focused on why the manufacturing organization should explicitly identify its manufacturing task to be consistent with and supportive of the corporation's competitive strategy and then organize manufacturing structure to accomplish a sharp focus for that task. Our approach so far has been more on "why" than on "how." The question that remains to be discussed is, "What is the method by which manufacturing policies can be analyzed and changed or developed to meet the requirements of the manufacturing task?"

To move from analysis to synthesis the focus of this chapter is on designing the production system. The design process is necessary either to develop a totally new production system for a new plant or, as is more often the case, to determine useful change for an existing system.

In designing a production system, what is being done essentially is to establish a set of manufacturing policies. Manufacturing policies are the means by which the basic structural elements of the system are made consistent and pulled together. Manufacturing polices can be thought of in two parts.

The first part has to do with bricks and mortar and machinery. This is hardware or "fixed assets"—the number, capacity, and location of plants and the equipment and process technology. The second part has to do with people and systems and procedures, or "infrastructure." In designing the infrastructure, decisions need to be made concerning the following manufacturing policy sectors:

1. What to make and what to buy, i.e., the integration issue.
2. Production planning, scheduling, and inventory control.
3. Work-force management.
4. Quality control.

5. The formal organization.
6. Controls, reports, and information systems.
7. Purchasing.

The most typical serious condition in most manufacturing plants is that of inconsistencies existing within the infrastructure. Different sectors of manufacturing policy are implicitly set up to accomplish conflicting objectives. It is as if an automobile engine were designed for Indy racing, the transmission for fuel economy, the tires for comfort, the suspension for road race maneuverability, and the trunk space for camping.

The same phenomena exist in factories when there is no clear design objective or set of priorities. Further inconsistencies also come about either because of growth, product development, marketing pressure, management, organizational changes, or the influence of professionals in the organization who earnestly seek to optimize their own traditional professional goals that are normally in conflict. Frequently lacking is a concept, scheme, or broad outlook that binds together all of the elements of the infrastructure.

A *manufacturing audit* is an approach to take in examining the production system and the infrastructure. *Exhibit 8.1* is a manufacturing audit checklist process that can be used in designing a production system or for analyzing an existing system to reveal inconsistencies and opportunities for improvements. Each element of the system must be examined from the standpoint of whether it is presently designed and operated to achieve the key manufacturing task. A useful procedure is to redesign each element of the system conceptually to provide focus on one task and then to compare the redesigned system with the present system.

Exhibit 8.1 Manufacturing Audit Checklist Process

I. *Make/Buy Choices*
    A. Examine the gray areas of items that could feasibly be made or bought.
    B. What does present make or buy position imply?
        High make _____? High buy _____?
        Impact on profitability
        Impact on cost structure (fixed vs. variable costs, investment level, breakeven point)
        Impact on ability to ride economic cycles
        Impact on quality
        Impact on risk (assurance of supply, downside risk of excess capacity)
        Ability to meet the manufacturing task

Exhibit 8.1 (*continued*)

II. *Capacity Decision*
   A. How does capacity compare with past, present, and future forecasted demand?
   B. Do we play capacity on the low side or high side? (Are we purposely low or do we try to be right on, or are we purposely careful always to have a bit extra?)
   C. What does this imply about
      Investment levels
      Costs, breakeven point
      Service levels, response times
      Risks
      Work-force management
      Quality
      Ability to meet the manufacturing task

III. *Plant Decisions*
   A. Number of plants
      One
      Some
      Many
   B. Size of plants
      Large
      Medium
      Small
   C. Location of plants
      Near raw materials
      Near customers
      Other rationale for location _____
   D. Focus and organization of plants
      Work allocated by
         Products
         Process/technology
         Scale, volume
         Other _____
   E. What does this imply about
      Costs
      Risks
      Service levels
      Organization
      Control
      Work-force management
      Production scheduling and inventory management
      Ability to meet the manufacturing task

Exhibit 8.1 *(continued)*

IV. *Equipment and Process Technology*
    A. Relative to the industry and stages of existing technology describe the extent to which
        We are mechanized
        We are ahead or behind competitors in use of latent technology
        We are sharp and aggressive in
            Tooling
            Equipment
            Process/manufacturing engineering
            Industrial engineering
    B. Describe key processes on dimensions of
        Set-up and changeover requirements
        General purpose versus special purpose capability
        Process capability versus product performance and quality requirements
        Mechanization-labor intensiveness
        Skills required
        Maintenance requirements, skills, and costs
        Supervision needed
        Flexibility for volume changes
        Internal balance of capacities and bottlenecks
        Maintenance requirements, skills, and costs
        Supervision needed
        Flexibility for volume changes
        Internal balance of capacities and bottlenecks
        Technology: mature, slow changing versus new, uncertain, fast changing
        Cost of equipment and facilities in P & L (high or low) relative to other costs
    C. What does above imply about
        Competitive ability
        Service levels
        Investment levels
        Production planning and scheduling-inventory management
        Risks
        Quality
        Work-force management
        Organizational needs
        Cost structure/breakeven curve
        Opportunities
        Ability to meet the manufacturing task

V. *Key Concept*
    A. A key concept in the manufacturing audit is that the choices of make or buy levels; number, size, location, and capacity of

Exhibit 8.1 (*continued*)

plants; equipment and process levels either determine or greatly
influence nearly everything else. These are brick and mortar,
structural, hardware, expensive, long lead-time, and difficult-to-
change decisions. Once made, decisions on other elements of the
infrastructure inevitably are restricted in range. By the same
token, the decision process on the various elements of the
infrastructure is made easier by having made the hardware group
of decisions first.

Turn now to the other elements.

VI. *Production Planning and Control*
    A.   Describe the present systems for
        Forecasting and planning loads and capacities
        Establishing customer promises
        Ordering production/releasing work to the plant
        Order quantities
        Size and location of inventories
        Balancing inventories
        Coordination and timing/expediting/correcting falldowns
    B.   What does each imply about the implicit manufacturing task?
    C.   What alternatives would focus better on the actual manufacturing task?

VII. *Work-Force Management*
    A.   Describe the present systems and choices for
        Selection of employees
        Training
        Job content—big, rich jobs or narrow, specialized jobs
        Pay systems—how pay is determined
           What we are paying for
           Opportunity for upward mobility
           Pay ranges
        Safety, industrial health, housekeeping
        Supervision
        Communications with employees
    B.   What does each imply about the implicit manufacturing task?
    C.   What alternatives would focus better on the actual manufacturing task?

VIII. *Quality Control*
    A.   Describe present systems and choices for
        Explicitly choosing quality levels
        Quality levels chosen
        Designing/engineering quality into product
        Process design and control

Exhibit 8.1 *(continued)*

Training and supervision for quality
Monitoring
    B.   What does each imply about the implicit manufacturing task?
    C.   What alternatives would focus better on the actual manufacturing task?

  IX. *Manufacturing and Industrial Engineering and Maintenance*
    A.   Describe present systems and choices for
        Improving processes
        Improving equipment and tooling
        Keeping up with technological developments
        Level of effort
        Influencing product design engineering for producibility
    B.   What does each imply about the implicit manufacturing task?
    C.   What alternatives would focus better on the actual manufacturing task?

   X. *Cost and Information Systems*
    A.   Describe present system and choices for
        What is monitored
        What is budgeted, forecast
        Setting standards, goals
        Selecting who gets what information and when
        Taking action when standards are not met
    B.   What does each imply about the implicit manufacturing task?
    C.   What alternatives would focus better on the actual manufacturing task?

  XI. *Purchasing*
    A.   Describe present approaches to purchasing management
        Purchased part design/value analysis
        Use of competitive bids
        Vendor selection
        Vendor assistance/training/communications
        Manning, organizational emphasis
        Control systems
    B.   What does each imply about the implicit manufacturing task?
    C.   What alternatives would focus better on the actual manufacturing task?

 XII. *Formal Organization*
    A.   Describe the present formal organization
    B.   Rank the functions in the order in which they are given
        organizational emphasis
        Manufacturing supervision
        Production planning, scheduling, inventory control

Exhibit 8.1 (*continued*)

      Maintenance
      Manufacturing engineering
      Industrial engineering
      Quality control
      Purchasing
      Personnel, labor relations
      Cost control
      Product/program management
      Design engineering
  C. Describe the system for performance measurement and evaluation
  D. What does each imply about the implicit manufacturing task?
  E. What alternatives would focus better on the actual manufacturing
      task?

A manufacturing audit can reveal which of eight "cardinal sins" may have been committed in the production organization. It can also suggest specifics for revised manufacturing policies and new procedures that would cleanse the organization from those sins. The sins are as follows:

1. Manufacturing implicitly has a new manufacturing task but continues the old manufacturing policies and structure.
2. Managers in manufacturing have no clear, consistent definition or understanding of the manufacturing task facing the organization.
3. The manufacturing policies and the infrastructure being employed are inconsistent. Taken together, there is a distortion in coordination.
4. The organization lacks a focus. It is attempting to cover too many technologies or too many products and markets, too wide a range of volume, and more than one manufacturing task.
5. The organization has the wrong equipment and process technology for the present manufacturing task.
6. The organization uses only economic hurdles for capital investment instead of also considering what the manufacturing organization must do to become a competitive corporate weapon.
7. The organization's decision orientation is based too much on achieving economies of scale (i.e., low costs from high volume or large scale) instead of looking at total performance along the full range of criteria marking success.
8. Selection of products and processes for each plant in a multiplant setup results in mixing together, somewhat at random, a product organization, a process organization, and a volume-focused organization (or any two of the three) instead of focusing around one type of organization.

Each can have a disastrous effect on the manufacturing organization's ability to make manufacturing a strategic weapon.

The basic premise implicit in the manufacturing audit approach to designing the production system is that each part of the fixed asset structure and the infrastructure provides many options in design. There are many different ways, for example, to use inventories and to schedule production. The manager doing the audit or redesigning the production system may look at each option and make a choice among a variety of trade-offs. Each choice will have a different impact on the seven major criteria for production success. The objective in designing the production system is to design each element of the system so that each has a positive impact on the firm's ability to meet the manufacturing task.

An example may clarify this point. A machine tool manufacturer made a strategic product decision to shift to a new line of modular machine tools, so that instead of producing conventional, standardized milling machines, the firm would be able to provide milling, drilling, turning, boring, and other machine capabilities in one machine tool in accordance with specific needs of customers. With that decision in its basic product policy, a manufacturing audit revealed the necessity of changes in much of its manufacturing structure.

For example, the existing formal organizational chart of the plant showed a typical functional organization. But with the manufacturing task changing from producing a large volume of fairly standardized conventional machine tools to the new, modularized, customized product line in which most customer's orders would be different, the organization would now have to be more effective at introducing new products and handling many customer specials. This placed a new emphasis on production planning, scheduling, and control. Emphasis on problem solving at relatively lower levels in the organization would be needed. For this reason, the organization structure had to strengthen production control and establish project management or product managers, giving them authority across the organization to get new products into production. Similarly, changes were necessary in the work-force management, moving away from incentive wages and toward enlarged job content on a fixed wage or salary basis.

Another illustrative example concerns a cosmetics firm. *Exhibit 8.2* is a one-page description of that company. The new owner's objective was to groom the company for sale by sprucing up the product line. The manufacturing task required rapid introduction of new products in a very seasonal business, demanding particularly effective production planning, scheduling, and control.

Strategically, at this point in company history, Dierdre Desiree required above all else low costs for a high earnings per share, heavy product development costs, and the preservation of the company's high quality

Exhibit 8.2 Deirdre Desiree*

Deirdre Desiree (DD) is well known for its broad line of high-priced women's cosmetics. DD had a slightly lower share of the market than its five or six main competitors and had been losing market share slightly for five years. Products were sold by exclusive sales to leading department stores and a few company retail stores. Advertising and reputation, effective retail salesmanship, and demonstration appeared to be critical. Business was highly seasonal with peaks at Christmas and Easter.

DD's strategy is to reverse market share trend by adding a new 10% to 15% of new products to its line of about 50 items while replacing about 10% of existing items and improving advertising effectiveness. Products consist of lotions, powders, lipsticks, and mascaras in equal proportions. Average unit price at factory is about $6, ranging from $2 to $12. Twenty percent of the products account for 50% of the dollar volume. Cost of direct labor averages $0.50, materials $2 of which $1 was for packages and boxes. Advertising represents about 25% of sales. Factory sales total about $72,000,000 per year.

The technology consisted of adding materials in bulk in large mixing kettles and drums and filling small-sized product containers (bottles, special packages, boxes) and then packaging. Automatic filling and packaging machines were available and generally economic at volumes exceeding 100 units per hour. Changing over an automatic line from one product to another required the line to be shut down for about five hours and a crew of five set-up men to do the work. Shelf life at the factory or in distribution channels generally caused no problems. FDA standards for cleanliness and bacteria counts were increasingly strict.

The location of DD's one manufacturing facility is in the New York City area at Long Island City.

Financially, DD is in a somewhat weak condition due to occasional unprofitable years over the past six years and large cash withdrawals by its recently deceased owner for her hobby of a stable of race horses. Ownership is presently in the hands of her estate, a large New York bank that had as its objectives eventual sale of DD as an acquisition target.

---

*This case was prepared as the basis for class discussion rather than to illustrate either effective or ineffective handling of an administrative situation. Copyright © 1977 by the President and Fellows of Harvard College.

image to enhance its value on the market. These objectives seem inconsistent, even impossible. The latter is accomplished at the expense of the former. How can both be done?

The economics of the industry indicate a cost structure in which materials and labor loom larger than plant, equipment, indirect labor, and other overheads. Storage, inventory, and handling costs are larger items. Costs are relatively flexible with volume. Transportation is not critical, but packaging and certain raw materials are substantial cost elements.

The technology of the industry is not complex. Compounding, blending, and mixing the parts are relatively simple batch processes requiring substantial precision and care for the most part only in the weighing out of ingredients. In contrast to many chemical and pharmaceutical processes, relatively little judgment and training are required of operators. Filling and packing can be substantially mechanized. Operations can be standardized, operators trained, methods engineered. Cleanliness and bacterial control are important but demand the mastery of no new technologies to handle adequately. Shelf life control requires good records in a simple system. Competent R&D work and packaging equipment are keys to success, but these functions are best handled outside the plant.

Perhaps the only difficult problem relative to many other industries is that of production planning, scheduling, and inventory management. Here the technology and the economics meet head on, for problems in bacteria control and shelf life collide with the economic advantages of long runs. And here, too, the problem of seasonality, forecasting consumer demand, new products, and changes in distribution policy meet the substantial costs of investing in and handling inventory. These problems are what require some management sophistication in the cosmetics industry.

Putting this all together provides an answer to the question, "What is necessary to be successful in manufacturing high quality cosmetics?" At Deirdre Desiree, our answer is, "A production system designed to achieve low losts and consistent quality and reliable delivery." This can be accomplished by the following:

1. A low cost location.
2. Inexpensive labor.
3. Thorough and competent, precise industrial engineering.
4. Careful and demanding training, especially in cleanliness and careful handling.
5. Development of reliable, well-accepted, and relatively tight (vs. loose) time standards.
6. Close, exacting supervision.
7. Alert, aggressive, hard-nosed, and sophisticated purchasing.
8. The maximum in mechanization via capital budgeting procedures designed to mechanize whenever possible (for low cost and high, consistent quality).
9. Skillful long-range sales forecasting.
10. Careful, top level, sophisticated aggregate scheduling and inventory costs.
11. Considerable economic analysis to minimize total setup and inventory costs.
12. Cost controls that weekly identify key costs against control standards with clear accountability.

The plant organization in this industry has to be heavily "top down." The simplicity of the technology, the heavy labor, materials, and inventory costs, and the problems of production scheduling require the key management skills to be in a small, closely knit, well-coordinated group at the top. The key thinking and all key decisions can be made by a handful of able, sophisticated managers at the top. (Contrast this with, for example, the electronics industry where judgment and technical skill are critical at nearly all levels or with the steel industry where the right equipment and capacity decisions make the difference.)

Each industry has its own "name of the game." In this industry it is *standardization, planning, and control* from the top down. Strength is developed in a few top people and in a rather formal system. This should be Deirdre Desiree's manufacturing philosophy; the manufacturing policies that can be keys to making manufacturing a competitive weapon at Deirdre Desiree are the 12 listed above.

If this seems obvious, or these manufacturing policies appear at first to be too general to be useful, let us emphasize the point by contrasting the present manufacturing policies observed in the Deirdre Desiree operations. These 12 are listed in the same order as those previously listed.

1. Locate the plant convenient to Manhattan for close personal control.
2. Employ relatively experienced labor, with considerable longevity, and with a strong union.
3. Minimize costs of plant (industrial) engineering.
4. Place little emphasis on training; rely instead on experience and longevity.
5. Use time standards only for general estimating purposes.
6. Employ experienced supervisors, who know products and workers well, and leave them on their own to exercise considerable judgment.
7. In purchasing, place the emphasis on quality and vendor reliability. Foster longstanding vendor relationships.
8. Keep capital equipment costs low.
9. Emphasize manufacturing flexibility and ability to respond quickly to changes in sales demands.
10. Handle inventory planning and scheduling at a relatively low level in the organization with least expense. Keep it closer to the foremen so that it will be practical and feasible.
11. Handle length of runs and inventory decisions at a low level based on experience and convenience rather than economic analysis.
12. Have an ordinary standard cost system to develop annual cost data.

The present manufacturing policies would be perfectly reasonable in some industries or at an earlier period in Deirdre Desiree's history. But they are in sharp contrast to the new set of manufacturing policies that were developed from the economics and technology of the industry and Deirdre Desiree's current strategy and needs.

In contrast to the recommended manufacturing philosophy, the present one appears to be to keep operations flexible and versatile and make decisions as low as possible in the organization. This might be appropriate in high-technology industries such as aerospace or electronics, but in cosmetics it causes high costs. Deirdre Desiree is in an industry where to achieve both low cost and high quality, centralized controls and standardized operations are necessary. Management strength and decisions must be concentrated at the top, where they can be closely coordinated with marketing, packaging, and sales.

Exhibit 8.3, Alternative Choices in Production System Design, is a further step in making a manufacturing audit. Exhibit 8.1 was largely an

Exhibit 8.3   Alternative Choices in Production System Design

I. *Criteria for Judging Manufacturing Performance*

Cost/efficiency/productivity	_____	
Quality/product reliability	_____	
Short delivery cycle	_____	
Dependable delivery cycle	_____	Rank in order of value to the
Return on investment	_____	company from the
Flexibility for volume changes	_____	achievement of exceptional
Flexibility for product changes	_____	performance under each
Other (describe)	_____	criteria. (1–8)

II. *Statement of the Manufacturing Task*

A.   At what must manufacturing be especially capable to satisfy strategic, financial, and marketing requirements over the next one to three years?

B.   What will be most difficult—the particular challenge?

C.   What, in the above, is changing from the past?

D.   Product life-cycle stage

Exhibit 8.3 (*continued*)

Low volume, low standardization, one of a kind   ____   (Check one.)
Multiple products—many ECOs   ____
Multiple products—few ECOs   ____
A few major products   ____
High volume/standard/commodity products   ____

III. *Desired Economic Structure*
  A. Cost of goods sold:
    Labor   ____
    Overhead   ____
    Depreciation   ____   (Fill in desired percentages.)
    Material   ____

    Total   ____

  B. Fixed Costs—Variable Costs
    Low variable   High variable
    and $\longleftrightarrow$ and
    High fixed   (Mark preferred point on spectrum.)   Low fixed

IV. *Equipment and Process Technology (EPT)*
  A. Integration (make or buy)   Make little $\longleftrightarrow$ Make much
    Forward (to end items)   Make little $\longleftrightarrow$ Make much
    Backward (to suppliers)   Make little $\longleftrightarrow$ Make much
  B. Number and size of plants: Few, big $\longleftrightarrow$ Many, small
  C. Capacity versus market forecast
    Barely enough capacity $\longrightarrow$ Comfortable capacity
  D. Location of Plants
    Locate near
      Raw materials/supplies   ____
      Customers/markets   ____
      Labor supply   ____
      Other (specify)   ____
  E. Focus of Plants
    Focus by
      Product   ____
      Process/technology/stage   ____
      Volume (long run vs. short run)   ____
  F. Degree of Mechanization
    Process Stage

	High	Low
1	____	____
2	____	____
3	____	____
etc.	____	____

Exhibit 8.3   (*continued*)

G. Choice of equipment
   Degree of specialization   General purpose ⟷ Special
   Set-up/changeover time   Low ⟷ High
   Technological risk/uncertaintly   Low ⟷ High
   Flexibility to volume change   Low ⟷ High
   Dedication of equipment   Pooled ⟷ Dedicated

H. Process Structure:
   Jumbled flow (flexible)   ____
   Disconnected line flow   ____
   Connected line flow   ____
   Continuous (systematic)   ____

V. *Manufacturing Infrastructure*

A. Production Planning and Control   (Circle your choice.)

Investment in forecasting	Low		High
Produce	To order		To stock
Inventory			
RM's	Low	Medium	High
W in P-decoupling	Low	Medium	High
Finished goods	Low	Medium	High
Schedule	Chase	Smoothed	Level
Reorder via	Reorder point		MRP
Track/monitor/expedite	Low		High

B. Subcontracting   Little   Much

C. Purchasing—investment in aggressive, sophisticated
       purchasing   Low-High

D. Quality Control

	Low		High
Inspect at	Receiving	In process	Final
Inspection frequency	Infrequent	Sampling	100%

E. Work-force management   (Circle your choice)

Worker discretion	Low	Average	High	
Wages versus community	Low	Average	High	
Incentive wages	None	Some	All	
Job content	Narrow		Broad	
Cycle time	Short		Long	
Pacing via	Supervision	Schedule	Standards	Machine
Training	Little		Much	Paced

F. Controls/Reports   (Circle your choice)

Focus:	Time	Quality	Investment	Cost
Investment in controls		High	Medium	Low

G. Manufacturing Organization
   Organizational emphasis   (high/medium/low)

Operations	_____	Note that only a
Production control and		few functions can
planning	_____	be given
		organizational
		emphasis

Exhibit 8.3 *(continued)*

Personnel (labor relations)	_____	
Industrial/manufacturing engineering	_____	
Maintenance	_____	
Purchasing	_____	
Quality control	_____	
Control of costs/controller	_____	
Functional organization versus project/product versus other type of organization		(Circle one.)
Centralized vs. decentralized control		(Circle one.)
Role of a central staff group	Small	Large
Coordination with		
Marketing:	Loose	Tight
Engineering:	Loose	Tight
Customers:	Infrequent	Continued

analytical process, whereas Exhibit 8.3 is a step-by-step approach for redesigning or synthesizing a production system. It takes the management through the criteria for judging manufacturing performance, the statement of the manufacturing task, and the desired economic structure by using a set of approximately 15 choices to make in designing the equipment and process technology and about 30 choices of manufacturing infrastructure. The list can be used first to indicate what ought to be and then the present manufacturing system can be compared.

The manager should be constantly asking which criteria in overall success (see Chapter 5) will be maximized by each choice made. The production planning control system, for example, shows eight basic choices in the design of a production control system, and the system designer must make each choice with the objective of designing a production system that in total best meets the criteria in line with the key focus required by the manufacturing task. Similarly, in work-force management, the analyst can ask, "If our manufacturing task is, for example, to produce a customized set of low-volume customer specials in a high-technology set of productions, what type of wages system makes sense?"

Subjecting the production system to this type of manufacturing audit uncovers inevitable inconsistencies and helps the manufacturing team to focus every element of the system on achieving the organization's current manufacturing task.

Since the first edition of this book in 1978, the new microprocessor-based manufacturing technologies have begun to be diffused into industry.

The questions around these new equipment, process, and control technologies center not on whether they will have an impact, but on what that impact will be—how to harness it to competitive advantage and speed it along while prudently managing the substantial risks involved. The next four chapters focus on these issues, beginning with the question of how the manager can develop understanding of manufacturing technologies sufficient to form the basis for making competent choices in a rapidly changing technological world.

THE IMPACT OF NEW MANUFACTURING TECHNOLOGY

These four chapters focus on the new manufacturing technologies, including robots, lasers, CAD, CAM, flexible machining centers, and computer-integrated manufacturing, and the opportunities and challenges they present. Chapter 9 makes the point that managers cannot afford to be technology aversive and suggests some basic ways for managers to gain vital understandings of equipment and process technologies. Chapter 10 examines some of the reasons that these new technologies are penetrating industry slowly, in contrast to their apparently superb advantages. Chapter 11 looks in more depth at the human resources implications of new technology. Chapter 12 points out that to strategic planners the new technology offers a whole new set of possibilites for using manufacturing as a competitive, strategic tool.

CHAPTER 9

Technology and the Manager

A persistent pattern seen in the autopsies of the major operating crises of large corporations and of the final failures of many small companies is the inability of one or more key managers to understand and to manage the technologies* of their businesses. Analysis of the careers of executives who topped off their advancement in positions lower than those that their education and basic abilities should have allowed often reveals a similar pattern: lack of knowledge, skills, and/or personal confidence in their competence to deal with and manage the technologies of their firms.

In an age dominated by technology and technological change, technology demands on managers are substantial and growing. But many managers are negative, reluctant, or simply untrained in their attitudes regarding the technologies on which their businesses are often based. Similarly, many managers work toward mastering basic skills and techniques in finance, marketing, control, and human relations, while openly expressing their lack of interest or confidence in building strength in the technology relevant to their work.

The importance of technology to corporations is evident. Corporations that make products or offer services must make decisions involving their technologies when they design products or plan services, choose equipment and processes, and devise operating facilites, distribution, and information systems. Because these decisions involve large commitments of funds and, often more important, large blocks of irreplaceable time, they are some of the most vital and critical of management decisions. Once made, their reversal or even a major shift is apt to be difficult or even impossible. Unwise decisions on technological issues are frequently fatal in a small business.

*In this chapter, *technology* denotes the set of physical processes, methods, techniques, tools, and equipment by which products are made or services rendered.

In many industries, product and process technologies are changing so fast that technological forecasting is a key skill. Entire industries are vulnerable to almost overnight technological revolution. And for U.S. industry as a whole, forced to compete against low-cost foreign labor with strategies often based on product superiority and constant new product and process development, it appears that management of operations, manufacturing, and engineering—and hence, technology—is growing more critical.

Although many factors contribute to individual and institutional aversion to technology, at least five assumptions appear significant:

1. It is usually assumed that technological decisions can best be delegated to technical experts, such as engineers.
2. It is often believed that many years of training are required to become competent in a technology.
3. It is often believed that only engineers and scientists can cope with technology-based decisions.
4. Most managers who are neither engineers nor scientists feel somewhat inadequate in matters of technology: they fear to appear stupid or foolish before managers "who know"; they stay away from things they don't understand; they defer to "experts"; they don't try to learn the technology either because others are already too far ahead or they feel it would take too much time to keep up.
5. Conventional wisdom about managing exalts the delegator, the manager who is never caught up in details. Many managers are reluctant to engage in learning technology that may not seem to be part of his or her job.

Such technology-aversive behavior may result in serious business problems and risks of personal obsolescence, and such behavior unfortunately compounds itself because lack of knowledge breeds lack of confidence.

Technology-averse top managers face a dilemma: They cannot escape exposure to technological change. Yet, they can seldom delegate choice of technology decisions to lower levels or to technical specialists because such decisions are so pervasive in their effects on product, markets, finance, and ability to compete that few lower-level managers have the breadth of facts and skills necessary for making wise decisions.

Individual executives who are technology aversive are dangerous to themselves and to their employers. Yet competence in understanding and handling technology appears difficult to acquire, risking exposure of one's perspective to the bottomless pit of seductive specific knowledge. What to do?

It is the thesis of this chapter that an intelligent manager can learn to understand and to deal effectively with technology and that this process is by no means difficult when approached from a managerial viewpoint. Experience shows that essential skills can in fact be readily developed. What is usually sufficient is a framework consisting of a few basic concepts and a set of questions, which can lead to the acquisition of that knowledge and those insights needed by a manager.

How can a manager "master" a technology to which engineers and scientists devote their professional lives? The answer is that a manager's mastery consists of basic understandings that are far less detailed than those required by engineers and scientists and that are quite different in kind. Managers need to know the answers to certain limited questions about a given set of equipment or a process technology. These questions can be identified and placed in a useful conceptual framework.

The balance of this chapter will be devoted to the development of a "basic technology framework," which managers might use as a start in understanding and dealing with the equipment processes and technologies of their industries.

A MANAGERIAL APPROACH TO EQUIPMENT AND PROCESS TECHNOLOGY

The manager needs to acquire and use three concepts or ideas or understandings about equipment and process technology. These are stated briefly here and dealt with subsequently in the same order.

Idea No. 1—The Pervasive Influence of a Technology

Because a given equipment and process technology (EPT) creates demands and requirements on all other elements of an operating system, all parts of the system must be designed and managed so as to be congruent and compatible with the chosen EPT. The choice of EPT is, therefore, the primary determinant of every operating system.

Idea No. 2—A Manager's Understanding of Technology

For the purpose of management decision making, any EPT can be described and understood in terms of four basic parameters:

1. What it costs.
2. What it will do.
3. What it requires.
4. The degree of certainty of the above information.

Idea No. 3—Technology, Economics, and Operations Management

A given EPT largely determines the economics and limitations of an operating system. These, in combination with the competitive strategy of the firm, determine those few particularly difficult factors or problems that are keys to success or failure of the operating system.

These three ideas form the basis of an effective managerial understanding of equipment and process technology. They can provide a framework useful for decision making, while relieving anxieties concerning the subject of technology, building confidence, and eliminating technology-aversive behavior.

Each of these three ideas will now be developed in further detail.

THE PERVASIVE INFLUENCE OF A TECHNOLOGY

Most products can be manufactured in more than one way. Choices usually exist in the selection of the equipment and the process. One alternative or set of alternatives must be chosen from a variety of possibilities.

An ordinary flashlight casing, for example, may be machined out of a metal bar; formed from sheet metal and soldered to form a tube; deep drawn on a press using a die; die-cast with a light metal and a mold; poured into a mold in a foundry and subsequently machined; cut out from brass, steel, aluminum, or copper tubing; blow-molded in polyethylene; or injection-molded in a variety of plastic materials. A company in the flashlight business has many choices and, once chosen, the EPT has a massive influence on the entire manufacturing system. The most obvious difference, of course, is in the production equipment itself, but that is only the beginning. Compare a deep-drawing EPT with injection-molding EPT: both use metal dies, but there are major differences as shown in the table (p. 117).

This comparison of EPTs suggests how different would be the skills, the management systems and approaches, and the problems involved in a metal-flashlight-casing operation as compared to a plastic-based one.

Two features are particularly striking. First, the scheduling and inventory system is vastly more complex in the metalworking plant where several operations must be performed on the same part. Paperwork must be provided to take care of moves from machine to machine, and capacity must be planned and scheduled. In plastics—one operation.

The second major contrast is in the entire area of the work force, skills training, and supervision. The lighter, cleaner, more automated work in the plastics plant will allow for a lower-skilled, lower-wage-rate job structure, with key technical and personnel administration skills lodged in a relatively few, more highly paid employees.

	Metal Drawing	Plastic Molding
Equipment	Massive press	Press size depends on capacity
Raw Materials	Metal sheets	Many plastics
Tools	Die set—male and female	Split halves
Building	Heavy foundations to handle weight and impact	Ordinary floor
Engineering Mfg.	Mechanical, metal expertise	Plastics, hydraulics expertise
Maintenance	Mechanical	Mechanical, hydraulic
Operator	Heavier work, higher skill	Lighter work, relatively lower skill
Supervisor Skills	Managing fairly skilled workers	Lower skilled work force and machine troubleshooting
Inventory	Sheet metal and in-process	Plastic powder and finished goods
Operations	May require several and finishing step	One
Scheduling	Potentially complex	Simple
Safety	Dangerous	Safer
Quality/Precision	Depends on die and machine physical setup	Depends on die and machine timing and cycle
Costs	Depends especially on die condition and setup	Depends especially on short cycle and changeovers
Flexibility- product change	Die change necessary	Die change necessary
volume change	Adds dies, machines, shifts or moves to higher speed equipment	Adds dies, machines, shifts; cycle limited
Potential for automation	Combine operations with transfer dies, install part location sensors, etc.; expensive to mechanize	Largely automatic. Not so expensive to mechanize

The Pervasive Technology

Each EPT brings with it its own demands and characteristics. The effects of an EPT may be seen as taking place on three levels:

PRIMARY Direct effects on the product, costs, investment and basic requirements.

SECONDARY Demands on the operating system infrastructure.

TERTIARY Effects on the performance ability of the operating system.

These three levels are illustrated in Table 9.1 and subsequently in Chapter 11.

Table 9.1. The Influence of an EPT on an Operating System

INFLUENCES Operating System Elements	Costs	Quality	Investment	Flexibility Product Change Volume Change	Customer Service
PRIMARY Direct Effects	Operator skills Labor Labor and material costs Set up and changover Supervision Maintenance skills	Precision Reliability Appearance Maintenance	Capacity Original Cost Economic life Inventory Utilities and building Certainty–stability of technology	Product range producible Setup and changeover time Lead times	Cycle time Total lead time
SECONDARY Systems Requirements	Purchasing System Burden rates Cost control system Work force management Mfg. eng. reqs. Mfg. organization structure	Maintenance system QC system Supervision Mfg. eng. reqs.	Inventory control system Capacity planning system Capital budgeting system	Production planning and scheduling system New product capacity and lead times	Customers promise system Organization for introduction of new product into mfg.
TERTIARY Performance Ability	Total costs Cost flexibility with volume change Product change	Quality performance Reliability	Return on investment	Ability to compete on profitable basis with change in volume and products	Ability to compete

Note: This table, somewhat modified, is also discussed in Chapter 11.

At this point, it may be clear how a given EPT choice spreads its effects from the workplace to the entire operating system and, finally, to the ability of the system to perform in a competitive environment. The necessity for all parts of the system—the system infrastructure—to be congruent and mutually consistent follows.

This may seem simple. In actual practice, however, perfect internal consistency is difficult to achieve. There are many subtleties involved, as well as ambiguities, and real administrative difficulties in achieving a total operating infrastructure that is wholly consistent with the EPT employed. Several examples may illustrate the problem:

Plant A

PRODUCT   Medium-priced pine and birch furniture.
OLD EPT   Individual assembly and finishing of each piece of furniture.
NEW EPT   Conveyorized assembly and finishing.

When the process technology was changed, the wage system based on individual incentives was no longer appropriate because the conveyorized system paced the worker; one stoppage or problem slowed down the entire group. Lower skill levels were required, because the individual jobs became narrower in content and more specialized. Demands on the supervisors shifted from scheduling and checking production records to providing supplies, handling technical problems that slowed the line, and quality controls.

Thus work-force management, cost and quality controls, scheduling, and inventory-control-system requirements changed overnight with the adoption of the conveyor. The production-management group had to recognize the need for and carry out all these system changes simultaneously.

In practice this proved difficult—difficult to foresee which old system would be inappropriate and to make many changes all at once. The net result was almost two years of less than fully satisfactory operations. During that time, the new conveyor was considered something of a failure, because each one of the incongruent systems individually made the new operating system less than fully effective.

Plant B

OLD PRODUCT MIX   Low volumes of many different semiconductors.
NEW PRODUCT MIX   Higher volumes of fewer semiconductors combined with old
                   product mix.
EPT   General-purpose equipment with functional plant layout.*

*Equipment located by groups of similar functions, for example, all grinders in one location.

Here the product mix changed. The EPT and all system ingredients did not.

The general-purpose equipment and processes were very flexible, in essence, changing from one product to another was quick and easy. But no economies of scale were possible, for example, holes were drilled individually rather than punched en masse with a die. Wires were soldered by hand instead of by a programmed wire wrapper. The result was high costs, long cycle times, long queues at operations that were bottlenecked by large orders, and late deliveries. Separate EPTs were needed for the old products and for the new ones; so also were different wage systems, supervisory skills, and production and planning systems. But the management was reluctant to tamper with the system, because they were uncertain about the content of the future mix of business. At the same time they feared that setting up two separate systems would cause worker discontent and perhaps interfere with deliveries in both kinds of business and would require a major investment.

To summarize, the EPT is important and its choice is usually critical. Now how about some basic questions that managers might ask and answer in order to understand an EPT and to choose wisely among alternatives?

A MANAGER'S UNDERSTANDING OF TECHNOLOGY

Consider a simple example of equipment technology, a process for cutting grass, a lawn mower.

A lawn mower could be described to a prospective purchaser as follows: "It costs $228. It has a gasoline engine and cuts a 24-inch wide swath of grass and is well made by a well-known manufacturer."

A technology-aversive prospective buyer might say, "I'll take it," only to get home to the 8-inch grass and find that:

- The cutting technology was based on a reel moving past a cutter bar. It could not handle grass much higher than one-half the reel diameter. It simply pushed the 8-inch crop forward and down.
- It was self-propelled but had no effective free-wheeling device, so that it was not possible to work close to and around a formal garden.
- It took 30 minutes to change the cutting height so that hillside grass could be cut longer (to cut down on erosion) than lawn grass.
- It was not powerful enough to cut wet, thick grass going uphill.
- It did not mulch leaves.
- It had a two-cycle engine, which meant that oil had to be mixed with the gasoline each time the little tank was filled.

This buyer should have purchased an extra-powerful, four-cycle, self-propelled rotary mower with easy handling for tight maneuvering and with a simple height-adjustment mechanism.

Understanding the equipment and process technology of lawn mowing in order to make a wise purchase of machinery would have required the owner-manager to develop an accurate mental concept of the process of cutting grass, with the machine operating on the hillside and on the level, under a variety of conditions, with consideration for the operator's time, money, and skills. The most crucial mistake, of course, was in the choice of a reel mower rather than one with a rotary blade. But for a house with low, big glass windows and with close-by neighbors' houses that were similarly constructed, the buyer would have also needed to consider the danger from flying stones propelled by the rotary mower. In either case, a reasonably good conceptual approximation of the actual grass-cutting action might have suggested enough of the right questions to lead to other useful questions. Choosing EPTs in manufacturing or service industry operations has many parallels to the lawn-mower problem.

Basic Choices in EPTs

What are the basic choices in EPTs? What are the basic factors involved? In fact, the EPT decision must deal with four EPT characteristics:

1. *Size and Capacity.* Do we want one big machine or three smaller ones? Do we want extra capacity for contingency and growth and flexibility?
2. *General Purpose Versus Special Purpose.* A general-purpose technology will handle a broader range of products and/or materials with a simpler changeover from one to another. A special-purpose technology will handle one product or operation very well but is of limited flexibility, for example, an automatic screw machine versus a simple engine lathe.
3. *Precision and Reliability.* We must determine the degree of precision of product specification that the technology must produce and know the probabilities with which the technology will meet those specifications.
4. *Degree of Mechanization.* In general, the more mechanized and automatic an EPT, the more its original cost, with less dependence on operator energies, skills, and judgment, and with more dependence on maintenance, engineering, and supervision for its care, adjustment, and repair.

These four characteristics pose a set of trade-offs between operating costs and different performance capabilities. They also imply trade-offs and frequently difficult decisions about the choice of the entire operating infrastructure. Consider, for example, the effect on the number of workers and kinds of workers imposed by each of the four characteristics above. Then recognize that the numbers and skills of production workers in turn have major implications for the wage system, labor agreements, recruiting, selection, supervision, and so forth. The all-pervasive effects of EPT decisions radiate out in all directions.

The same range of effects and trade-offs would affect cost and quality controls, production planning and scheduling, plant engineering, and every other ingredient in a factory system. The complexity of the problem of choosing an EPT or operating with a given EPT is further compounded by the fact that size and capacity, general versus special purpose, precision and reliability, and degree of mechanization often place conflicting demands on various elements of the operating infrastructure that may be difficult or impossible to overcome. So where do we start in making EPT decisions?

Making EPT Decisions: Where to Start?

The place to start is with the actual physical process that takes place in the technology. What actually happens to the raw material itself? How does it happen? How does it work? What does the operator do? The executive needs to be able to draw or graphically describe for others what goes on in the equipment process. What are the machine's motions and actions?

If the manager's equipment is a machine tool, he or she must acquire the concept of the moving tool, the machine-held workpiece, the chip-making action—or whatever does the job. If his or her business depends on an electronic black box, hydraulic or physical analogies will often do: "This box regulates the electrical pressure that it sends out, smoothing its variations into an even, steady flow." In chemistry, a visualization of molecular particles combining or breaking apart under conditions of temperature or pressure can lead to sufficient understanding to sense accurately the kinds of things that might go wrong or that must be carefully controlled. The concept, for example, of a plastic resin being formed by molecules joining together in chains of varying lengths leads to an understanding of the polymerization process and its demands on the operator for precise, skillful, "sixth-sense" control of the reaction.

To summarize, *the first step is to acquire a fairly accurate analogy or visualization of the actual physical process taking place.* The manager who does not have this sense of what happens to the material in the EPT will never have any real perception and grasp of the EPT. A homely or familiar analogy is usually enough.

To acquire a working understanding of an EPT, it usually helps to draw a diagram and describe a physical analogy concerning what happens to the material during the process. How is it changed? What motions and actions take place in the equipment? What does the operator do? What must be done before the EPT can function? What must be done after the EPT operation? What can go wrong? What is most apt to go wrong?

Armed with a conceptual image of what happens in and around the EPT, a manager is well prepared to develop what she or he needs to know about the EPT. Four basic questions derived from *Idea No. 2*, cited earlier, usually will suffice.

1. What will it cost?
2. What will it do?
3. What will it require?
4. How certain are the above?

Every machine (or EPT) can be described within these four general parameters. Each may be elaborated somewhat, but the notion is simple. Taking each element in turn:

What Will It Cost?

EPT costs in general consist of initial investment cost, installation, debugging, and operating and continuing labor, material, maintenance, utilities, and other overhead costs. The economic life of the EPT may be used to annualize the initial investment costs, or they may be handled in a more sophisticated manner. All of this is simple and straightforward.

What Will It Do?

This may be more difficult but not necessarily so. A given EPT will perform certain physical activities that can be predicted and measured. They can be described in terms of the materials it will handle, the production output per hour (capacity), the range of product variations that can be produced, and the qualities of the product (e.g., specification, performance characteristics, tolerances, and reliability).

What Will It Require?

Every machine (or EPT) must be operated, started, stopped, loaded, unloaded, changed over from one product to another, maintained, repaired, and speeded up or slowed down as volume requirements change; its waste products must be disposed of. These are "operating requirements." Every machine or EPT also creates a set of "people require-ments"—human skills, which are largely determined by the technology. The numbers of operators, setup men, maintenance mechanics, or engi-neers are basically functions of the technology.

Any EPT has other basic requirements for space, utilities, and raw materials—needs that may often be routine but are sometimes critical to its performance.

How Certain Are the Above?

Another type of information and understanding vital to managerial com-petence in choosing and operating an EPT—the degree of certainty or uncertainty attending the cost, performance, and requirements data de-scribed to this point—will complete the basic four parameters of an EPT.

Old, well-proven EPTs in general have relatively few uncertainties re-garding their costs, performance, and requirements. The opposite is apt to be true of newer EPTs, particularly those "crowding the state of the art."

Critical uncertainties may be involved in the following factors:

TIME How long will this technology be superior to competitive EPTs? How long will this EPT last before it wears out or needs major maintenance?

RELIABILITY How often will the EPT produce the desired product quality? How often will the EPT produce at its expected capacity?

INFORMATION How sure are we about all the pieces of knowledge we have about the EPT?

These are sometimes the most difficult questions a manager must face in deciding about a new EPT. They are normal issues, because "newness" is a normal part of the problem: Do we or do we not adopt this new EPT? Buy this new machine? If it is new to the company, it immediately intro-duces uncertainties in the form of a learning period for company personnel to master its idiosyncrasies. If it is new to industry, there are apt to be many engineering and scientific imponderables to which time, effort, and expense are the only answers. In either case, a debugging process for working out the uncertainties and overcoming the problems as they emerge is a critical element in planning and organizing for a change in EPT.

Seasoned top operations managers learn that any intelligent and ener-getic management team can master an EPT over a period of time. Smooth-running facilities are apt to have had ample time to be debugged, improved, and systematized. But look out for change in an EPT! Established un-derstandings, operations, and systems are apt to be immediately undone;

production is interrupted, costs skyrockets, quality runs berserk. Abilities to predict, organize for, and handle these disruptions due to uncertainties in a change EPT separate the few fully successful managers from many others.

What particular skills and techniques are useful for the manager in dealing with the uncertainties of new or changed EPTs? Is scientific or engineering training essential to the manager because of these uncertainties? Is technology aversion perhaps the better part of wisdom when the uncertainty level creeps up?

In fact, the answer is still "no," because in many respects the professionally trained manager is at his or her comfortable best in coping with the uncertainties in EPTs. This is so because management training deals with uncertainties, applying useful techniques such as PERT, CPM, decision trees, sensitivity analysis, simulation, and the varieties of probabilities and statistics. Most uncertainties can be quantified and their outcomes evaluated; as a result, not only the risks (the "what ifs") but also the organizational mechanisms to minimize risks come clearly into focus. Furthermore, managers are in a position to demand and insist on the best technical and economic information available, and to be more impartial and objective about it than involved scientists and engineers.

Exhibit 9.1 summarizes the foregoing ideas about how a manager can learn to understand and work with EPT.

There remains now only the third and final "idea" to discuss. It deals with the inevitable connections between technology, economics, and the key problems in technologically based operations.

TECHNOLOGY, ECONOMICS, AND OPERATIONS MANAGEMENT

Idea No. 3 attempts to put the pieces together. Repeating it: "A given EPT largely determines the economics and limitations of an operating system, which, in combination with the competitive strategy of the firm, determine those few particularly difficult factors or problems that are keys to success or failure of the operating system."

Technology works in two ways:

1. The way it sets costs and outputs determines the basic economics of an EPT:
    a. Total costs
       Capital costs (equipment, facilities, and inventory)
       Direct costs (labor and material)
       Indirect supporting costs (utilities, maintenance, supervision, planning and scheduling, engineering)

Exhibit 9.1 Technology and the Manager:
A Manager's Understanding of Equipment and Process Technology

---

Step 1. Explain, Diagram, and Analogize the Physical Operation:
Why is the process necessary?
What happens to the material during the process?
What motions and actions take place in the equipment?
What does the operator do?
What must be done (load, make ready) before the EPT can function?
What must be done (unload, clean up) after the EPT operation?
What can go wrong?
What is most apt to go wrong?

Step 2. Identify Precisely Available Knowledge Concerning:

What the EPT Costs	What the EPT Will Do	What the EPT Requires
Original cost	Output/time	Materials
Economic life	(cycle,	Labor: skills, numbers / set up, operate, load, unload
Direct operating costs	capacity)	Supervision
	Range of products	Technicians
Indirect support costs	(specs, quality)	Maintenance
		Space: equipment, inventory
		Utilities: power, etc., waste, environmental impact

Step 3. Identify the Degree of Certainty/Uncertainty of the Knowledge in Step 2:
What is known for sure? How do you know?
What is the range of possible outcomes?
What would be the effect of each?
What is the best estimate of the probabilities of each?
Use managerial techniques for dealing with uncertainties and linked effects,
such as the following:
- PERT/CPM/network techniques,
- Decision trees,
- Simulation,
- Linear programming,
- Sensitivity analysis,
- Probabilities/statistics,

to quantify effects of alternate decisions.

---

b. The cost mix is critical

c. Costs versus volume (breakeven, fixed, and variable costs)

d. Economies of scale

e. Cost effects of product changes and changeovers

f. Paybacks—cash flow versus equipment costs

2. Technology also largely determines the set of constraints within which the equipment or process must operate. These are the *requirements* and the *what it will do* items of Exhibit 9.1. These abilities have, of course, a reciprocal, namely, *what it won't do* or the limitations of product range, output, quality, tolerances, and versatility—in a word, flexibility. Once the EPT is chosen, these factors, as well as the economic effects, are fairly well set.

How a Choice of Technology Impacts the Operating System

What is the effect of these constraints or inflexibilities on the firm and on the operation? Essentially, they place limitations and they create organizational or system demands, such as a particularly strong scheduling and inventory-control system or a maintenance system or a quality-control system. Take, for example, a new, highly automated auto-engine-block machining center:

Basically a general-purpose machine, it could produce only a very few ranges of engines without extensive changeover, had very high setup and changeover costs, and was very expensive to buy but required only a small labor force of highly skilled technicians to operate. This EPT brought with it certain "musts" for the operating system:

- There must be good forecasting, scheduling, and inventory control to minimize changeovers.
- There must be well-trained technicians available to minimize downtime.
- There must be a steady, dependable flow of uniformly high-quality castings to ensure high-volume operations.

The EPT also created a set of economics with high fixed costs, low variable costs, considerable savings with high volume, a high breakeven point, high costs for product changes, and a good cash-flow payback of volume stayed high and product changes were kept low.

The net result of these constraints and economics defined the key difficulties, focal manufacturing problems, and "the name of the game," in essence, what the management must be good at to succeed with this technology. In this case they had to be especially good at production planning, forecasting, scheduling, and inventory control. But since the firm's competitive strategy was to offer a broad, flexible, product line of engine options, it meant that the "name of the game" in their engine business was to handle product changes quickly and effficiently. Success depended on it, once that EPT had been adopted. Engine-plant organization reflected the requirements for good scheduling and inventory control plus special task-force teams set up to minimize downtime in product changeovers.

How an Industry is Affected by Its Basic Technology

One other example shows how technology in combination with competitive conditions determines the industry "name of the game," or what difficult tasks must be done well to succeed.

The steel industry is characterized by high capital costs, relatively low variable costs, few pieces of equipment (versus man, as in a machine shop), high transportation costs, considerable "art" versus science in the EPT, and high volumes of tonnages. These combine to produce the following manufacturing features of the industry:

- Great risks involved in a few pieces of equipment.
- Long and difficult start-ups.
- Very sticky costs.
- Emphasis on balance and integration.
- Considerable dependence on the skills of direct labor.
- Limitations on product mixes that can be efficiently produced by any one plant and manufacturing team.

These features in turn make the following elements of steel manufacturing critical:

- Choices of equipment and processes with particular regard to sizing-capacity-product capability.
- Plant location.
- Number and size of plants.
- Balance of equipment.
- Timing of choosing a new techology/technological uncertainty.

One particularly difficult problem in the industry is internal balance. There is the problem of maintaining balance at one integrated facility between blast furnace, steelmaking, and finishing capacity, while:

- Technology has steadily offered significant improvements in each stage.
- Changes in product mix are being demanded by the markets.

- Market demands are changing over geographical areas.
- Equipment changes are extremely expensive, risky, and time-consuming.

There is the further problem of changes in cost and product flexibility over the span of four stages: raw material, blast furnace, steelmaking, and steel finishing. By and large, the process is less flexible for cost and volume and mix and more flexible for product flexibility in the early stages and conversely in the later stages. A given plant can handle only certain products and certain volumes economically.

CONCLUSION

Exhibit 9.1 summarizes the ideas discussed in this chapter. In times of rapid technological change a manager cannot afford to be technology aversive. Managers increasingly compete with their own personal skills and attitudes concerning technology.

Technologies can be analyzed and characterized systematically by the nonengineer/scientist. Analogies can be worked out to develop conceptual understandings. The relationships among (1) an EPT, (2) its resulting economics, and (3) constraints are generally straightforward. These three factors largely determine the especially difficult aspects of managing any operations.

We turn now to a discussion of the new manufacturing technologies. The highly mechanized, automated "factory of the future" has been touted by its proponents for several decades as just about to happen. But the penetration of these technologies has in fact been modest and pedestrian and, to many, very disappointing. In the next chapter this phenomenon is examined as to both the specific content of the factory of the future and the economic and managerial factors impeding its progress.

CHAPTER 10

The Factory of the Future—
Always in the Future?

For 35 years the "factory of the future" has promised a new era in manufacturing. But that new era has remained continually in the future. The postwar promise of sweeping technological progress has yet to materialize. Neither in competitive advantage nor in attractive and satisfying quality of work lives have the hopes born in the 1940s been realized. Yet year after year, futurists have continued to predict substantial changes just ahead. But the fact is that changes of that sort have not come about.

This is not to say that the factory of 1985 is entirely like the factory of 1945. There have been changes in equipment, working environments, and managerial controls. But for the most part these changes have been modest and evolutionary, inching along year after year. Thirty-five years ago the expectation was that the factories of the future would be not only clean, relatively quiet, attractive places to work in, but, equally important, the uses of servo-mechanisms and of a whole new age of machine tools and industrial equipment would result in factories that were more economic and able to produce at lower cost and better quality. The ongoing promises of wholesale automation, mechanization, robotry, computerized, hands-off decisionmaking, and a radically improved quality of industrial working life (QWL) have remained just around the corner.

Meanwhile, the U.S. factory has come under increasingly severe pressure of foreign competition; it has frequently proved noncompetitive; it repels many capable young people; it seethes with a discontented labor force. As an institution the factory is failing the nation. It is surprising and, indeed, ironical, therefore, that such urgently needed change is coming about so slowly.

Will the American factory establishment reform itself before it dies? The question, however dramatic, is beginning to force itself into the open. Some observers are predicting that the bulk of U.S. manufacturing will gradually move to Asia as the U.S.A. and Canada continue to slip until they can no longer produce competitively in many industries [1]. So the paradox today is that unless the "factory of the future" is finally but quickly made a reality, the institution's future may be perilously and drastically impaired.

The purpose of this chapter is to examine some of the reasons for this surprisingly slow progress in the face of mounting needs for change, and to identify managerial and technological possibilities for breaking the present logjam so as to create factories that can compete and survive. A principal premise of this chapter is that the "factory of the future" must be competitive and it must be socially viable or there will be no such institution in the future as we know it today.

The paper will first focus on certain dilemmas faced by American manufacturing management, including our limited technological progress, QWL, and competitive strength. Following this, we seek to identify the causes of these past and present blockages. The paper then turns to look at the near term future, which, in fact, now appears to be drawing close to offering solutions to the roadblocks of the past, leading us to the perhaps surprising conclusion that the "factory of the future" may finally become a reality in the next decade.

TODAY'S DILEMMAS

In an age known for technological miracles technological progress in the factory has been startlingly and disappointingly modest. The average age of machine tools is in excess of 18 years. Even factory buildings by the thousands are old and obsolete. Our productive equipment is typically years behind our international competitors.

The promise of high degrees of mechanization and automation has been slow to come about. The much heralded "robot" barely made its appearance in 1980, albeit with much publicity [2]. Assembly lines are little different from what they used to be, and while there have been gradual increases in productivity, even this modest rate of increase has slowed considerably.

Even numerically controlled machine tools and numerically controlled servo-mechanisms in the factory have been surprisingly slow to be adopted. Numerically controlled machines, while making a gradual penetration, still only account for a relatively small percentage of machine tools and a minute proportion of production. Process control computers have made a large penetration in some industries, but even this remarkable tool has been adopted slowly relative to the number of possible applications. We hear a great deal about the computer in the factory, and yet computerized production controls are in their infancy and the literature is rich with data citing disappointing results, far from the full potentialities of this equipment [3].

On all these counts, technological progress has been much slower than might have been expected. But it is equally clear that the availability of equipment and the existence of the essential technological ideas, concepts, and mechanisms have far outrun the ability of the modern factory system to absorb these new technologies. Somehow management in the manufacturing world has apparently been unable to assimilate fully the new technologies that engineers and scientists have made available.

Similarly, in working conditions, environment, and the perceived quality of work life, progress has also been disappointing. While certainly factories are cleaner, quieter, and generally more pleasant to work in than they were 30 years ago, the attractiveness of the manufacturing plant to our able young as a place to work is very low. And at this time there are more than 200 documented experiments in improving QWL, but research shows that a large proportion of these experiments are given up as failures after 3–4 years. There are three national institutions that are working at research and experimentation in improving productivity and the quality of work life. But the existence of these institutions is simply another piece of evidence that a serious problem exists. Meanwhile, the factory as a place to work continues to have a low appeal to the outstanding young, future-skilled technicians and managers urgently needed as attested by widespread shortages in technicians, skilled maintenance workers, setup and skilled machine operators, and in high-potential supervision.

The management of today's factories also poses substantial dilemmas to corporate management. These dilemmas center on not only issues of quality of work life and managing human resources better, but also encompass serious economic problems in many industries. In industries with old and stable technologies and mature product life cycles and products (such as steel, textiles, electrical equipment automobiles, paper, and appliances and furniture), managements have been faced with the financial problems of needing expensive new equipment and processes simply in order to survive. Yet manufacturing managers have been unable in many cases to secure the necessary funds from their managements for investing in new plants that might offer lower costs, better quality, and the ability to compete more successfully.

The final set of dilemmas centers around competitive strength in many

U.S. industries. The bottom line is simply that foreign competition has increased its share of sales in many industries where U.S. factories are less able to compete than they were in the past. It is important to note, however, the declining competitive strength is due not only to high costs. It is often due to factories being unable to produce adequate quality levels or to match the ability of foreign factories to introduce new products quickly and handle change flexibly.

TODAY'S PARADOX

The net result of this combination of circumstances is that today the factory is seriously damaging the nation's well-being. It has been a disappointing institution, disappointing not only to its customers but also to its employees, to its owners, and to its management. It is an institution that has not only failed to move ahead as promised 30 years ago, but is, in fact, in many corporations decadent and decaying.

The surprising fact of this gradual decay of an institution long at the heart of national economic progress and prosperity is hard to understand. Here is an institution in which engineers and technology have made available remarkable machinery, equipment, processes, and controls. But this institution only seems able to adopt new technology very slowly. And its organizational processes and ability to absorb new technology are apparently marginal, such that the process is nearly always accompanied by "bugs," delays, and many failures that frequently are blamed on the technology. But technology has apparently far outrun the ability of the factory as an institution to use it. We have machine tools and processes, computers, controls, numerical control, direct numerical control, computer-aided design in manufacturing available, far in excess of its being purchased, applied, and successfully used. And all of this is developing at the very time that the factory institution appears to need new technology in equipment and processes and controls far more than ever in its history.

The paradox is illustrated by the picture of many industries floundering and losing market share to foreign competition because of high costs, low quality, and inability to compete while at the very moment engineers, technologists, are offering machinery processes and equipment that would appear to answer many of manufacturing's problems. Furthermore, in foreign plants such technology is typically adopted years in advance of North American manufacturing facilities.

As a result of all this, we have the ironic situation of industry loaded with unused technology yet in trouble in terms of competition, costs, flexibility for volume and product change, return on investment, ability to attract young, able people, "blue-color-blues," worker discontent, lay-offs, unemployment, strikes, plant closings, and a gradual shift in the economy from manufacturing to service industries and from exports to imports.

It would be simplistic to blame these problems on manufacturing managers, workers, unions, technology, or engineers, or, indeed, any single major source. And it would be wrong to generalize about all industries when the problems clearly vary from one industry to another. Nevertheless, it does seem clear that U.S. manufacturing industry is beset with competitive, economic, and managerial problems as never before while technological progress and technological opportunities and possibilities are at an all-time high. What is going on in manufacturing management that contributes to such a paradox? Let me turn first to look at recent history.

MANUFACTURING 1945–1980

The causes of the present industrial malaise and set of dilemmas are by no means simple, but it is clear that many changes are affecting the performance of the factory as an institute. Externally, the first major change is a vast increase in competitive pressures. The rise of the diversified corporation has resulted in more companies competing in more markets and more industries. International competition and international trade have been steadily rising. Not only is manufacturing volume increasing long-range in Europe and the Common Market countries, but also in Asia, particularly in Japan, Singapore, Korea, and Taiwan. As a result, no industry has been immune from the threat of foreign competition, now even including the semi-conductor industry in which America had such an enormous head start.

Another set of changes has had a considerable impact on the factory, namely, shorter product life-cycles. Here, engineers and technology can take the credit or the blame. The onrushing changes in technology and products in almost every industry have combined with increased competition to bring about shorter product lives, more products, more competitive products, more products being introduced, more products phasing out, exponentially increasing management, and operations complexity in manufacturing.

Outside the factory, in management, there have also been many changes. In the 1950s more companies adopted modern marketing methods, focusing on new product development and product management. The firm's responsiveness to markets and customers was improved through more scientific market research and information systems. In the 1960s, modern management methods also came to be developed and widely adopted in financial management. The age of dominating financial controls, yearly operating plans, and monthly budgets and sharp-eyed controllers arrived. Companies grew to be managed on a divisionalized, decentralized basis with annual budgets, quarterly budgets, and strict monthly controls against these budgets. Profit centers proliferated. To reduce top management surprises and increase a sense of management control, strict financial controls and measurement systems were gradually perfected. They now reign supreme.

Measures of return on investment and return on assets came to be vigorously applied to the factory with more demanding pressures not only on inventory controls but also on paybacks on new machinery and equipment. When these new controls were combined with high interest rates, the net result was that the factory manager faced ever more administrative hassle and difficulty in justifying the purchase of new machinery and equipment. The hurdle rates in many industries climbed to 35–50%, meaning that new machinery and equipment were often simply not purchased.

These problems, external to the factory, gradually resulted in a whole new set of internal factory management problems. Not only did there come to be more products and shorter product life-cycles, more customer specials and lower order quantities, but at the same time financial pressures were applied to factory management as never before. Then entered a new set of problems.

Rising from the factory floor came determined employee demands and heightened expectations for job content and fulfillment. In the late 1960s and 1970s there developed new pressures from workers, sometimes called "the blue-collar-blues." The work force frequently began to show its discontent in the form of low quality, productivity, and lessened cooperation. Different age groups acted differently. More pressure was placed on factory managements to keep workers "happy" and productive. And so factory management was squeezed down for lower costs and better products while the unions (or strong motivation for union avoidance) pressured upward.

But in factory management itself there was generally only the slowest awareness of the forces and realities of these external pressures. Most factories were not managed all that differently in the 1970s as compared to the 1940s and 1950s. By and large, manufacturing management was dominated by engineers and people with technical training and a technical point of view. But the problems in their factories grew much more broad, complex, and more multi-dimensional than strictly technology- and engineering-based. Manufacturing managers faced economic problems, control problems, workforce problems, and confounding dilemmas of satisfying top management on a multitude of conflicting performance criteria [4].

These problems require a new kind of manufacturing manager. In the past management issues centered largely on industrial engineering and manufacturing or process engineering, for the emphasis was on efficiency, productivity, time-and-motion, and methods. In the 1970s the issues shifted more toward managing large numbers of demanding and often strident workers, and required the ability to handle more complexity in product mix, production inventory, and cost controls and scheduling, the ability to introduce more new products and change products and volumes flexibly, the ability to compete successfully in a much more difficult competitive environment, impacted with not only international competitors but also with a new mix of domestic competitors.

In this sense, the age of mass production and industrial engineering as we once knew it, is gone. In most industries, there are fewer products produced strictly on a mass production basis, and the "principles" of efficiency and productivity are no longer adequate as the basis for successful competition. Nor are merely technical skills and insights sufficient to cope with strong-minded, top management applying the new and demanding financial tools, ratios, and performance measures that are in use today. Factory managers are too often outgunned and outmanned by sophisticated professional managers at the top, while frequently outmaneuvered by labor and worker groups within. The factory manager educated primarily in terms of engineering disciplines is frequently unable to compete and hold his or her own.

Seen in this sense, the world has now moved away from and beyond many engineering-educated and oriented factory managers and their ability to handle problems successfully in factory management. But the situation today and in the 1990s will undoubtedly continue to grow in complexity. The conflicting pressures of today will not go away for we can see no diminution of the ingredients: (1) more sources of competition; (2) technological change; (3) top management sophisitication and controls, and (4) worker demands for better QWL.

What does all this imply to manufacturing management? One clear conclusion is that there is a necessity to get out ahead of the problems— away from a reactive mode. The factory has long lead-times. For the whole system to be able to cope all of its long time-frame ingredients must be "right." If the factory has the wrong equipment, or is in the wrong place, is the wrong size, or has the wrong organization, production control, or human resource management practices, it will not survive successfully. But note that these are issues of structure and policy rather than operation. And factories have been operated for 100 years with an *operating* point of view, focusing on short term issues.

For these reasons, the emphasis in successfully managed manufacturing firms is gradually shifting to long-range structure and manufacturing policy issues. Manufacturing managers who are focusing on operations, on daily, weekly, monthly, or even yearly bases now find themselves in impossible one-down positions when they end up with the wrong structure in their facilities. We have moved into a new era in manufacturing in which an engineering education and the engineering point of view are no longer adequate. Management of manufacturing now has to make decisions not on an annual basis, but typically looking ahead 5–10 years with a more strategic point of view.

So manufacturing management focus must shift from operations to manufacturing strategy and structure. This is a new and fundamentally different way of looking at manufacturing management than conventionally applied in the past [5]. More change is called for, not less. But if manufacturing has been so slow in adapting and reforming itself in the past 30 years, what hope is there of now making the urgent, yet fundamental changes in self-governance that appear vital for survival? What is it that has made it a slow organism to adapt to change?

WHY THE FACTORY HAS BEEN SO SLOW
TO ADAPT AND REFORM ITSELF

1. Four major causes for slow adaptation appear influential.

   The factory has been dominated from the top by a short-term financially oriented point of view, developed and carried out by financially dominated top managements. This has resulted in hurdle rates for justifying new equipment and processes that have been so excessive that our factories have been growing steadily older. The short-term financial point of view also dominates decisions in making investments in quality of work life, improving working environments, developing better organizations for managing and attracting people, and, indeed, in making difficult long-term investments in systems for quality and production control. So the financial, short-term point of view has been seriously at fault.

2. Slow progress in mechanization and automation has also been a result of manufacturing management that has been strong on operations but short on strategic, long-term planning. The emphasis has been, quite naturally, on industrial engineering productivity, meeting schedules, and maintaining efficiency on a month-by-month basis. We have been unable, often enough, to look at total, complete factory systems and

to make the broad, whole-cloth changes that are necesssary. Changes are made one by one, piece-meal. When one part of the system is changed, it throws another into disequilibrium. And as each change takes a year or two to make, such as a change in equipment or inventory control or organization, the whole is never quite right.

3. The major criteria for manufacturing success has been on "efficiency" rather than on ability to compete. But a manufacturing plant may be measured on at least seven criteria rather than merely productivity and efficiency:

   a. Cost and efficiency
   b. Quality/product reliability
   c. Delivery cycle
   d. Delivery reliability
   e. Investment
   f. Flexibility for product change
   g. Flexibility for volume change

   The criteria themselves are trade-offs. The manufacturing system is technologically limited (such as an aircraft, a machine tool, a boat) in its performance. It cannot be superb in one performance characteristic without hurting another. Choices must be made. The system must be designed for excellence on one or two of these criteria and the others done as well as possible after that excellence is achieved.

   How to choose the one or two criteria for excellence? Leading manufacturing executives choose their area of outstanding performance based on corporate strategic needs. This is the process of developing manufacturing strategy.

4. Finally, it seems clear that management has not been offered the right equipment, systems, technology, and tools by engineers. The engineering profession has been superb at developing individual technologies (for example, automated machine tools and direct numerical control). But when these magnificent new innovations have been applied, they have usually proven slow to be effective and economic. For example, in advanced computer-based production control systems, research makes it clear that very few of these systems work out to be nearly as economical or as useful as originally expected. They take years to improve and the payoffs in most cases are quite different from those projected (not necessarily worse, but different).

   Equipment and process technology that often looks great to the engineer goes unsold or is adapted very slowly because it does not match or mesh with existing equipment or is so radical as to cause managements to be prudently chary.

EPTs available therefore are generally far in advance of those accepted and put in place. The reasons for this are complex but they surely include the following:

a. Management, caution based on experience of failures, delays, and fiascos;

b. Offering components rather than systems;

c. Payoff/capital budget systems that focus only on quantitative and usually dollar-identified ingredients;

d. Technology that does not offer what is needed (more on this later).

All of these factors and certainly others have kept the factory of the future always in the future.

WHAT IS NEEDED

But while the factory of the future is needed now, it is simply not being established. The rate of change is too modest to meet the competitive needs of the times. For the economic needs are substantial; even the survival of some industries and the possible revival of others already very sick are at stake.

The requirements for change in factories are obvious and, while industry by industry specifications are beyond the scope of this article, on a generalized basis factories that can survive competitively in the future will meet the following needs:

- Competitive production costs for reduced run lengths and increasing product mix complexity.
- Reliable, consistent quality.
- Ability to reduce costs with decreased volumes.
- Ability to introduce new products quickly.
- Ability to change over products without excessive delays.
- Adequate return on investment in equipment and inventory.
- Competitively short delivery cycles.
- Ability to meet delivery promises, i.e, be predictable.

In many companies and industries factories today fall short on one or more of these criteria. In most cases advanced technology is available yet not being used. In metalworking, for example, completely mechanized, computerized systems of machine tools and transfer machines are available for a near hands-off operation operated and monitored by direct numerical control and a series of real-time factory-located mini-computers. But aside from some partial, experimental pilot operations there is little to see of such plants in operation today. In the process industries more progress has been made, but the truly advanced installations are limited to large plants with limited product mix.

Meanwhile, in the face of available technology waiting for acceptance and installation, today's factory must change if it is to attract capable people and hold them with an adequate level of perceived quality of working life. Here technology lags rather than leads.

Few technologies are designed to improve QWL (quality of work life). Some have been developed to provide minimal or improved safety and health conditions (e.g., paint spraying booths, and coal mining equipment), but factory production equipment is developed 99% for reasons of product, economics, and technology. Studies of QWL show that the workers' perception of life at work is influenced not only by factors of supervision and social interrelationships but by the actual processes involved in doing the work. Important factors concern repetition, physical stress, use of judgment, and skill levels required [6].

We turn now from why change in the factory has been so slow to consider whether and how a more radical pace of change might take place. Some or all of the numerous negative factors that have been holding back change would have to be eliminated or moderated. These roadblocks can be grouped into four principal areas:

1. Inadequate technology.
2. Backward managerial assumptions and processes.
3. Unfavorable economics.
4. Negative worker reaction.

INADEQUATE TECHNOLOGY

The equipment and process technology (EPT) offered during the past 30 years has been inadequate to equip the factory of the future because the EPTs have simply not met the needs of business. New and modern EPTs have moved in a grand scale in certain process industries such as chemicals, paper, steel, plywood, and petro-chemicals, where giant economies of scale have been offered. But in some industries—such as metalworking, assembly, electronics, furniture, textiles, construction, shoes, apparel, plastic modeling, printing, packaging, electrical machinery, transportation equipment, boat building, foundries, toys—the new EPTs have been evolutionary and typically creeping in their progress. There has been more mechanization, to be sure, but the factories still have many people, while fewer direct labor personnel, a higher fraction of indirect labor, a great deal of man-handled loading, unloading, adjusting, setup, scheduling, and record-keeping.

This slow progress has been limited by the technology available. By and large, the new EPTs for sale have typically failed to meet the strategic needs of the business because of one or more of the following sets of problems:

- Too costly, relative to their benefits.
- Inflexible, in terms of product and material variety, changeovers, setups.
- Designed to be efficient only on long runs and high daily volumes.
- Full of "bugs" and the problems inherent in new processes.

Companies have typically spent money freely for product innovation, but generally have been more reluctant to invest in process innovation. The EPTs that have been developed have generally been offered by specialized equipment producers, each doing one part or step in the process. As a result, the individual EPTs may have performed satisfactorily but they did not coordinate, mesh, or span over enough process steps so as to eliminate people and overhead and produce major economies. Machine tool companies, for example, concentrate on their specialities: milling, turning, drilling. Some firms have offered machining centers but few have offered fully integrated and coordinated total operations sequences, including transfer mechanisms and computerized controls for low volume manufacturing and sufficient product and volume flexibility.

So the EPT industry has seemingly been unable to always read customer needs and develop their product lines accordingly. With the age of mass production behind us, in addition to shorter runs and more customer specials, EPTs have not been offered to solve the cost, quality, and technical problems in any but the high volume process industries.

This is at first a mystery in itself, but the reasons are probably based on the following:

- Slow-moving technical capabilities.
- Excessive specialization.
- Fragmentation in EPT manufacturing industries.
- The cyclical nature of equipment buying.
- Limited and narrow engineering capabilities.
- The economics of EPT design and production that make new, integrated general purpose equipment expensive, risky, and time-consuming to design and build, requiring virtually assured markets.

And much of the above is due to excessive specialization among engineers as well as equipment firms and inability to design fully integrated manufacturing facilities.

So a major key to slow progress has been inadequate technology, which has offered high cost, large-scale economy, mass production, process-type EPTs with insufficient flexibility for product and volume changes and inadequate systems for integrating whole, coordinated facilities, and generally with 2–4 years of continuing development necessary prior to meeting design specifications consistently. What promises to be different in the future?

The answer is—a great deal! Perhaps even radical, spectacular, order of magnitude changes in EPTs are ahead. The new technology that is already starting to make a major difference is in micro-electronics, which is offering a whole new wave of EPTs in virtually every industry. EPTs, which can think, react, self-correct, adjust to product and volume changes, offer general purpose flexibility and special purpose economies, coordinate with other process links, reduce scheduling, paperwork, indirect labor, and overhead costs, and offer a whole new range of versatility and even cost reduction, are now becoming available. And micro-electronics is only a part of the picture.

Goldhar and Avakian [7] have compiled a list of what they call "trends in technology," which capture not only these sweeping changes in micro-electronics, but related changes in industrial technologies as well:

- Computers of all sizes.
- Micro-electronics.
- Robots and automated assembly.
- Advanced computer-controlled machine tools.
- Lasers and other "exotic" processing techniques.
- New materials and increased understanding of their behavior during processing.
- The embodiment of process design in software rather than hardware.
- Data-intensive production tasks.
- Systems optimization techniques.
- Integration of physical conversion activities with information and control systems.
- Distributed processing capability for both data and materials.
- New joining techniques.
- More sophisticated sensors (especially optical).
- Nondestructive testing.
- Low-cost video and telecommunications.
- Improved software capabilities.

- Multi-purpose machines and manufacturing "cells" (flexible manufacturing).
- Dedicated systems (product family/group technology).

These changes offer new generations of EPTs that are advanced by orders of magnitude. They offer potential answers to many, if not all, of the above mentioned drawbacks and problems in EPTs offered in the past.

The new technologies are, of course, no panacea. They require more knowledge and sophistication to select, acquire, and implement. They will test the abilities of engineers and managers and rapidly make outdated a generation of technical people who cannot cope. Furthermore, they demand as well as offer more in the way of a systems approach: poorly designed or based on only partially complete information, new integrated technology and systems will be as disastrous as ever.

Nevertheless, the conclusion is, for the first time now, that essential technology is available and probably finally ahead of other factors such as managerial and economic. We turn now to these other factors.

Managerial Factors

Six key managerial factors have held back investment in the factory of the future.

1. The previously cited short-term financially dominated point of view in top and manufacturing management, with reward systems based principally on performance against annual budgets and profit returns from proliferating numbers of profit centers.

2. High hurdle rates for investment paybacks.

3. Top management inexperience in manufacturing and a more typical financial/marketing orientation. To many such executives, manufacturing and the production function is a necessary nuisance—it soaks up capital in facilities and inventories, it resists changes in products and schedules, its quality is never as good as it should be, and its people are unsophisticated, tedious, detail-oriented, and unexciting. All of this has led to a poor and unreceptive climate for major innovation and financial investment in many industries.

4. Risk aversion by corporate executives relative to major new innovative investments. They have seen too many new pieces of equipment gather dust and not be utilized fully, not work as well as expected, and require further investment in support facilities and overhead burden (usually un-anticipated) to be jumping with enthusiasm about anything for the factory that is not well tested and proven out by somebody else. "Let my com-petitor take the risk" is the common outlook, and such an outlook is difficult to criticize. Why be number one in taking big risks in new EPTs of "factories of the future"?

5. Managers in the manufacturing sector have typically not been suffi-ciently innovative, daring, or shown the leadership necessary for pro-posing major new high-risk factories, or to break away from the safe, tried-and-true. Again, this behavior is not irrational, considering the facts of experience. This is a principal focus of Chapter 20.

6. Too many manufacturing managers focus on the short-term: meeting the monthly schedule, bogeys for quality and delivery, and labor/personnel problems. They lack a strategic point of view. They struggle with existing structure of EPTs and basic in-place systems, not seeing alternatives, and lacking the perspective of what is possible or even what other companies are doing, often in the same industry. Manufacturing strategy is a new art, often unknown.

These problems center around issues of corporate experience and attention, focus, short-term outlook, risk-aversive rather than innovative behavior, and availability of a new breed of professional, sophisticated managers. What changes are in sight?

In manufacturing management, the changes under way are less obvious and sweeping than in available technology, but there are certain clear signs that some of these problems are at least now being recognized. Management analysts are, for example, repeatedly citing the existence and damaging effect of the emphasis on the short-term, and the pressure on managers for meeting budgets and current profit goals at the expense of innovation and longer-term development of resources. *Businessweek*, in fact, carried such an article [8], and my colleagues and I have been beating this drum for some time [9,10]. Such giants as TRW, certain General Electric divisions, and American-Standard have recently trained their top executives in the new, manufacturing strategy approach to man-ufacturing management.

This kind of development is promising, for it is not just "management development": it is also an effort to change a corporation's basic man-agement approach in manufacturing from short-term to long-term, from operations to policy, and from tactical to strategic. It focuses on structural decisions—those decisions such as EPT choices, number and size of plants, capacity policy, and make or buy decisions that in the long term can make manufacturing a competitive weapon—instead of focusing, as most production managers do, on costs and short-term productivity. Its premise is that with improper, unwise, or unplanned structural decisions, no amount of able, diligent, and dedicated production management can achieve competitive results.

So this is promising. But it is small in scale. For while many companies are taking this new approach, it is a small proportion of the U.S. manufacturing world. The balance still works along on cost, efficiency, quality, inventories, and delivery, apparently oblivious of the fact that these criteria are inherently in conflict with each other and that a great factory is designed to focus on the few criteria that are most critical.

But recognizing the problem and doing something about it are different. A few companies and a few top managements and a handful of academics hardly change U.S. industry. Nevertheless, these signs of recognition and concern are being seen more often now. The problem is ever more widely recognized as very serious.

The industrial crisis in the U.S. is being discussed in widening circles [11] for the first time in years, and there is a clear recognition in the country that manufacturing productivity must be improved, and that concern is being echoed and reechoed in boardrooms, business schools, and top management training. And the focus in many companies is clearly moving back to manufacturing after 20 years, moved by the engine of change, of high cost, slumping productivity, poor quality, unstable labor relations, and the inability to compete. The pressures are economic, and there is leadership being developed and momentum being created.

There does appear to be a new breed of manufacturing manager on the scene, gradually expanding his or her influence (see Chapters 19 & 20). This new breed is competent not only in technology but also in management. She or he, who focuses on design *and* operations with equal facility, has a broad viewpoint that copes not only with technology but also with coordination, systems, and people. They focus on entire interrelated systems and operations and not just on individual equipment or departments or functions. They have a general management point of view rather than a functional outlook, yet are tough-minded, self-disciplined, and can identify and handle the essential critical daily details that can make or break an operation.

Such people are a small minority, but their strength and their future is in their competitive ability; they are rendering obsolete more narrow technicians and strictly technical, functional, departmental people. They will inherit the power of managing the factory of the future. The question is not whether, but when. More on that later.

Economics

The economics have generally not favored major manufacturing investment of substantial innovative content.

1. Risks are high, demanding a high return.
2. Interest rates and capital shortages demand a quick payback.
3. The corporate tax climate, even improved by a lower income tax rate and the investment credit deduction, requires higher paybacks than in many countries to make investments attractive.
4. Limited capital availability in many firms have held investment to virtual necessity.
5. Well written-off facilities look more profitable on paper, and the managerial reward system in most companies promotes this point of view: "Meet the plan, hit the ROA budget, and you'll get your bonus." In other words, keep assets low, don't invest.
6. Investments are reviewed in *quantitative* terms instead of projecting their *nonquantitative* effects such as the following:
   a. Flexibility for product change.
   b. Flexibility for volume change.
   c. Effects on quality and reliability.
   d. Impact on morale, spirit, attitude, pride and employee relations.
   e. Impact on ability to compete.
   f. Impact on ability to survive long-term.
7. Corporate emphasis on economics has been for better financial performance relative to industry competitors or industry data, not long-range survival.

But the economic situation, too, is changing and changing very fast. What has happened is that the U.S. is suddenly waking up to the stark economic reality that the industrial sector of our economy is in near-desperate straits. The pendulum has swung from the view that the right financial policies and good marketing was the universal formula for success, to the realization that noncompetitive manufacturing ruins an otherwise successful manufacturing business. Rising imports, declining exports, cheap high-quality foreign goods, and quality, reliability, and consumer liability problems have brought home the truth that manufacturing can be a competitive weapon used for or against the firm.

The result has been congressional study, a flood of nationwide articles in such publications as *Businessweek*, *Fortune*, *Time*, *Newsweek*, *Harvard Business Review*, and the *New York Times*, focusing on productivity, QWL, and the viability of the U.S. manufacturing industries. The rise of national attention is an economic as well as a social fact for it is bringing to the public view and concern the many negative economic problems industrial managers face:

- Taxes that discourage investment.
- Excessive, often conflicting government regulations and enforcement.
- Rising costs of energy.
- OSHA, EPA regulations, consumer court decisions.
- Difficult and often inimical labor relations.
- Oppressive state and local taxing structures.

Many top managements are beginning to demand nonquantitative long-term and annual goals of their managers in an effort to build superior competitive resources for the long-term. They are developing yardsticks that are not limited to dollars but measure performance in terms of developing people, EPTs, QWL, morale, and competitive assets and structure. This, too, is promising.

On the less positive side, inflation, conventional payback/hurdle rate capital budgeting, capital shortages, high interest rates, and considerable economic uncertainty continue to pose high negative drawbacks that deter the factory of the future and continue to reduce the pace of change.

Work-Force Factors

Even the work-force environment during the 30 years has not encouraged the factory of the future. Attitudes of labor leaders and employees as a whole have favored the "here and now" in pay increases, rather than "job enrichment," QWL, and/or improvements in the work environment.

Workers have not been insisting on or urging new EPTs. Research shows that they want better supervision, better wages, and better benefits, but nowhere does the literature or case experience show workers urging technological change other than for reasons of safety and industrial health. On the contrary, changes in the status quo are often looked at with suspicion or resistance because they may reduce the number of jobs, dislocate skill needs, and downgrade high seniority employees.

Looking at changes going on and projecting the near future, the work force factors balance out on the positive side. Unions concerned over membership and sheer survival of jobs in a stagnant and declining industrial climate are slowly reducing their opposition to new and more radical industrial equipment and processes. The present fear of declining employment and the existence of the 1980 recession, 9% unemployment rates, the public outcry and wide awareness of weaknesses in our industrial system, and the competitive advantages of our more modern-equipped foreign competitors are all bringing about an improved climate and less resistance to new EPTs.

New emphasis on the industry side of QWL, better, more interesting jobs, and improved human resource management are growing wide spread. There is growing attention, too, on designing improved total working environments. The new, more highly-mechanized factory can and usually is a better place to work, and this fact is increasingly well accepted by employees at all working levels.

The work force environment, therefore, is no longer as negative and resistant to more rapid change as it has been in the past 30 years.

CONCLUSION

We have examined these changes sector by sector and considered their potential influences on the future. The final question is—are these changes now going on sufficient to suggest a decade of more rapid development and change in manufacturing?

It seems to me that there is, in fact, at the present time, an extraordinary amount of change going on in each of these sectors, which have been so negative since 1945. The changes going on simultaneously imply a potential order of magnitude set of change in the manufacturing world that have never been seen occurring so concurrently.

It would not be hard to conclude that the "factory of the future" at last is about to become a reality. The new technologies that allow EPTs to become more versatile and flexible are available in most industries. The basis of technological advance over the past is in making job shop, short-run, product-specialized factories more like process-type long-run, high volume factories, in essence, fewer setups and changeovers, less indirect labor, and easier scheduling and sequencing.

In this sense, the new technologies appear to supply the answer to the most fundamental manufacturing dilemma of the 1960s and 1970s, namely, that manufacturing *techology* was moving toward offering even more mass production scale economies while *markets*, driven by economic and competitive pressures, were moving away from mass production technology and management practices in many industries. The new technology offers the "economics of flexibility" needed.

So the technology is ready. Management practices, under the duress of recession, industrial decline, and stagnation, are beginning to change. The rate of that change is the question now, but not its direction. It is being speeded by economic pressures, but it will be restricted by the inertia of decades of archaic practices and outlooks, short-term pressures, and a very limited number of managers who can bring a strategic point of view and developed skills in manufacturing policy to the scene. The work force factor in the equation is at the worst neutral, but probably, indeed, positive.

The economic side of the picture is still perhaps the major drawback to much more rapid change. The availability of equity capital for higher risk, innovative investments is one key, inflation another, and changes in the tax and regulatory structure another. Successful leadership by some larger companies developing models of technological and commercial success of truly innovative factories can be an engine for change via the competitive process. Several companies successful with new factories in an industry will transform that industry and their competitors must go along to survive. For these reasons, the future will beyond doubt show a rapid period of growth and change in the factory.

I conclude that we may have ahead of us in the factory over the next 15 years, the most rapid change in any of our major institutions. It will be held back by too many factors to be a five-year revolution, but the rate of change will probably be five or ten times faster than any reindustrialization or reequipment or renewal of a major social institution in the past 35 years. Driven by competitive economics, supported by available and fast developing technology and concerned employees, while held back until government taxes and regulations change, the critical ingredient in this whole puzzle, positive or negative, is the manager.

The "new breed," as described, will be an enormously positive driving factor. But the "old breed," limited by many tenets of professional management and the skills of short-term management control learned in many schools of business, is still predominant. The "new breed" is too limited in number and youthful in age and organizational level in most companies yet to tip the scale.

American industry and the factory of the future are now poised for rapid change. The key to the rate and timing of this change is the manager. Managers are now in a position, for the first time in industrial history, to make the "factory of the future" more than an ever-elusive dream. This is the subject of the final chapter of this book.

The next chapter takes up in more depth the factory of the future as it might affect the working environment. What are the probable effects on job content, skills, supervision, and quality of work life? It turns out, not surprisingly, that these are complicated questions. The answers depend not only on the technologies but on the whole range of implementing activities, ranging from operating procedures to employee selection to communications. The bottom line is not complex, however: the impact of the new technologies on the working environment can be whatever managers or workers want it to be. It can be managed.

REFERENCES

1. Hayes, Robert, and William J. Abernathy, "Managing Our Way to Economic Decline," *Harvard Business Review*, July–August 1980.
2. "Robots Join the Labor Force," *Businessweek*, June 9, 1980, p. 62.
3. Miller, Jeffrey, "Fit the System to the Task," Harvard Business School, Division of Research Working Paper #80–29.
4. Skinner, Wickham, "Manufacturing—Missing Link in Corporate Strategy," *Harvard Business Review*, May–June 1969.
5. Skinner, Wickham, "Reinventing the Factory." *Issues: The PA Journal for Management. Vol 1. No. 2,* 1984, pp. 3–11.
6. Walton, Richard E., "Quality of Work Life: What is it?" *Sloan Management Review*, Fall 1973.
7. Goldhar, Joel, and A. Avakian, "Managing Change in Manufacturing Systems," Discussion paper for the National Research Council, Washington, D.C., 1980.
8. "How Companies Can Lengthen their Sights," *Businessweek*, June 30, 1980, pp. 92–94.
9. Banks, R. L., and Steven C. Wheelwright, "Operations vs. Strategy: Trading Tomorrow for Today," *Harvard Business Review*, May–June 1979.
10. Lauenstein, M., and Wickham Skinner, "Formulating a Strategy of Superior Resources," *Journal of Business Strategy*, July 1980.
11. "Curing Ailing Industries," *Time*, July 14, 1980.

CHAPTER 11

The Impact of Changing Technology on the Working Environment

In the 1980s technological changes will undoubtedly affect working environments massively, powerfully, often unpredictably, often perniciously. In these ways, technology will run according to form. Nevertheless, some new forces may begin to alter the consistent historical pattern, a pattern in which technology has been an irresistible prime mover that inevitably defines working tasks and working environments.

Many companies have recently begun to try to manage this process instead of simply letting it happen. As they do, and as the purposes for which technology is developed expand, these companies are likely to have an increasing variety of technologies from which to choose. For example, the need for technologies that save materials and energy is rising relative to the traditional labor-saving motive. At the same time, management assumptions, values, and techniques may be shifting in the direction of no longer taking for granted that the quality of working life (QWL) must be subordinated to the choice of equipment and process.

These are interesting developments with potentially far-reaching consequences. But they are new, and their imminence and future impact are both uncertain, so that, as we look ahead, some important questions arise. Can industrial managers cushion or manage the impact of technological change for the benefit of working environments, and how? Are there inherently inevitable and difficult choices between equipment and process technologies (EPTs) that benefit the working environment, and EPTs that are more productive and economical? Finally, can technological development be influenced or managed in order to produce EPTs that improve the working environment and QWL?*

In trying to look ahead a decade, we must form some judgment on these questions. But the subject described by the title is a complex one even before facing these challenging questions. Its complexity derives from the many interdependent issues that are involved. For example, what technological changes will take place? How will these changes bear on the working environment? What is the process by which technology affects the work environment? When these impacts take place, what will be the result? To begin to explore these issues, this chapter first focuses on the basic relationship between a firm's equipment and process technology and its working environment.

TECHNOLOGY AND THE WORKPLACE

A given EPT places demands on a company's operating policies and practices that are often rather difficult to overcome. For example, a plant using a basic oxygen steel process is apt to be a hot, noisy, and potentially dangerous place in which to work. In an oil refinery, where most work involves a team effort, an individualized incentive pay scheme would be hard to develop. And in a clothing factory, rich, broad jobs, such as making entire shirts, are hard to arrange. Jobs tend to become specialized because shirts have so many parts, making it difficult to keep them separated by size and fabric, and because the sewing operations are so varied. These kinds of constraints, by and large, have made the working environment dependent on technology throughout industrial history. But more is involved in the quality of working life.

A steel mill is a different place in which to work than an electronics plant, that is clear enough. But working in a computer factory for Honeywell might be perceived by some workers as quite different from working in a computer factory for Burroughs, because although the two companies (let us assume) may be using the same EPTs, a worker might feel that one of these plants had nicer people, a better pay system, kind

---

*Throughout this chapter, I use "working environment" and QWL (quality of working life) nearly interchangeably, but with the implicit intention that QWL is a value judgment (by workers or anyone else making the judgment) of the working environment. The term "working environment" represents all that a worker observes and feels at his or her workplace, including the job tasks, physical conditions, the impact of the supervisor, unions, colleagues, pay schemes, pay rate, controls, work rules, pressures, and discretion, to name a few examples.

and understanding supervisors, more chances to use one's judgment, or more interesting jobs.

So the QWL depends not only on the EPT, but on what I will call "operating policies and practices," that is, the web of procedures, such as work rules and pay systems, followed in the factory. A "good" EPT with "poor" operating policies and practices might not make a good working environment, and vice versa. The working environment, therefore, is a function of both the EPT and the resulting network of operating policies and procedures, which must be designed and managed so as to be internally consistent with and supportive of the EPT.

Because of the EPT's influence on operating policies and practices, as well as its impact on jobs and the workplace, the process of choosing an EPT can also change in the future. This choice is a management decision process depending on the premises, ideology, and strategy of the company on the one hand and the available technological alternatives (and management's awareness of these alternatives) on the other. Since the development of new technology depends partly on the needs and demands of business, informed managers, who are beginning to make the quality of working life a criterion in choosing EPTs, may influence the efforts and directions of scientists and engineers who design technology.

Any and all of these actors, factors, and processes will influence QWL during a decade of changing technology. And to add just one more variable, the quality of a work environment is a human perception dependent on each worker's personal sense of what makes a good working life. Exhibit 11.1 attempts a simple graphical picture of the dynamics of these elements in a changing work environment.

Our assignment is the decade ahead, but we must first see what we can learn from the past. The balance of this chapter discusses conventional and present practices first, then the future, and finally puts the two together for some conclusions.

HOW TECHNOLOGY AFFECTS THE WORKING ENVIRONMENT

Basic to the study of technology's impact on future working environments is an understanding of the mechanisms by which technology has affected jobs and work in the past.

Equipment and process technology has been the prime determinant of working environments for several fundamental reasons. The first is the pervasive effect of an EPT on the whole operating system. The second is that the process of developing and selecting from the stock of existing technologies has generally left the working environment as a dependent

Exhibit 11.1   Technological Change and the Working Environment

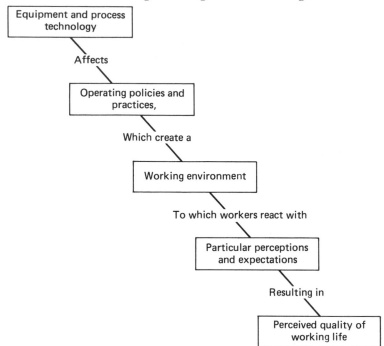

variable. The third reason is that, until very recently, operating policies and practices have not been developed to cushion or modify the impact of an EPT.

Because a given equipment and process technology creates demands on and requirements for all other elements of an operating system, all parts of the system must be designed and managed to be congruent and compatible with the chosen EPT. The choice of EPT is, therefore, normally the primary determinant of every operating system, and its influence pervades the system.

Since most products can be manufactured in more than one way, choices generally exist in the selection of the equipment and the process. Once a new choice is made, however, virtually every element in the superseded production system is apt to change. At the center is the workplace, where the technological changes are physical and tangible. Changes then ripple out into the entire system, the institution, and sometimes an entire industry.

The pervasive impact of equipment and process technology is illustrated by the differences between plastics-molding technology and metalworking. Making flashlights of plastic instead of metal, for example, is entirely different for the worker, the supervisor, and all support groups.*

The ordinary flashlight casing may be made in many ways. One would be by drawing metal out in a tubular shape on a press using a die, another by molding plastic resin by injection. Exhibit 11.2 suggests the different skills, the management systems, and the operating problems demanded by a metal-flashlight-casing operation compared to a plastic-based one. Two distinctions are particularly striking. The first is that the scheduling and inventory-control system is vastly more complex in the metalworking plant, where several operations must be performed on the same part. Paperwork is necessary to take care of parts removed from machine to machine, and capacity must be planned and scheduled. In plastics, with but one operation on one press, production scheduling is much simpler. The second difference is in the working environment; the job content, skills, training, and supervision. The lighter, cleaner, more automated work in the plastics plant would ordinarily be suitable for a less skilled, lower-paid employee, with key technical and personnel skills lodged in relatively higher paid employees.

Thus, each EPT brings with it its own demands and characteristics. A given EPT choice spreads its effects from the workplace to the entire operating system and, finally, to the ability of the system to perform in a competitive environment. This comes about because of the powerful economic advantages that occur when all parts of the system reinforce one another. An alert management recognizes the requirements the EPT places on the various management systems by its initial impact on the basic manufacturing process, and then develops an appropriate structure. The usual practice is to choose the EPT and then to design or adjust the system's operating policies and practices. The effects of an EPT, then, take place on three levels:

PRIMARY   Direct effects on the work, worker, working environment, product, costs, investment, and basic requirements.

SECONDARY   Demands on the operating system infrastructure: wage and work force management, production planning, scheduling, and control, quality control, production organization.

TERTIARY   Effects on the performance ability of the operating system; that is, what the system can and cannot do well.

These three levels are illustrated in Exhibit 11.3.

The same ripple effect seen in one company from a change in technology

*To make the same point, but in a different context, this page and Exhibit 11.2 are largely repeated from Chapter 9, Technology and the Manager. Exhibit 11.3 is based on Exhibit 9.1 but with an additional column: "working environment."

Exhibit 11.2 Contrasting Production Systems for Manufacturing a Flashlight Casing: Metal versus Plastic

	Metal Drawing	Plastic Molding
Equipment	Punch Press	Injection molding machine
Raw materials	Metal sheets	Plastic resin pellets
Tools	Die set—male or female	Split halves of a mold
Building	Heavy foundations to handle weight and impact	Ordinary floor
Manufacturing engineering	Mechanical, metal expertise	Plastics, hydraulics expertise
Maintenance	Mechanical, hydraulic	Mechanical, hydraulic
Operator	Heavy work, higher skill	Lighter work, lower skill
Supervisory skills	Managing male work force, scheduling	Mixed work force, machine troubleshooting, quality checking
Inventory	Sheet metal and work-in-process	Plastic powder and finished goods
Operations	May require several plus finishing	One
Scheduling	Potentially complex	Simple
Safety	Dangerous	Safer
Quality/precision	Depends on die and machine setup	Depends on molds; timing set into machine
Costs	Depends especially on die conditions and setup	Depends especially on short cycle and changeovers
Flexibility-product change volume change	Die change necessary	Mold change necessary
	Add dies, machines, shifts or move to higher speed equipment	Add dies, machines, shifts; cycle limited
Potential for automation	Combine operations with transfer dies, install part location sensors, etc.; can be largely automatic	Largely automatic

Exhibit 11.3   The Influence of an EPT on an Operating System

Operating System Elements INFLUENCES	COSTS	QUALITY	INVESTMENT	FLEXIBILITY product/volume change	CUSTOMER SERVICE	WORKING ENVIRONMENT
PRIMARY Direct Effects	Operator skill level Labor cost Material Energy requirement Setup & changeover Maintenance Skills Mgt. scheduling Control	Precision Reliability Appearance Maintenance	Capacity Original cost Economic life Inventory Utilities & buildings Certainty-stability of technology	Product range producible Setup & changeover time Lead times	Cycle time Total lead time	Physical conditions Job content Skills & experiences needed Safety Industrial health Pace required Social elements of job
SECONDARY Operating policies & practices	Purchasing system Burden rates Cost control system Work force mgt. Mfg. eng. reqs. Mfg. organization structure	Maintenance system QC system Supervision Mfg. eng. reqs.	Inventory control system Capacity planning system Capital budgeting system	Production planning & scheduling system New product capacity & lead times	Customer promise system Organization for new product introduction into mfg.	Wage system Supervision Labor contract Personnel policies Grievance procedures Knowledge needed at workplace Communications
TERTIARY Performance ability	Total costs Cost flexibility with volume change, product change	Quality performance Reliability	Return on investment	Ability to be profitable with changes in volume and/or products	Ability to compete by short lead times & reliability of delivery promises	Productivity Morale Effort Ingenuity Creativity Flexibility Competitiveness Responsibility assumed at working level

usually spreads out over entire industries as each business firm gains cost, delivery, quality, or product advantages.

What have been the effects of technology's classic historical dominance of the workplace? Often the results are seen as harmful to QWL. Mass production, for example, usually means repetition and, therefore, potential boredom. Assembly lines, conveyors, and automation generally reduce skills and narrow job scopes. Because machinery does its work faster, humans are paced and pressured to keep it producing.

On the "good" side, however, most people would probably agree that life in both manufacturing and service/office industries is a great deal better in 1985 than in 1935. Industrial history is full of examples of technologies developed for such conventional objectives as improved profit potential and a better product, which have also resulted in better working environments and improved QWL. For example, most new mechanization for the reduction of labor also reduces or eliminates repetitive human tasks or actual physical work. Offices and factories are cleaner, quieter, lighter, and more comfortable than they were fifty years ago.

This reduction of tedious, repetitive work has probably been the major fringe benefit of mechanization and automation. Numerically controlled machine tools, computers, word-processing systems, containerized shipping, automatic testing, wave soldering, and automatic component insertion (in electronics), mechanical fruit picking, the bulldozer, and direct telephone dialing are examples of technologies that have reduced tedious and/or strenuous operations. Yet, none of these technological innovations, it seems safe to say, were developed primarily for the purpose of improving working environments.

Nevertheless, that turned out to be a major and primary effect of these new EPTs. Job contents were changed from specialized, narrow tasks, low in skill and sometimes physically demanding, to tasks requiring more skill and experience. Low-level operating skills were replaced by setting up, maintenance, troubleshooting, and other high-skilled operations. True, a residue of very low-level repetitive jobs remains, such as loading and unloading automatic machines, but these jobs are substantially fewer.

The disappearance of messy carbon paper and blue reproduction fluid in office work came about largely as a side effect of the development of copy machines for cutting labor costs. Coal-mining equipment, which mechanically claws out coal, was developed because the high wages of unionized miners offered mining firms an incentive to find savings. The chief beneficiary, however, was the miner himself, whose physical work was much reduced.

Although the history of technology abounds with such examples of serendipity, the working environment has been determined by EPTs selected for reasons other than their influence on QWL.

Why is it that consideration of the working environment has come last in both the development and selection of EPTs? Some of the assumptions implicit in the corporation's traditional method of choosing an EPT are as follows:

- Someone will turn up able and willing to do nearly any job if the wage is right.
- People are adaptable to a wide variety of tasks and conditions.
- People match themselves with acceptable jobs.
- Problems with any negative job reactions can be handled with the following:
  - Careful selection.
  - Adequate training.
  - Wage adjustments/monetary incentives.
  - Proper supervision.
  - Good discipline.
  - Open communications.
  - Proper grievance procedures.

These assumptions boil down to one idea: namely, that an otherwise successful and profitable EPT may present personnel problems, but such problems can be overcome. These assumptions appear to have been valid much of the time and, indeed, have held factories together for many generations.

In the last decade, however, these premises have grown vulnerable. Workers' perceptions of what is acceptable are clearly changing, and their expectations of working life are more demanding. Today our society is generally suspicious of single, overriding motives such as "growth," "profits," "efficiency," and unmanaged technological innovation.

For these reasons, many managers are now asking some new questions about EPTs: Are a good working environment and highly competitive, profitable EPTs mutually exclusive? Granted that the corporation must profit and compete successfully to survive, cannot EPTs be designed and selected, and operating practices developed for the purpose of better work environments? These questions are now explored.

If good QWL and productive EPTs are mutually exclusive, then we must choose between them, and where poor working environments would result, cushion the impact with better operating practices, such as job restructuring, better tasks, pay systems, communications, and others. If they are not mutually exclusive, we can learn to develop EPTs that improve productivity and QWL and also develop better operating policies and practices for the workplace.

To explore these questions, we need to be more precise about the elements of a high-productivity EPT and its effects on the workplace. An attempt to describe the characteristics of a high-productivity EPT is shown in Exhibit 11.4. The left column lists 20 common descriptors of an equipment and process technology that, it is conventionally assumed, produces high productivity. Not all readers will agree with the author's asessment of the effects on productivity, nor with the effects of each quality on the working envioronment and QWL. Nevertheless, the two right-hand columns with the author's comments point out the uncertainty of the effects.

Several conclusions can be drawn from this analysis:

- There are many myths about technologies and QWL that need more precise and contextual thinking. For example, assembly lines are not always necessarily highly productive. It depends on worker reactions, product mix, the physical elements of production, and 1,001 other factors. And assembly lines are not necessarily bad for QWL either, depending on job content, pace and rate of flow, particular workers, use of buffer inventory, and another 1,001 factors.
- Many of the assumed positive productivity effects of certain EPTs depend substantially on worker reaction to the EPT and, indeed, to the whole working environment. Hence, old "principles" of industrial engineering must now be seen as dependent on workers, management, and the situation. High productivity cannot be automatically achieved or guaranteed by any technology if worker cooperation and effort are negative.
- Similarly, many of the presumed negative effects of so-called high-productivity EPTs on working environments and QWL need not take place, depending on how EPTs are structured, managed, and accepted. For example, a mature, dependable, low-maintenance EPT can be boring if the operator only watches it, or interesting if the operator has complete charge of scheduling setup, changeover, and maintenance. The operator's expectations, interests, skills, and attitudes partly determine the impact of the EPT. Conversely, "job enrichment" policies, as demonstrated by many researchers, do not guarantee high QWL.

The answer to the basic question, therefore, is that there is no inherent conflict between high productivity and high QWL. Both working environment and productivity are dependent on the technical, human, and workplace infrastructure. The fact that conflicts have surfaced so often between the EPT and the working environment is due to the social and personal impacts of industrialization per se, the low priority given to the effects on the work environment in both EPT development and selection, and operating policies and practices.

Exhibit 11.4 EPT Descriptors Related to Productivity, Working Environment, and QWL

EPT Descriptor	Conventionally Assumed Effect on Productivity	Conventionally Assumed Effect on W-E and QWL	Comment	
			Re: Productivity	Re: W-E and QWL
1. Large volume, scale	Good	Bad	Generally true	Not necessarily bad
2. Standardized product	Good	Bad	Generally true	Not necessarily bad
3. Highly mechanized, automated	Good	Bad	Depends on worker reaction	Can eliminate boring jobs
4. Highly fixtured, maximum use of fixtures and tools	Good	Bad	Depends on worker reaction	Can make jobs easier
5. Easy to maintain	Good	Bad	True	But if easy, operator can maintain
6. Dependable, predictable. mature technology	Good	Bad	True	But if so, operator can take charge
7. Special purpose (vs. general purpose)	Good	Bad	Depends on product mix or cost of changeover	Can be more interesting
8. Easy to set up and change over	Good	Bad	Generally true	But if easy, operator can do it
9. Straight-line layout	Good	Bad	Easier to control but may cost more in space and inventory	Workers may like ease of control if given more latitude

163

Exhibit 11.4 (*continued*)

EPT Descriptor	Conventionally Assumed Effect on Productivity	Conventionally Assumed Effect on W-E and QWL	Comment	
			Re: Productivity	Re: W-E and QWL
10. One-level building	Good	Bad	Easier to control but no major advantage in materials handling	Depends on architecture, noise, social groupings
11. Requires little skill to operate	Good	Bad	Depends on worker reaction	O.K. if matches worker interest and skill to job
12. Continuous vs. batch	Good	Bad	Depends on product mix and technicians	Not necessarily less interesting
13. Automatic material handling load, unload	Good	Bad	Depends on its reliability and flexibility	Can make jobs easier
14. Paced operations	Good	Bad	Depends on consistency, balance	Depends on rate and pace
15. Specialized, narrow, job content	Good	Bad	Depends on worker reaction	Not bad for everyone
16. Little worker discretion	Good	Bad	Depends on worker reaction	Not bad for everyone
17. Low in-process inventories	Good	Bad	Depends on absence of problems and variations	Depends on pace, variation, and problems
18. Standard methods	Good	Bad	Depends on worker reaction	Not bad for everyone
19. Requires little knowledge of other operations	Good	Bad	Depends on steady flows	Not bad for everyone
20. Central scheduling	Good	Bad	Depends on what knowledge is needed for good scheduling	Not bad for everyone

To conclude, technology has been powerful in its effects on work environments in the past and, more often than not, has had a negative short-term impact.

However, poor work environments are not inevitable in the future, for any or all of the factors affecting work environments are susceptible to change. For example, the analysis so far suggests the following possible influences that can change the future impact of technology on the workplace:

- Scientific and engineering knowledge and skills leading to new technologies.
- Sociological/ideological forces including new technologies.
- Economic forces including new technologies.
- New objectives for management selection of EPTs.
- New criteria for management selection of EPTs.
- New weighting of criteria in management selection of EPTs.
- New operating policies and practices to cushion or improve the impact of existing EPTs.
- Legal and governmental influences on EPT choices and operating policies and practices.
- New perceptions of existing workers about what makes a good work environment.
- Perceptions of new workers about what makes a good work environment.
- New worker reactions to working environments they perceive as poor.

These factors and their interrelationships are pictured in simplified form in Exhibit 11.5. We turn now to the future.

NEW FORCES THAT MAY ALTER THE FUTURE

Although our view of industrial history shows how the work environment has been the slave of technology and management operating policies and EPT selection decision processes, it also shows the way to future change. We saw three critical factors in the technology/work environment interface:

- How the impact of technology on work is managed.
- What motivates and influences the development of new EPTs.
- How EPTs are selected by management.

All three of these key factors now appear to be undergoing changes that will affect the future.

Exhibit 11.5   Factors Influencing Future Impact of Technology on the Workplace

PRESENT		NEW		CHANGE
EPTs	+	"Mothers of invention"	=	NEW EPTs TO CHOOSE FROM
MANAGEMENT DECISION PROCESS	+	Objectives, ideologies, premises, processes	=	DIFFERENT, MODIFIED EPTs SELECTED
				These will produce NEW EPTs and with
OPERATING POLICIES AND PRACTICES	+	Techniques, concepts, objective, legal requirements	=	REVISED OPERATING POLICIES AND PRACTICES
				NEW WORKING ENVIRONMENTS will result. These will combine with
WORKER PERCEPTIONS, MOTIVES, AND REACTIONS	+	Changing values, expectation, and goals of workers	=	NEW WORKER ATTITUDES AND PERCEPTIONS OF QWL

Improved Techniques for Managing the Impacts of Technology on the Working Environment

Although the future will be determined by new technologies influenced by a variety of changed forces and revised managerial decision apparatus, let us assume for now that the working environment continues to be the dependent variable of technology that it has been in the past. Also assume for the moment the classic premise of corporate managers and scientists/engineers that whatever working environment may result can be managed or contained.

Perhaps because new EPTs were designed and selected without regard to the work environment in the past, a new body of knowledge and set of techniques have emerged over the past 10 years or so that are now assisting some managements first to cushion and then to improve working environments.

Driving this new thrust for better management at the working level are various engines of change, most of which are described elsewhere in this book in detail. For example, corporate profits can become an incentive to develop better ways to manage the impact of technology when a firm's large investments in facilities are threatened by worker dissatisfaction and unrest, for these conditions have a multiplier effect and can render such investments disastrous. Changed social attitudes toward working environments, widespread shortages of qualified workers, or militant unionism will lead managers to develop new techniques for improving the working environment. Federal and state laws, such as OSHA regulations, as well as industrial problems, such as low productivity, inflation, and foreign competition, are spurring the development of new techniques.

As a result of these forces that affect profits, industry is learning to manage the working environment, and to manage it better. More management and staff attention is being placed on "people." Many companies have hired top-level corporate officers, called "managers of human resources" or the equivalent. An increasing number of these officers are listened to and exert power and influence as never before.

These forces are inducing the development of important new intellectual and analytical concepts that are providing useful frameworks for management to develop tools and techniques for improving the working environment. In particular, a rich literature has grown up describing how work may be "restructured" within a given technology.

Work restructuring generally includes changing job tasks and content, compensation schemes, the scope of workers' responsibility, social structure, status hierarchy, and procedures for vertical and horizontal mobility. Knowledge is growing about indicators of and ingredients affecting QWL, and strategies are being devised for diffusing successful work restructuring into the organization. Professor Richard Walton has identified eight criteria for a high QWL, which can motivate such strategies:

- Adequate and fair compensation.
- Safe and healthy working conditions.
- Immediate opportunity to use and develop human capacities.
- Future opportunity for continued growth and security.
- Social integration in the work organization.
- Constitutionalism in the work organization.
- Work and the total life space.
- The social relevance of working life.[1]

The results of work restructuring experiments are receiving attention in the literature as a result of a large number of pilot programs that have taken place in the United States and in Western Europe. Experiments in work restructuring have been carried out in companies such as Corning Glass, General Foods, General Motors, General Electric, and Cummins Engine.

The experiments have involved the following: nonsupervised work groups; new pay systems; increased participation in decisions affecting group teams; job enlargement; group-developed tools, systems, procedures, and work methods; and the provision of additional information for cost analysis and cost control. Although these experiments have generally been considered successful, their diffusion into broader usage has sometimes proved difficult.

All in all, it is growing clear that many managements are making modest but increasing progress in learning how to improve poor working environments created by technologies that were developed or chosen without regard to the working environment. It is now reasonable to assume that this promising work will continue, will be gradually diffused into new practice, and that the small nucleus of existing experiments and new work structures will grow at least modestly over the next decade. Progress will be gradual rather than revolutionary, it appears, because these experiments now cover only a tiny fraction of the work force and will take years to gather more momentum.

It is important to define what progress in work restructuring means. Although the goal of restructuring work is to improve work environments, the process is essentially one of adapting the tasks, rules, and practices affecting work to improve the status quo under existing technology. That is, the EPT is given, and the job of improving QWL is one of scrambling to adjust human work to the technology in the best way possible. But since, as we saw earlier, a given EPT determines to a great extent the entire operating system and sets up physical and technical constraints, the benefits of work restructuring are severely limited in many cases. When the EPT dictates a poor QWL, as in the case of the typical foundry of the 1950s, work restructuring is little more than a Band-Aid. At best, when the technology of the process is more neutral, as in electronic assembly work, work restructuring can result in substantial imrovements.

These notions lead to the next question. Since a given EPT is typically so pervasive and, therefore, the benefits of better operating policies and practices such as work restructuring so limited, can we expect to come across or develop new technologies which themselves may be more conducive to better working environments?

Factors Influencing the Development of New Technologies

Increasing the Stock of Available Technologies.   The flow of new technologies available for selection is stimulated and directed by a variety of forces (Exhibit 11.6). Some have effects that can be fortunate.

One quickly developing technology appears to show promise for a favorable effect on QWL—that is, the explosion of computers, minicomputers, and communications. The effect is fortuitous, for the main purposes of such technology are improved production and inventory controls, cost and quality controls, and information systems. But side effects are already beginning to be seen at the workplace.

Until now, the machine operator has generally been servant to hard-and-fast orders, specifications, and decisions. He or she is given an order,

Exhibit 11.6 Factors Affecting Innovation in Equipment and Process Technology

1. Scientific knowledge
2. Engineering skills
3. Corporate investment
4. Government investment
5. Corporate objectives
6. Productivity
7. Economics/cost mix
8. Resource availability
9. Product changes
10. Product quality
11. Safety and health
12. Environment

material, and equipment typically set up and ready to go; inserts the material; runs the machine; stacks up the finished pieces; and gets another order. The parts produced will either pass inspection or be rejected, and if rejections are high or sales improve rapidly, another order may have to be produced right away. With the minicomputer, workers can be given the opportunity for intelligent participation; in effect, they can have an ongoing discussion with an advisor, the computer. They receive feedback from the computer about the quality of the work being produced, can make adjustments to improve quality, and can give the computer suggestions for improved operations.

In effect, workers can respond intelligently to information they need for doing their jobs better and more easily. Classical "supervision" is superseded by an information system that answers questions and gives rapid feedback for the workers' own improvements of performance. Currently, the best trained and most well-intentioned supervisor is forced by lack of time and the limited information one person can possess to issue definitive orders. The intelligent worker sees other alternatives and raises many questions to which the supervisor now must give a limited, narrow, and often hurried response.

The "system," then, seems arbitrary or downright stupid to the worker who sees firsthand, for example, that yesterday he or she was pressured all day for production and today has to stretch the work out to make it last. The use of minicomputers can change the supervisor's response to workers from a blunt "don't ask questions—do as you're told" to an accomodating, "here's what we need—please work it out your own way, use your ingenuity, and ask us any questions." The supervisor becomes a helper, colleague, teacher, or coach. His or her task of disciplining workers to follow orders can be reduced or eliminated.

So once again, some technologies that come along benefit the workplace. But another question now arises: Are there new or different forces at work that may develop substantially new equipment and process technologies from those currently available?

Changing Factors Motivating New EPT Development

There are many "mothers of invention" besides necessity, and it looks as though some new motivating forces, in fact, will result in a flow of EPTs to the workplace that may differ substantially from those of the past. At least seven changes are already working:

- Until recently it seems safe to say that saving labor has probably been the most common and powerful motive of technological development in equipment and processes. In many industries, however, materials are now the greatest expense, and, therefore, the new target for cutting costs. The United States has drifted toward becoming a material-short nation; we export fewer materials, import more, and move more materials longer distances. We are increasingly guarding our supplies of iron, cotton, copper, wood pulp, water, and petrochemical feedstocks. Costs of materials have outpaced and fueled inflation and, as a result, new technologies in metalworking, construction, chemicals, and cryogenics have developed, to mention but a few.

- A second major change in the economics of many industries has been the substantial increase in overhead costs relative to direct labor. As labor-saving technologies have been introduced and managements have invested more in overhead, the ratios of these costs to direct labor have gradually increased so that now overhead is a prime area of cost savings.

  A growing portion of overhead costs is, of course, energy. Energy not only represents a rising cost, but, in fact, is becoming such a scarce resource that the present level of consumption could again result in the shutdown of entire factories and industries, as in the winter of 1976–1977. For this reason, many of the large and well-managed companies are going through their entire EPTs step by step and reprocessing with energy-saving technologies.

- A third new factor resulting in new technologies is the increased emphasis on asset management (in contrast to cost management). Increased costs of capital, combined with more opportunities for putting capital to work than can be financed, are resulting in a search by management for technologies that use assets more effectively. Increased capacity per dollar invested is one goal of asset management. Others are EPTs that are faster and thereby require less inventory, or those that offer improved flexibility for producing more product varieties with fewer pieces of equipment.

- Law and the courts are of growing importance in EPT design. The Environmental Protection Act and the Occupational Safety and Health Act are typical. For example, companies mandated by law to cut pollution are developing new EPTs rather than pay fines and risk being shut down.

  Enlarged protection for consumers by the courts has begun to have an effect on EPT development in many industries, as companies attempt to produce safer and more reliable products.

- "Mature" industries, such as steel, textiles, automobiles, and chemicals, are generally becoming less competitive in the United States, whereas industries characterized by a high rate of technological change and innovations, such as computers, industrial electronics, specialized plastics, cryogenics, and industrial and construction equipment, are holding unique competitive advantages. Assuming this trend will continue, we can foresee more emphasis on EPT development, characterized by higher skills, more information, more on-the-job problem solving, shorter runs and order quantities, greater product varieties, and hence a changed working environment, which most analysts would predict to be an improvement.

- According to Abernathy[2] and Hayes and Wheelwright,[3] productive units in less mature industries tend to have small-scale capacity with a low level of backward integration, flexible but inefficient general-purpose equipment, skilled labor, and a loose and entrepreneurially based form of organization. Productive units in firms with low unit volumes or large numbers of multiple products tend to have disconnected or jumbled flows, as in a job shop, compared to the connected line flows of assembly lines. Therefore, technologies motivated for this kind of industrial product and process matching will tend to produce working environments that require less monitoring, more skill, and a higher judgment level.

- Supporting this conclusion, although arriving at it differently, some economists observe that U.S. capital spending over the past five years has tended to lag behind GNP growth, particularly in the construction of giant-scale plants needed to achieve competitive cost levels in bulk-process industries. High cost of capital, combined with the enormous capital investment and risks inherent in such ventures, has caused this slowdown relative to development and investment in EPTs in the non-commodity industries.

- A force gradually becoming more powerful in influencing technology development is society's beliefs and values. Our period of history is frequently called "postindustrial," with business no longer predominating over government or allowed to neglect human values, and with reduced confidence in science and technology to solve problems. We feel a new need for the development of human capital. The service-industry sector, which is more dependent on people than machines, has been growing faster than manufacturing. New ideologies are replacing individualism, property rights, competition to satisfy consumer desires, the limited state, and scientific specialization. One of these, communitarianism, which focuses on the rights and duties of membership in the community, community needs, the active planning state, holism, and interdependence, is already having an influence on workers and working environment.[4] Earlier chapters deal with these changes in values and the work ethic, and our task here is limited to noting that ideology, values, and societal objectives are bound to influence EPTs. This influence will be felt in many ways.

The Possibility of Developing and Selecting Technologies for Better Working Environments

There is no question that managers, engineers, and scientists can develop and select technologies that produce better working environments, for this is already being done in isolated instances today.

We are not talking about "work restructuring," which we noted earlier is adapted to a given equipment and process technology. But in situations in which the working environment is considered intolerable, as in paint spraying, coal mining, and nuclear power installations, EPTs have, in fact, been designed around the human operator. Not only was tooling, for example, usually "human-engineered," but the basic technology of the operation was developed from the start with the working environment in mind.

In these examples, work environments were so potentially harmful that improvements were essential. This illustrates that design objectives are critical and that if a satisfactory environment is given a high priority in the design and selection process, the EPT will meet these objectives. In the Volvo Kalmar plant, the EPT and engineering of the car itself were specifically designed in part for a team assembly process. The same thing occurred in the General Foods pet-food plant in Topeka, where the EPT design was influenced from the start by the prime objective of making the plant a good place to work.

To be successful, however, this process takes more than a new ideology, a firm policy, good intentions, new objective functions, and design criteria that are heavily weighted toward a good work environment. Also necessary are several other management skills that are still rare: an ability to anticipate the effect of a technology on the working environment and the skills to design EPTs, which produce favorable working environments without sacrificing conventional objectives of cost, delivery, and quality. Our only knowledge base for these skills derives from experiments in restructuring work. There managers are learning which factors in an EPT cause problems in the working environment.

At Cummins Engine Corporation, managers, assisted by Professor Richard Walton, have set forth some principles for the design of EPTs, which result in better work environments:

Some Work Restructuring Criteria in the Design of Machines and Plant Layouts[5]

1. Knowledge and skill will be required (not eliminated) by complexity and challenge in the task.
2. Variety will be allowed in operations performed, skills required, physical location, and working conditions.
3. Judgment and discretion will be permitted.
4. "Free space," that is, time, is created, for example, by buffer inventories between stations, permitting meetings, self-pacing, action independent of others, teaching-learning interchanges, and so on.
5. Operations will be grouped so as to allow team responsibility for an integrated task, incorporating support activity such as scheduling, maintenance, and inspection.
6. Jobs will be similar to avoid a hierarchy of jobs and to allow a pay scheme based on "what you know."
7. Interpersonal contact and communications will be facilitated by layout, noise level, and "free space."

So the necessary knowledge is developing although this is a new art. Certainly many years of experimentation and refinement will pass before EPT designers will be as capable of producing good working environments as they are at reducing direct labor and increasing volume and quality.

Several other impediments stand in the way of the development of better EPTs. One important and particularly sticky problem results from the disaggregation of many industries. For example, a small electrical equipment manufacturer must figure out how to get machine tools that have been designed, let us say, so that operators can do much of the maintenance, setup, and sharpening. In such a disaggregated industry, the EPTs are usually purchased from suppliers who are not easily influenced by a small fraction of their customers, so until enough manufacturers specify that they want equipment providing better work environments, it will be a slow process.

Furthermore, the nearly universal practice in large divisionalized corporations of budgeting and controlling on a monthly basis, according to an annual plan, induces a cautious, low-risk, short-term approach on the part of division managers. This attitude is hardly conducive to experimental development of new technologies to improve working environments.

With regard to another obstacle, we may be more optimistic. Until the 1970s, conventional manufacturing decision making was done by factory specialists. Decision criteria were dominated by a strongly technical, "nuts and bolts" productivity point of view. This resulted in manufacturing policy decisions that were often in conflict or simply out of touch with corporate strategy and competitive marketing requirements. Dominated by cost and efficiency, manufacturing policies often resulted in plants that become corporate problems, limiting a firm's ability to compete flexibly as markets changed because bricks and mortar and the wrong expensive equipment in place had to be amortized over many years. Narrow thinking resulted from the isolation of manufacturing as a function, and from policy decisions made to optimize functional rather than corporate objectives.

In the 1970s one new emphasis in corporate management is on a strategic, integrated approach to the management of all functions. There has been a steady trend to multiproduct, divisionalized, corporate organization and recently some firms have adopted a new approach to manufacturing that links it to the corporate strategy. These factors may be leading manufacturing managers to new decision criteria and processes in forming manufacturing policy.

This new approach to manufacturing policy recognizes the inevitable trade-offs in designing and operating technology-based systems and requires that managements be more explicit in recognizing and choosing trade-off positions in the achievement of a "manufacturing task" that is derived from corporate strategy. A major contribution of this new approach toward the improvement of working environments is the promise it offers of movement away from the single dominating goal of cost or efficiency. The new approach is better able to handle, sort, weight, and balance a multidimensional set of criteria. As the old limited approach largely neglected the human factors (as well as many others) in choosing EPTs, the new approach can include consideration of the working environment, with appropriate weighting.

On balance, then, what is the likelihood of managers and engineers moving proactively to increase the stock and influence the choice of available EPTs that improve the working environments? On the positive side it is happening, albeit slowly and cautiously. The technology is developing as well, although it is still in its infancy. New forms of decision making in corporate manufacturing policy may provide a vehicle for the consideration of many objectives, while at the same time the trend toward decentralized corporate divisions has weakened the excessively function-oriented organizational structure of the past.

On the negative side, there are still barriers between suppliers and users of technology that make more difficult the task of managements in improving working environments. Furthermore, the state of the art is that it *is* an art and not a science. We do not know how to do it: Managements and engineers are surprised by "good" designs that do not work and by side effects of ordinary EPTs that unexpectedly do work. It is still too mysterious and complex for most companies to risk more than experimentation.

It appears that public pressure and the new interest in QWL on the part of managements and employees are becoming a pivotal factor. For to improve QWL will take more firm involvement on the part of top management than the effort now receives. More labor crises, skill shortages, sick industries, and stalled productivity, on the one hand, and glowing examples of profit improvement from the intrepid, on the other, may also speed the process.

For these reasons, we judge that the proposed development of new EPTs conducive to better work environments is in an early experimental stage with no clear trend in view. At least five years of proven results, diffused widely across a substantial number of leading companies, will be necessary before industry reaches the takeoff stage where "everybody's doing it."

Changes in the Management Decision Process for Choosing Equipment and Process Technologies

Exhibit 11.7 lists factors involved in these management decision processes. As stated earlier, many of these factors are changing or are apt to change.

In particular, a powerful influence in management selection of EPTs favorable to QWL will be the expectation of profitable results. In other words, an efficient worker who obtains more production out of a given investment in fixed assets is a profitable worker. The changing cost mix moving toward a lower percentage for labor and a higher percentage for

---

Exhibit 11.7   Factors Involved in the Management Decision: Choice of Equipment and Process

1. Ideology—values
2. Objectives
3. Risks/uncertainty
4. Choice of criteria
5. Weightings of criteria
6. Judgment of anticipated results
7. Costs
8. Investment
9. Capacity policy
10. Resource reliability
11. Cycle—delivery

overhead and materials will induce the same effect. The ancient clash over production and pay on the part of management and workers, respectively, will cool when there is a higher multiple of value added per employee, and when both parties are pushing for better utilization of material, overhead, and energy. Such considerations would indeed induce a manager to choose an EPT that provides a favorable working environment.

SUMMARY AND CONCLUSIONS

When changing technology moves across an industry, its effects on operating systems are usually pervasive and powerful. The choice of an EPT is the single most influential decision a management makes in determining QWL in a manufacturing or service-operations system. Once made, many other elements of the system are adapted to serve the EPT, or, if left unchanged, become incongruent and dysfunctional. The working environment is similarly affected by a change in EPT. All systems of work, including job content of individual jobs, pay schemes, the role of managers, and decision-making processes, are influenced and constrained by a choice of EPT. For these reasons EPT has been the major factor in determining QWL in a given work situation.

A second but always critical factor that acts as a modifier of the impact of EPT on the work environment is the set of operating policies and practices surrounding the workplace. A third and also critical factor is the decision processes by which managers choose an EPT. The fourth critical ingredient is that of worker perceptions, both individually and in groups. Exhibit 11.4 suggested the relationship of these four factors acting together. (The following paragraphs summarize the conclusions developed in this chapter.)

For most of the industrial history, technology has dominated the working environment. The effects have been good and bad. Machines replacing labor do not, in themselves, produce poor working environments, for machines may remove drudgery and monotony as well as create them. Some technologies help and others hurt, and the working environment has been a haphazard result of the choice of EPTs from whatever stock of EPTs has been available.

An unusually rapid enlargement of EPT stock may now be forthcoming because of the changing mix of cost factors now taking place, emphasizing material, energy, and capital and deemphasizing labor costs. A possible, indeed probable, effect is a work environment in which the goals of labor and management may be less in opposition than they have been.

Some managements are developing skills and experience in adapting to

EPTs, largely through restructuring the work content and infrastructure governing work and workers. Experiments have generally worked out well, but diffusing the innovation usually has proven difficult. Unions usually have been cautious and skeptical concerning these experiments.

A few managements are attempting to influence the stock of EPTs for the better by intentionally developing EPTs that may be conducive to better work environments. This takes new knowledge and judgment that are only beginning to be developed.

The management decision processes for selecting EPTs are being changed in some corporations by objective criteria that include anticipated effects on the work environments and the weighting of these criteria more heavily relative to traditional economic criteria. The new manufacturing policy/corporate strategy approach to EPT decisions facilitates the use of broader criteria related to longer term strategic considerations and may move traditional manufacturing management thinking away from a functional and toward a strategic corporate viewpoint.

Changes in ideology, worker insistence on participation, and management belief in the potential of better management of human resources will further the whole process, including better adaptation to existing technologies, affirmative development of new technologies, and more decisions influenced by QWL in choosing EPTs.

Disaggregation of industries and EPT suppliers, and inadequate knowledge of cause-and-effect relationships between the EPT working environment and the monthly divisional performance focus still cause substantial barriers to development of better EPTs.

Altogether, these conclusions add up to a scenario in which we can expect incremental change in the form of more new EPTs, more experimentation, more risk taking, and more management investment, concern, and involvement in EPTs and the work environment. Probably the greatest single factor that is beginning to change the process at many points (Exhibit 11.7) is managers' premises and objectives—premises about people and their potential and objectives that include better development of human resources. The choice of technology is now beginning to be influenced by these considerations.

There are many signs that a growing number of U.S. managements are no longer willing to let the working environment just happen. Some will try to manage that sector of their business just as they attempt to manage markets and finance, costs, and assets. The profit motive will be the driving force largely because of the multiplier effect that a turned-on, released, and cooperative work force can have on production.

What will be the effect of changing technology on working environments in the 1980s? Managements will slowly begin to react to existing technologies and to whatever technologies come along with better operating policies and practices; they will gradually produce better working environments. Many will not be content merely to react, however, and will instead begin to select and innovate new technologies that offer advantages for the working environment. They will be stimulated, partly by the ongoing change in factory costs, material and energy, partly by changes in ideology and intention, and, finally, perhaps most of all by the recognition that achievement of profitable competitve productivity is steadily demanding a more competitive, dedicated, and committed work force, free of the resentments that fester and restrain in a poor working environment.

We have now dealt with the impact of changing technology on the manager, on the factory as a whole, and on the work force. There is a fourth impact as well, and it is the subject of the following chapter. The fourth impact is quite new, in effect. It is that operations technology can become a powerful strategic lever.

This should not be new or in fact is not new at all. Henry Ford's assembly line formed a devastating strategic weapon, as did continuous casting in the steel industry, and interchangeable parts for Isaac Singer in the last century.

But what is new is that practically none of the modern writers on corporate strategy take up this enormously powerful tool, in spite of its effect throughout industrial history. Technological breakthroughs in equipment and processes are dramatic, but strategic advantage may be created by careful choices of existing processes, such as in the case of the success of mini steel firms. The fact is, in modern day strategic thinking, operations technology is more often than not a blind spot.

NOTES

1. Richard E. Walton, "Quality of Working Life: What Is It?" *Sloan Management Review* (Fall 1973): 11–21.

2. William J. Abernathy, *The Productivity Dilemma* (Baltimore: Johns Hopkins University Press, 1978).

3. Robert H. Hayes and Steven Wheelwright, "Matching Manufacturing Process Structure to the Product/Market Structure," Working paper, Division of Research, Harvard Business School, Harvard University, 1977.

4. George C. Lodge, *The New American Ideology* (New York: Alfred A. Knopf, 1975).

5. Internal document of Cummins Engine Company. Also adapted in Richard E. Walton, "QWL Indicators—Prospects and Problems," *Studies in Personnel Psychology* (Spring 1974).

CHAPTER 12

Operations Technology: Blind Spot in Strategic Management

Innovation in operations equipment and process technology can be used strategically as a powerful competitive weapon. It can bring to bear many other strategic factors besides achieving low costs—superior quality, shorter delivery cycles, lower inventories, lower investment in equipment, shorter new product development cycles, and new production economics. The potential of aggressive innovation in operations equipment and process technology is frequently a blind spot in strategic management. This powerful competitive weapon is generally unused, neglected in both corporate operations and the professional literature. In fact, conventional practices in strategic management nearly inevitably doom technological development in equipment and processes to take place in a reactive and pedestrian mode.

In employing equipment and process technology (EPT) as a strategic tool often only one concept is considered: that of becoming "low-cost producer." But even that strategy, while listed as "generic" by Michael Porter [1980], is generally employed for protection and seldom used as an integrated, offensive strategy. Usually, it is perceived as a fortunate byproduct of having already achieved (somehow) a high market share, success, growth, and thereby, volume production. And it is the volume which delivers the mathematics of the learning curve and, hence, low production costs. This nice set of dominoing events is well known and it often seems to happen. But seldom do these events result from a proactive strategy, one which would say, "let's invest enough in EPT research and development to gain a competitive advantage from creative technological innovation'' (and not just from sheer volume). But even this is a limited view of the strategic possibilities that await discovery in operations technology.

Planned, aggressive innovation can bring to bear many other strategic factors besides achieving low costs. Competitively unique EPTs can also produce superior quality, shorten delivery cycles, reduce inventories, minimize investment in plant and equipment, cut down the new product development cycle, make possible entirely new products, shift economies of scale so that short production runs are feasible, and create new production economics, allowing for a richer product mix, more product proliferation, and more customer specials.

One of the outstanding examples of the achievement of strategic advantage by investment in innovative equipment and process technology is in operation at John Deere's new tractor manufacturing complex in Moline, Illinois. New computer controlled machining, assembly, and inventory processes are enabling the company to shorten lead times, economically offer customers unique products, and lift quality levels to new highs.

Each of these potential achievements can offer distinctive competitive advantages around which the corporation can plan its strategy (see Chapter 13).

With this rich array of potential contributions it is surprising that production or operations technology is so little used in strategic management. Why is it given a back seat to new product development and marketing management as a competitive resource? Why is investment for research and development usually focused on *product* development rather than on *process* development?

The current situation in many US manufacturing industries offers some insights into these questions. I have been studying twelve American industrial firms, focusing on some of the new manufacturing technologies such as robots, computer-aided design (CAD) and computer-aided manufacturing (CAM), lasers and the like, in an effort to understand the ''factory of the future'' and whether, when, and how it is to come into being. The twelve firms I selected are all large-scale leaders in advanced manufacturing in the forefront of their industries. I believe they offer good examples of the best, current practice. From this research some tentative explanations have begun to emerge as to why equipment and process technology continues to be a blind spot in strategic management, and why in spite of the enormous strategic potential of the new, largely microprocessor-oriented technologies, progress toward creating new competitive advantages through EPT development seems slow.

INDUSTRIAL TECHNOLOGY–1982

The US factory has come under increasingly severe pressure from foreign competition; it has frequently proven noncompetitive; it repels many capable young people; it seethes with a discontented labor force. Nevertheless, wholesale automation, mechanization, robotics, computerized, reduced-cost operations, and a radically improved quality of industrial working life (QWL), remain promises that have been just around the corner for 30 years.

Now that manufacturing performance is clearly critical to competitive survival in many industries, it is surprising and ironic that we still find ourselves with outdated factories and obsolete equipment. Worse, we are strangely slow to adopt the promising new manufacturing technology that could reverse or at least begin to improve the inferior strategic positions of many US industrial firms. In a few instances operations executives have developed new process technology that could become the foundation of a changed, competitive strategy. But these instances are few and far between.

Why is the American factory establishment so slow to adopt new manufacturing technology? Some predict that we will continue to slip in our ability to produce competitively and will end up as a nonindustrial nation. Yet many technologists argue that the "factory of the future" can still save us. Both sides of the debate agree that the US factory is in peril.

The tantalizing promise of advanced mechanization and automation has been an elusive hope for a long time. Now, finally the much-heralded "robot" is making its appearance, but with more publicity than impact. Even numerically controlled machine tools and numerically controlled servo-mechanisms are being adopted by factories surprisingly slowly. Process control computers are widely used in some single-product industries, but even this remarkable tool has been adopted reluctantly and slowly in light of the number of possible applications. We hear a great deal about the potential of the computer in the factory, but the literature about computerized production controls is replete with disappointing results. Technological progress has been creeping instead of galloping as we might have expected in this era of exploding scientific and product technology.

It is abundantly clear that the equipment available and today's powerful technological ideas, concepts, and processes have far outrun the ability of the factory system to absorb them. We have available advanced machine tools and processes, computers, controls, numerical control, direct numerical control, and computer-aided design in maufacturing far in excess of our ability to purchase and successfully use them. Somehow, management in the manufacturing world has not been able to fully exploit the new technologies that engineers and scientists have developed.

Over its history the factory institution has seldom been able to adopt new technology quickly, perhaps because absorbing new technology is as much an organizational problem as a technical problem.

INDUSTRIAL HISTORY 1945–1982

What has been happening in our factories since 1945 helps us to understand why the factory has seldom made operations technology a strategic resource. The economic and societal factors which structured the factory affect its current ability to take advantage of new operations technology. One major change in this period is a vast increase in competition. The rise of the diversified corporation has resulted in more companies competing in more markets and more industries. International competition and international trade have been steadily rising in most industries. Manufacturing has increasingly spread all over the world, and Asian nations have gradually penetrated the traditional Western markets. As a result, no industry has escaped foreign competition. Instead of sharpening industrial competence, however, in many cases this competition has dulled it. A generation of dispirited "losers" has been created; investment funds have been withheld; and growth, new technology, and innovation have been dampened.

While losing its share of the worldwide market and running down its equipment, the factory has been forced to cope with a trend toward shorter product life cycles.

This combination of increased competition and shorter product life cycles has affected the factory in many ways. It must produce more customer specials and shorter runs; order quantities are lower; set-up costs rise as a percentage of total costs; and problems of managing inventories of parts and materials have become more critical. The result has been more stress and complexity in operations management.

Adding another straw to the camel's back are sweeping changes at the corporate level. In the 1950s companies began to adopt modern, scientific marketing methods, placing more emphasis on new product design, development, product management, and advertising. In the 1960s, modern financial management methods came into use, featuring accurate and eagle-eyed financial controls, yearly operating plans, and strict monthly budgets, quarterly budgets, and precise monthly controls against these budgets. Exacting financial controls and measurement systems with the loopholes closed one by one became a central force of corporate management affecting executive behavior and providing a dominant yardstick for factory performance, not only for inventory control, but for making investment decisions where paybacks on new machinery and equipment were set by corporate goals. The financial orientation at the top caused operations managers more administrative hassle and difficulty in justifying the purchase of new machinery and equipment. The hurdle rates in many industries climbed to 35–50 percent, meaning that new machinery and equipment were often simply not purchased.

The late 1960s and 1970s saw the appearance of strident employee demands and new worker expectations. The work force frequently demonstrated its discontent with low quality, low productivity, and lack of cooperation. Different age groups required different supervisory tactics. More pressure was placed on factory managers to keep workers "happy" and productive. As factory management was squeezed from above to lower costs and make better products, employees and unions pushed upward. Factory managers were caught in the middle.

But there was scant recognition of the forces behind these pressures on factory management, and few, if any, new management tools and concepts were developed to cope with these new waves of problems and demands. Most factories were managed in the 1970s very much as they had been in the 1940s and 1950s. Manufacturing management was dominated by engineers and a technical point of view. This may have been adequate when management issues largely centered on efficiency and productivity and the answers came from industrial and process engineers. But the problems of operations managers in the 70s had moved far beyond mere physical efficiency.

Operations managers' jobs had become much more complicated. Once simply charged with "efficiency," operations managers now had to manage more demanding workers, to handle more complexity in product mix, production, inventory, cost controls, and scheduling, to introduce more new products, to change products and volumes flexibly, and to successfully compete in a more intensive competitive environment. Manufacturing managers faced economics problems, control problems, work force problems, and confounding dilemmas trying to satisfy top management on a multitude of conflicting performance criteria, mainly financial in orientation.

These issues required a new breed of multidimensional manufacturing managers but the factory system had produced too few such people. The age of mass production and industrial engineering is over. Today, fewer products are produced strictly on a mass production basis, and a single-minded focus on productivity is no longer adequate. Technical skills and insights are no longer sufficient to cope with strongminded, top management applying the new and demanding financial tools. Many previously successful factory managers have been outgunned by sophisticated professional top managers while being perplexed and hurt by the apparent alienation of a once-loyal cadre of workers.

Given 35 years of increasing pressures and declining competitive performance, it is little wonder that factory management has been in a reactive mode and hence unable to create and sell a corporate strategy to innovate equipment and process technology. If there is a blind spot in strategic management about operations technology, it is less because of myopia at the top than because of functional operations managers' inability to promote operations technology as their own competitive weapon. How is corporate top management to know about this promising but untried factor in competition if their own operations people do not burst out to proclaim and champion the new idea?

OBSTACLES TO CHANGE

Past history suggests that three roadblocks stand in the way of change for the future:

1. If operations continue to be measured mainly by short-term, financially oriented standards, they will stay in the dark ages, held back by excessive requirements for justifying new equipment and processes; our production technology will grow steadily older. The short-term financial point of view also dominates decisions concerning nonphysical investments in operations, those designed to improve the quality of life at work, and to improve systems for quality and production control.

2. A second roadblock to change is top management's perception of operations as a kind of "productivity machine" rather than as a potential strategic resource. Their view is that "efficiency" is the overriding criterion of performance. Top management asks "how can operations improve our financial results?" instead of asking, "how can operations make us a stronger competitor"?

3. Operations managers need to become better at long range planning. Operations managers are skillful at operations, but not at strategic, long-term planning. The conventional emphasis has been on productivity, meeting schedules, and maintaining efficiency on a month-by-month basis. Often we have been unable to look at total factory systems and make wholecloth changes. Instead, changes aremade one by one, piecemeal. As each part of the system is changed, it throws another into disequilibrium. And as each change takes a year or two to make (for example, a change in equipment or inventory control or organization), the whole is never quite right. Small wonder, then, that too few operations managers are effective contributors to corporate strategic councils.

These three roadblocks have been industrial facts of life; they have left the keepers of operations technology so impotent as to be unable to use operations technology as a strategic weapon.

In addition to these managerial roadblocks, history suggests that the aggressive use of operations technology for corporate strategy has been delayed by the state of the art as much as by any myopia of strategic planners. The equipment and process technology (EPT) available over the past 30 years in many industries has frequently been inadequate to form a competitive weapon. Too often the EPTs available have simply not met the needs of business.

Progress has been limited by the technology available. New and modern EPTs have moved in on a grand scale in certain process industries, such as chemicals, paper, steel, plywood, and petrochemicals, where they offered giant economies of scale. But in fragmented industries where enormous productive units have been a competitive impossibility (for example, metalworking, assembly, electronics, furniture, textiles, construction, shoes, apparel, plastic molding, printing, packaging, electrical machinery, transportation equipment, boat building, foundries, and toys), the new technologies offered have been merely evolutionary and creeping in their rate of progress. The new EPTs have generally failed to meet the strategic needs of the business because they have been:

- Too costly, relative to their benefits.
- Inflexible, in terms of product and material variety, changeovers, and setups.
- Designed to be efficient only on long runs and high daily volumes.
- Full of "bugs" and the problems inherent in new processes.

Operations management has not been offered the right equipment, systems, technology, and tools. Superb individual technologies have been developed (for example, automated machine tools and direct numerical control). But when these magnificent new innovations have been applied, usually they have been slow in becoming effective and economic. They take years to improve and the payoffs are usually quite a bit lower than projected. Radical new equipment often does not mesh with existing equipment. Managements have grown prudently chary.

It seems strange that market forces have not induced "better mousetraps.'' But the available EPTs have generally been developed by specialized equipment producers to one part or step in a process. The individual EPTs may have performed satisfactorily but they were not coordinated, nor did they cover enough process steps to eliminate people and overhead and thereby produce major economies. Machine tool companies, for example, concentrate on their specialities: milling, turning, and drilling. Some firms have offered machining centers but few have offered fully integrated and coordinated total operations sequences, including transfer mechanisms and computerized controls for low-volume manufacturing and for sufficient product and volume flexibility. Needed but not available is the kind of designer-contractor prominent in the chemical process industries offering the ''turnkey'' new facility.

For the most part, the industrial equipment industry has apparently been unable to interpret customers' strategic needs and develop product lines accordingly. In spite of the decline of mass production, and the trend toward shorter runs and more customer specials, too few EPTs satisfactorily solve the cost, quality, and technical problems found outside the high-volume process industries.

Finally, strategic investments in operations technology have been discouraged by conventional premises and practices:

1. Corporate performance and reward systems are based on performance against annual budgets. Well written-off facilities look more profitable on paper, and reward systems in most companies reinforce this view.

2. Capital budgeting is based primarily on return on investment, rather than on strategic analysis.

3. The inexperience of top managers in manufacturing makes them unreceptive to major innovations in factory technology. To many executives, manufacturing and production are necessary nuisances—they soak up capital in facilities and inventories; they resist changes in products and schedules; their quality is never as good as it should be; and their people seem unsophisticated, tedious, detail-oriented, or unexciting.

4. Manufacturing executives are averse to the risk involved with major new innovative investments. They have seen too many new pieces of equipment fail to be fully utilized and not work as well as promised (requiring further investment in support facilities and overhead) to be enthusiastic about anything for their factory that is not well-tested and proven, preferably by somebody else. ''Let my competitor take the risk,'' is a common, not altogether irrational outlook. Why be number one in taking risks for new EPTs when the penalties for failure are so high?

5. Manufacturing managers tend toward cautious conservatism. Typically, their careers have been insular and their attitudes and behavior are conditioned by years of vulnerability to criticism. They get the blame for falldowns and they bend every effort to be certain that things won't go wrong.

6. Manufacturing managers must focus on the short term to meet the monthly schedule, maintain good quality and delivery, and solve personnel problems. They find it difficult to develop a strategic point of view in the midst of their struggle with existing EPTs and the basic in-place systems; they do not see alternatives; and they often lack the perspective to see what is possible or even what other companies are doing. Manufacturing strategy is a new art.

To look ahead, how will the future differ from the past? Can and will operations technology play an enlarged and more strategic role in the industrial firm? What is changing?

SEVERAL PIVOTAL CHANGES

During the past five or ten years the operations technology available has begun to change enormously in nearly every industry. It offers new capabilities and no longer clashes with such marketing realities as short product life cycles.

Radical, order-of-magnitude changes in EPTs are now appearing. The new technology, microelectronics, is offering a new wave of EPTs in virtually every industry. EPTs that can think, react, self-correct, adjust to product and volume changes, offer general-purpose flexibility and special-purpose economics, coordinate with other process links, reduce scheduling, paperwork, indirect labor, and overhead costs, and offer a whole new range of versatility and even cost reduction are becoming increasingly available. In addition to microelectronics are new materials, advanced software capabilities, new optical sensors, and the increased effectiveness of employees armed with more information and offered more opportunities to participate; we begin to see potential answers to many of the drawbacks and problems in the EPTs available in the past.

Key to new strategic advantages are the new technologies that allow operations to become much more versatile and flexible through the use of microprocessor computers and controls. They make job shop, short-run, product-specialized factories operate more like process-type, long-run, high-volume factories, requiring fewer setups and changeovers, less indirect labor, and easier scheduling and sequencing. Complete printed circuit board facilities, such as those at Hewlett-Packard and Lockheed, for example, furnish evidence of the practicality and competitive leverage of self-contained, microprocessor-based new manufacturing technologies.

The microprocessor, coupled with computer-aided design and flexible machining and processing equipment, can make changes in products and materials in minutes rather than hours. Setup and changeover times are drastically reduced. They can make product proliferation and customer specials an affordable marketing strategy. The factory will have a whole new set of economics.

The new technologies appear to supply the answer to the most fundamental manufacturing dilemma of the 1960s and 1970s, namely, that while manufacturing technology was making greater economies of scale possible with mass production, markets, driven by economics and competitive pressures, were moving away from mass production towards more specialized products.

Greater knowledge and sophistication are required to select, acquire, and implement the new technologies. They test the abilities of engineers and managers and rapidly outdate a generation of technical people. They require a systems approach; if a system is poorly designed or based on only partial information, the new integrated technology systems can be disastrous. Organizational power will shift to managers who understand these systems.

With the new technology at hand, are the associated management problems going to disappear? Probably not, but these problems are at least being recognized. Management analysts are stressing the damaging effect of emphasizing the short term at the expense of innovation and long term development. In an effort to broaden their perception of the strategic potentials of operations functions, many large firms, such as General Electric, TRW, American Standard, and Hewlett-Packard, are now training their top executives in manufacturing strategy.

This is not just "management development," but an effort to shift the corporation's basic emphasis in manufacturing from operations to policy, and from tactics to strategy. By focusing on structural decisions—EPT choices, the number and size of plants, capacity policy, and make or buy decisions—instead of on costs and short-term productivity, manufacturing can become a competitive weapon. With poor structural decisions, no amount of able production management can achieve competitive results.

Another change in some companies is promising. At the Copeland Corporation, one of the world's largest refrigeration compressor manufacturers, instead of projecting only their investments' quantitative effects, they are beginning to assess investments in nonquantitative terms, such as:

• Flexibility for product change.
• Flexibility for volume change.

- Effects on quality and reliability.
- Impact on morale and attitude.
- Impact on the ability to compete.
- Impact on the ability to survive long term.

Many corporations, such as General Electric, are beginning to require such nonfinancial goals in order to build superior competitive resources for the long term. Their yardsticks are not limited to dollars, but measure performance in terms of developing people, EPTs, QWL, morale, and competitive assets and structure.

A final hopeful factor is the possibility that the new factory will be such a different place to work that its people will become a competitive resource as well as its technology. The movement for better quality of work life is gathering momentum and has brought about hundreds of experiments in new working environments. Better and more interesting jobs are being created and human resource management is being improved. Companies that accomplish a revolution in the work place will create a resource in their operations that strategic planners cannot ignore.

The ultimate question is, are these changes profound enough to make companies use operations technology as an element in strategy?

THE NEW INDUSTRIAL COMPETITION

An extraordinary amount of change is taking place in industrial operations. Factors that have had a largely negative impact for 35 years are changing. Changes in these factors may produce an order-of-magnitude change in the factory. It is no exaggeration to say that the factory is being reinvented in the 1980s.

The burst of new operations technologies that has occurred simultaneously with the new global industrial competition [Abernathy, Clark, and Kantrow, 1981] seems an extraordinary coincidence. But this competition is essentially technological. Operations technology and product technology are propelling vigorous new competitors to a larger share of the market. Industrial management today depends on managing technological change.

The flood of new products and operations technologies demands a new level of organizational performance for handling substantial change. Organizations must learn rapidly, adapt quickly, and solve a stream of problems without crisis. For example, the auto industry needs to learn how to bring out a new model in two or three years rather than six or seven.

Further, it needs to replace the massive, inflexible capital equipment that has kept its product strategy captive to its operations technology.

The auto industry is typical of many industries where economics and inflexible operations technology collide with the need for new products to compete with those produced by on-rushing technology. That a burst of global competition has coincided with the development of new operations technology is not a coincidence but two sides of a single phenomenon; the new competition is based on that technology. The question for corporate strategic planners is not whether operations technology can become a strategic resource, but how to make it one, just as rapidly as possible.

This being the case, we turn next to five chapters which detail how operations technology and the manufacturing function can become a competitive resource. The first step, I contend with co-author Milton Lauenstein, is to recognize that competition is above all a battle between resources—and the company with the best resources usually wins.

REFERENCES

Abernathy, W.; Clark, K.; and Kantrow, A. 1981. "The new industrial competition," *Harvard Business Review*, Vol. 59, No. 5 (September/October), pp. 68–81.

Porter, Michael E. 1980. *Competitive Strategy*. The Free Press, New York.

MANUFACTURING AS A COMPETITIVE RESOURCE

The five chapters in this part are particularly addressed to top corporate managers. The objective of this section is to offer three still unconventional concepts to directors and executives of manufacturing firms.

1. The company with the best resources wins, and manufacturing is usually one of the most important.
2. The obsession with productivity is wrong and leads to minor cost savings at the expense of major, strategic moves that can restore or create competitive advantage.
3. The physical side of the business is neither mundane nor merely "details". On the contrary, it is where the big dollars are, and where strategic leverage can be created.

CHAPTER 13

Formulating a Strategy of Superior Resources

The organization with superior resources—technology, knowledge, management, human skills, and finances—usually wins. A key objective of management is to develop those key resources to be better than those of competitors. This basic tenet of strategy is perhaps the one most frequently violated as managers so often spread and divert vital, limited resources instead of concentrating and focusing them so as to achieve a clear, overwhelming competitive advantage.

The advantages of focusing assets and energies on a narrow enough sector of objectives to be able to achieve competitive superiority are obvious enough in the management of both military and corporate operations. They are clear in personal careers as well. "Don't spread yourself too thin" is accepted as sound advice for managers. Rare is the executive who has not learned that trying to do too much at once usually results in success in nothing.

The disciplined corporate organization concentrates its resources and attention on a limited sector of technology, product, or market and, thus, gains a telling competitive advantage. Many such companies, in a successful reinforcing cycle, have grown even stronger and, gaining experience, financial strength, and market share, then develop even more powerful resources and a position of industry dominance. The unfocused company— with resources spread thin, talents stretched tight, and lacking a clear edge of superiority in key resource sectors—ends up struggling to survive. Its market share, profit margins, and cash flows are typically smaller than those of the dominant focused producers. The poor get poorer.

This chapter is co-authored with Milton C. Lauenstein.

Lucky or brilliant breakthroughs in technology or product or marketing may pull it out, but the firm plays catch-up ball when its resources are inferior.

Why, then, is the truly focused company or division so rare? There are, in fact, many factors that tend to scatter and diffuse a company's activities, skills, and resources and start it down the slide to a weakened strategic position. Analysis of companies whose results have deteriorated because they lost focus over a period of time suggests that identifying the causes for weakening resources can lead to a more positive posture for an effective strategy for developing superior resources.

THE TEMPTATIONS OF DIVERSIFICATION

The position of every company in each of its markets is subject to a continuing series of threats from competition, changing customer demands, new technologies, government regulations, and a host of other factors. Managers are usually properly sensitive to these vulnerabilities and are rarely completely sure that positions will not be eroded. When a company or division is primarily dependent on one market, product line, or technology, it is especially nervous. The results of losing its position would be so serious as to constitute a strong motivation to diversify.

Obviously, a disaster in any one area is less serious to a firm that operates in several. However, when diversification results in a company's resources being spread weakly over several areas, the chances that it will not be able to compete effectively may be very much higher in each area in which it participates. A study of the Fortune 500 companies indicates that nondiversified companies on the average not only achieved faster growth and superior return on investment but also were considered safer by a noted published investment advisory service.

Salter and Weinhold[1] cite the low capital productivity of widely diversified companies. The return on equity of a broad sample of such companies was 18 percent below the Fortune 500 average in 1975 and 20 percent below in the ten-year period 1967–1977. They state that

the acquisitive diversifiers had low price-earnings ratios. On December 31, 1977, the average P/E of the sample was 30% below that of the New York Stock Exchange stocks as a whole. The situation has changed little over several years. Even higher return-on-equity performers like Northwest Industries, Teledyne, and Textron have P/E's well below the market's average.

These facts suggest that the reduced vulnerability to reverses in any one sector was more than offset by the negative effect of diffusing effort in the diversified companies.

"MEETING THE PLAN"

In many situations where superior resources have not been built, current operating problems have dominated management thinking. Especially in the case of divisions of large corporations, results in the relatively short run are critically important to the careers of the division managers. Pressure to "meet the plan" (i.e., the annual and monthly or quarterly budget) is the engine of a short-term point of view. Immediate customer requirements, competitive moves, production and cost problems get priority attention.

As a result, planning efforts are typically concentrated on the current year. Strategic issues receive superficial attention at best, and the long-term development of resources needed to achieve leadership in a specific market gets almost none at all. Every effort is made to live within the short-term operating plan and to overcome variances occasioned by operating problems, economic conditions, competitive moves, or unexpected actions by customers. Identification of key resources is not made explicit, and investment in those resources is neglected.

Many chief executive officers were successful practitioners of that approach when they were at lower levels of management. They have learned through their experience as operating executives that advancement comes from improving profit margins, taking customers away from competition, meeting forecasts by squeezing out every dollar rather than from sacrificing current earnings to build the capabilities that may be more decisive in the long run. This leads to opportunism and scattered actions rather than effort focused on long-term objectives. If things are not going well, pressure is exerted to seek a "quick fix."

Equally common is the tendency in the large, portfolio-managed, financially dominated company to "dump the losers" and move to greener fields, without thoroughly considering what it would take to build the resources necessary for success. In the smaller or medium-sized company, the syndrome is to merge or acquire companies in new fields, reducing their focus and potential competitive advantage in the market they know best but about which they are discouraged or feel impotent.

UNDERESTIMATING OPPORTUNITIES IN PRESENT FIELDS

Many companies move away from a single-minded concentration on their present lines of business because, discouraged with their performance, top management concludes that their markets, products, or technologies have too-limited growth or profit futures. Sometimes this is a valid judgment. But often the real problem is a failure to manage effectively the present business. The failure may be derived from current marketing, manufacturing, or product design policies or activities. The difficulty may be more basic. The firm may have failed to develop the unique capabilities needed to compete successfully in its industry. When critical resources are already spread thin, it is easy to conclude that the future looks bleak—and that diversification is the only way out.

For example, a medium-sized inorganic chemical specialty company reached pessimistic conclusions about its future and subsequently embarked upon a lengthy program to diversify and grow in other fields. Over several years, it acquired four companies in a variety of growing industries. Ultimately, however, its original business began to increase in volume and profitability while its acquisition floundered along and finally fell by the wayside. This occurred after considerable time, capital, and management effort were consumed. The happy ending was delayed, in fact, for over five years while the management diverted scarce resources to the new fields, which seemed to offer attractive industry growth and higher profit than their own. But they learned that they were better off to compete effectively in a field they knew thoroughly than to come in last in several different growth industries.

BUCKLING UNDER THE PRESSURE TO GROW

Companies and divisions are usually under great pressure to grow. There are financial reasons, managers' ambitions, career opportunities, and rewards in the stock market. This set of forces constantly exerts inducements to expand and leads almost inevitably to a rosy view of opportunities for the company outside of its present sphere of activities.

A high-technology company waited patiently in a "crouching position" for several years as potential customers only slowly discovered and began to take advantage of its unique technological skills. Impatience set in for the managers, whose personal finances depended principally on market appreciation of company stock, believed the company to be too small to attract market attention. Growth itself became a primary objective.

For this reason the company made a large acquisition in a low-to-medium-technology industry that was totally different from the business it knew well. The acquisition doubled sales. The purchase price was modest, however, because the newly acquired company had not performed well in recent years. The new parent believed that it could turn matters around with its own management skills and superior technical competence.

The diversification proved disastrous. Management was poor and, hence, the company lost more money than the parent could earn. The parent's management was unable to be in enough places at once either to anticipate or to control the losses. After absorbing substantial management and financial resources, the acquisition had to be sold. Meanwhile, the firm's patient but thorough development of superior resources in its own high-technology field finally began to pay off as new, large, and profitable business was developed. Growth as a primary, overriding objective had proved dysfunctional when it led the management into a situation it could not manage.

THE OVERCONFIDENCE SYNDROME

When a company is doing well, its managers often believe that they have superior ability and can, therefore, succeed in almost any business. The merger candidate "only needs the good management we can bring it." They lost sight of the fact that their specialized knowledge of the particular practices, products, and people of their own industry, which took years to acquire, represents an important basis for the competitive success they have achieved. In a new market, where they do not have the background and experience-bred wisdom required for success, they often fail, or at best do not succeed. Worse still, by diverting attention from their main business, they may wreck or at least seriously injure it.

MISJUDGING THE SUCCESS REQUIREMENTS

A repeated cause of disappointment in investment in a new field by firms successful in their own traditional areas is simply miscalculation or poor judgment of a new area. Problems encountered in the new business often turn out to be more complex, knotty, and resistant to solution than originally anticipated.

Analysis of such problems suggests that these misperceptions occur most often when a clear connection appears to exist between the old business and the new—when there is a common customer or market, or a familiar technology or similar product. For instance, in the example given earlier of the high-technology firm, the parent company and the company acquired both served the same general market area, along with other markets. But such connections are often merely superficial. Managers hastily say, "We're familiar with that," only to find that even with the same customer there are often major differences in what it takes to sell a new product. Based on some familiarity, the company is overconfident, and fails to check deeply enough into the whole set of resources, knowledge, and expertise it takes to be successful in the new sector or business. What appears contiguous and realizable in one dimension may be far removed and difficult in other vital success elements.

THE RUSH TO USE IDLE CAPACITY

The factors mentioned above combine to create an almost overwhelming pressure to enter new fields if a company has idle capacity. This pressure may be most pronounced when the idle capacity is in unused manufacturing facilities, but it also occurs when the company perceives it has the marketing capability to sell other products, managers ready for promotion into new challenges, engineers without full workloads, or other forms of underutilized resources.

When a company is paying the fixed costs for production facilities that are not being used, the pressure for increased earnings is frequently acute and the incremental effect of putting the facilities to work is obviously modest. For these reasons a task force is then organized to find a product, to locate subcontract work, or to do almost anything to employ the excess capacity. Too often the result is an operation that does not fit the facilities, skills and style of current manufacturing. Run lengths may be different. Skill levels and wage rates that are appropriate for the new operation may be quite different from what the company has been doing. Ultimately, the intangible costs to the present operation may far exceed the incremental margin gained on the additional operation.

Similar phenomena characterize taking on new lines to sell. Almost inevitably there are new things for the sales force to learn, not only about the products and their uses but also about the way the new products are marketed. Efforts on the present lines are diluted. Sometimes the expected increased potency of having a broader line ultimately results in a new way for the customer to split his business with competition. Or the customers use the greater volume with the supplier as an additional lever to get lower prices.

Whether in manufacturing, marketing, or technology, taking on new activities usually involves unforeseen costs and often requires the development of additional capabilities at considerable cost. Thus, efforts to fill idle capacity, like the Trojan Horse, easily infiltrate an organization, but they frequently succeed only in absorbing a good deal of time and effort while diverting managers from more profitable activities.

THE SIREN SONG OF INTEGRATION

The managements of many companies have yielded to the siren song of integration, which very often sounds like a successful strategic approach. In concept, forward integration can help assure markets, broaden horizons, and get the supplier "closer to the customer." And backward integration promises to protect sources of supplies, save profit paid to vendors, and afford better control over quality and delivery.

Too often, however, the more highly focused supplier or customer has learned to do a job far more efficiently than the company which takes it on as part of an integration strategy. At the same time, management attention is diffused and the company moves into a position of managing businesses that it does not understand well and about which it must learn the hard way over time. Moreover, the company is probably carrying on these activities on a scale far lower than that of its suppliers and/or customers, which usually represents a built-in economic disadvantage. Keeping up with changing technology in these new fields often requires investments and resources not available to the company. Often enough, the final decision is a retrenchment.

LACK OF A SOUND STRATEGIC POLICY

The factors prompting diversification and diffusion of effort are particularly virulent in the many situations where companies do not have a well-thought-out strategy. Those companies that have analyzed their prospects and determined the field in which they are likely to grow fastest and make the highest return on investment are much less likely to be tempted into an unwise diversification. In contrast, those that have been simply concentrating their attention on operations have no real basis for resisting the lure of the various defocusing factors which push, pull, or seduce them away from effective focus.

When a firm lacks a sound strategy, it is vulnerable to whims and often tries to copy the patterns of the successful. Thus, small- and medium-sized firms are prompted to look at giant corporations as models to emulate. Since they are often diversified, it appears that entering new fields is a good way to expand.

Similarly, top management nearly always watches competitive moves closely. When a competitor takes a new tack, a company's management is naturally apprehensive lest that give the rival a telling advantage. As a result, one frequently sees the companies in a given industry play follow-

the-leader. The temptation to imitate a competitor often has a more decisive influence on the decision of whether or not to diversify than an
analysis of whether the move is sound and appropriate to the situation of
the company.

THE DANGERS OF PRIDE

When a chief executive has been responsible for a company's entering a
new field, it may become a matter of personal pride and identification and
prevent or delay an otherwise wise divestiture when it fails or does not
clearly succeed. Disposing of the unsuccessful new venture would, of
course, appear to reflect adversely on the reputation of the executive's management.

As a result of pride, many companies are held back from shedding
operations years after they have demonstrated that those operations offer
neither an attractive return on investment nor even a growth opportunity
for the enterprise. Thus, even when there are valid reasons for a company
to spin off sidelines and drop some unfocused activities so that it can
concentrate its resources on its better opportunities, the acquisition process turns out to be irreversible because of personal motives.

STAYING IN FOCUS: WHAT CAN BE DONE?

A company's operating resources—facilities, technology, distribution
channels, personnel, market knowledge, management skills, reputation—
have been designed and developed for the businesses in which the enterprise is already active. It will normally be able to earn the greatest
return on investment in those businesses in which its operating resources
are the most outstanding. Therefore, the first and usually the best place
to find opportunities for expansion and attractive returns is in the very
sectors where the company has already focused. Until top management
is satisfied that this has been thoroughly accomplished, it should not
permit other areas to be explored.

Often this is not done, simply because managers have grown stale in a
business area. They tend to conclude that their limited success should be
blamed on the business area and not on themselves. Managers lose ob-
jectivity about their own industry and business and "know things" which,
if analyzed or tested, are no longer, or perhaps never were, true. Sometimes this happens because the very familiarity with an area of business
(which should be an important asset) becomes a liability when it leads to

false assumptions of how things "must" be done and "what cannot succeed in this industry."

This occurs most often when business conditions, costs, consumer habits, or technology, for example, change from the situation in which the firm has been successful. Such changing conditions can make it more difficult to find opportunities to grow in the field in which an enterprise is already engaged as long as it retains its traditional approach to the business. The management becomes discouraged and begins to look for new fields instead of recognizing and overcoming the challenges in the present business area that have altered its earlier pattern of success.

The company's present scope of operations may be too broad for it to be able to achieve a leadership position. If so, the firm would be well advised to identify a segment of its present industry in which to focus its resources, rather than to continue to spread them thinly and across areas in which they are not better than those of competitors. The capabilities of a company are more likely to represent competitive strength in a narrow segment of its own field than in other areas.

Early success carries the seeds of future problems in other ways as well. Not only does a management become wedded to its particular winning approaches to business, but often the excellent results are produced for a period of time despite levels of efficiency and effectiveness that could not be permitted in more competitive situations. The high costs and low productivity that sometimes develop in businesses with an unusually strong proprietary position eventually catch up and hurt. Disappointing results deter the company's full exploitation of its current opportunities by inducing management to look outside rather than inside.

Recognizing this syndrome is the first step in counteracting it. Before abandoning an early success turned sour, the managers must determine whether the business requires a new approach or simply a higher level of operating effectiveness. While it may be difficult for a company already in the field to recognize its own problems, thereby leading it to falsely based discouragement, a strong dose of self-analysis may prevent the abandonment of a business area in which it actually has the basic elements needed for success.

ARE THE GREEN FIELDS REALLY GREENER?

In evaluating business possibilities outside of the fields in which it is already operating, a company must be doubly careful. First, it must be sure it thoroughly understands the requirements for success in the new field. Since the company has not been active there before, this may be an expensive and hazardous undertaking.

New business territories are often alluring. At first the venture seems so easy that to resist is difficult. "If we get only x percent of the market, it still looks like a good deal." Potential customers give encouraging reports to attract new suppliers. Once the commitment is made, however, the situation is different. Having succeeded in attracting a new supplier, the customer is now interested only in the best value it can get.

Now the new supplier finds itself pitted against well-entrenched competitors in an uneven contest. With greater volume, years of experience, and a depreciated plant, the established supplier often has lower costs. New competition often causes old high prices to disappear, so that only the low-cost producer can earn a reasonable return on its investment. With capital already committed, it is too late to withdraw without large losses.

For these reasons a company should determine whether or not its resources really do qualify it to compete successfully with the well-established firms already supplying the market. Often, present competitors have important strengths that are not readily apparent to the newcomer. As the newcomer enters the field, requirements for business success that were not immediately apparent rise to the surface. A field service organization may be needed. Large inventories may be essential. Discounts and special terms may make prices significantly lower than they appear to be. Continual technical development and new products a high cost may be an inherent feature of the business. Failure to meet any of these requirements may result in winning too small a share of the market to be profitable. The analysis and research required to surface these realities is expensive and painstaking. But there is really no other way to combat the "green field" temptation.

WHAT ARE THE EXPANSION CRITERIA?

To decide whether or not to undertake or expand in a given area, it is useful to have a list of strategic criteria against which to evaluate the opportunity. Such criteria should direct attention to factors influencing how attractive the new activity is likely to be in the long run. They may include:

- *Expected return on investment over the long term, with reasons.* It is important to analyze the reasons given to determine whether in fact they represent an adequate basis for anticipating attractive financial results.

- *Evaluation of the company's resources for being in the business compared with those of actual and potential competitors.* Such factors as manufacturing and distribution costs, technical competence, financial requirements, knowledge of and access to markets, raw material position, and business relationships must be reviewed. It is essential to identify those factors that are critically important for success in the business in question and to be sure that the company is adequately prepared in these areas. If other firms are better qualified for the business in question, it is not likely to provide an attractive return.
- *Anticipate share of relevant market segments.* Most often, the leading company in a market enjoys economies of scale and has inherent cost advantages. If a company is unable to identify one or more segments in which it has a good chance of gaining a leading position, it should be cautious about entering a new area. If "only x percent market share of the business even looks profitable," it is unlikely to remain a good opportunity in the face of competition from firms with larger shares.
- *Business trends.* A business area may be changing so as to become either more or less attractive to a given entrant. These changes may be in any phase of business: technology, market size, buying habits, marketing tactics, or whatever. Before investing in a new area, management should consider the impact of likely changes on results in the longer term.
- *Effect on other operations.* New business relationships can be either helpful or harmful to other divisions. Entering a new field inevitably draws management attention and often other resources away from other corporate activities. Nevertheless, companies diversifying often expect synergies to contribute to building resources, such as technology or marketing programs in one operation which could contribute to the success of other activities. More often than not, however, these synergies do not take place because they are simply very difficult to achieve in an administrative sense. People and cultures get in the way; they have different objectives; they have different reward systems. These factors result in focusing on their separate operations rather than on something of joint interest.

REWARDING MANAGERS FOR RESISTING SEDUCTIVE DIVERSIFICATION

Performance measures that reward executives for developing long-term resources are essential to provide incentives to spend more effort on activities that can be decisive with respect to longer-term results. Such a reward system is likely to lead to greater corporate focus and is less conducive to seductive diversification. For example, programs to develop outstanding depth in a technical field, to achieve market leadership, or to become the low-cost producer require a concentration of effort in relatively narrow areas rather than spreading efforts over a wide diversity of business activities.

But the reward and measurement system must identify and encourage these kinds of long-term investments, because the payoffs are apt to be beyond the tenure of the particular manager who pays the costs and makes the investment. That manager pays the definite cost for an indefinite outcome, usually years ahead. Therefore, only an unusually long time horizon reward system will encourage long-term behavior rather than a "meet the plan" mentality.

Using "resource development" as one element on which to base incentive compensation has been effective in motivating managers to give weight to building the capabilities that will make for long-term profitable growth as well as current results.

SUMMARY

The advantages of a strategy of superior resources are easy to recognize. However, many powerful factors lead to executive decisions that tend to diffuse efforts and resources so as to seriously impair the buildup of the corporate strength necessary to achieve leadership in any field.

Operating executives often tire of concentrating and simply "trying harder" to achieve attractive results in the execution of current programs. Performance, however, usually depends on the relative quality of assets available to the various competitors. A major determinant of success in the long run is the quality and quantity of effort applied to develop formidable personnel and organization, technology, marketing expertise, manufacturing know-how, brand name acceptance, sales techniques, and customer behavior. Instead of seeking "greener fields," therefore, managers would usually do better by investing in building resources in present fields or a segment of present fields. But incentives and performance measurement commonly reward executives primarily for current results. By encouraging the pursuit of short-term opportunities, these policies and procedures often discourage investments aimed at building the long-term resources needed to achieve competitive success.

Top management can secure the advantages of corporate focus by demanding full exploitation of opportunities in areas in which the company is already active, establishing strategic criteria for evaluating business segments the company might enter, and providing incentives to develop resources for the long term.

As to the manufacturing function's potential for development into a superior strategic resource, a frequent cause for failure is the mindset that continues to focus on "productivity" instead of that particular task necessary to support the firm's competitive strategy. The next chapter speaks to that issue.

NOTES

1 Malcolm S. Salter and Wolf A. Weinhold, "Diversification via Acquisition: Creating Value." *Harvard Business Review* 166–176 (July-Aug. 1978).

CHAPTER 14

Boosting Productivity Is the Wrong Focus

After 20 years of neglecting its factories, U.S. industry's current all-out, frenetic effort to restore productivity growth is generally falling short of what is needed to regain lost competitive positions in world markets.

What is now going on in industry is impressive. Underway for a year or so is a vast outpouring of aggressive and often creative responses to our industrial crises: productivity committees and czars, quality circles, renewal of work standards, sharpened cost controls, redesigned job workplaces, even novel human resource management experiments. Industrial management has gone back to basics. It's blocking and tackling again—the old game plan which led to American industrial leadership has been pulled off the shelf, dusted off and vigorously reapplied.

The only trouble is that this time the old game plan doesn't seem to be working as well as it used to. The focus in U.S. industry has always been "productivity," and for 75 years the basic management approach to achieving it has been to rationalize, streamline, simplify, cut, squeeze and apply the pressure. Top management is now returning to these basics. But the paradox is that the harder we seek and press for more productivity, the more elusive becomes the objective or recovering competitive strength.

The problem is that most productivity projects these days are only operational in scope and make savings only at the margin. They straighten out work flows and clean up inefficient operations and thus whittle off 10% savings, an hour here, a dollar there. For the inefficient, the first savings are easy. In well-managed plants, as most of our plants actually are, the savings are marginal yet take much effort and ingenuity to accomplish. Like squeezing an orange, it takes a lot more pressure to get the last few drops than the first. Applying pressure further alienates the work force and so squeezing out more output produces a backlash of resistance and resentment.

Even when such operational efforts succeed, they are usually insufficient to overcome U.S. cost disadvantages. Some examples are: Japanese cars cost $1,000 less than Detroit's. Japanese rejections of machined parts are 1% of those in their American counterpart plants. The cycle for developing and producing new complex commercial electronic products in Japan is three years vs. seven years for the U.S. Many Japanese plants turn over inventories 9–10 times faster than we do. The Japanese typically have practically no incoming inspection. Our quality costs run 10–20 times higher. Cost differences of these orders of magnitude cannot possibly be offset by conventional productivity efforts toward saving labor.

Furthermore, our productivity programs are typically cost oriented, while our competitive problems are by no means limited to cost inequalities. We are beaten more often by superior product quality, service and reliability than by lower prices. And foreign competitors are frequently able to move from idea to manufacturing to delivery in half the number of years it takes us. Asian firms' flexibility for product and volume changes is astounding. Productivity programs which focus on efficiency rarely improve a plant's ability to become a corporate strategic weapon.

What this amounts to is that we have *structural* problems which are not even dented by *operational* focus on the traditional goal of productivity, no matter how diligent. If the problems are structural and competitive, then we need structural and strategic changes, not merely operational ones. And large-scale problems generally require rather fundamental changes.

There is some reason to fear that our focus on productivity may get in the way of the rethinking that is necessary. It may be time, for example, to question much of the ancient wisdom about big plants. It has traditionally been argued that big plants spread overhead and take advantage of economies of scale, thereby boosting productivity. But from a strategic point of view, many American plants may well be too big; they attempt to make too many products, based on too many technologies, to meet the needs of too many markets.

Our obsession with productivity may also divert management attention from thinking about how to adopt advanced technologies and—just as important—how to restructure corporate incentives, which too often block investments in major technological change. Investments in new equipment and processes usually take a good three to five years to perfect, but in too many U.S. companies, capital budget systems demand an earlier payback—with the result that essential new technology is turned down.

Management reward structures that discourage risk taking also hold back the adoption of new technologies and equipment, particulary as needed investments grow even large in cost, scale, and interconnectedness.

In 1892, Frederick Winslow Taylor taught managers to divide up jobs and specialize, mass produce, standardize and squeeze out the pennies. But now all our competitors have learned to do that and many do it far better than we. And the individualistic American worker resents the pressure.

So the new challenge of industrial management is to learn to think about factories differently. Productivity or efficiency results are at best superficial indicators of industrial health. Beneath that surface is a whole set of vital strategic and structural concepts. It is asking a lot of industry to change a mind-set, and discard productivity as the ultimate criterion for manufacturing success. But what is needed is just that, for although productivity is undeniably a good result, as an aim in itself it is proving to be self-defeating.

The next chapter goes further into the same theme, that productivity is such a common obsession among top managers of manufacturing firms that it has become a disease. The productivity focus is a remnant in history, but is becomes malevolent when it preoccupies the manager and prevents the development of a more aggressive and imaginative operations-based competitive strategy.

CHAPTER 15

The Productivity Disease

Management, after 25 years, finally is getting interested in the function that employs 75 percent of their employees, and 80 percent of the company's assets. Companies are turning production people into top management counselors. Production people are getting much more involved; they are being listened to. And, of course, production managers are overjoyed because they are back in the heart of things.

But these managers also are under tremendous pressure from today's tough economics, tough competition, and fast-changing technologies. This pressure is accompanied by shorter product life-cycles, more products, and—driven by the consumer—a very competitive emphasis on quality.

How are these concerns being manifested? By far the most predominant aspect is that renewed focus on productivity. We see productivity czars, productivity committees, productivity staff groups, and productivity labs, not to mention productivity projects and research. Productivity competitions and plant-by-plant comparisons in productivity are common practices, along with new approaches to management, new controls, and new performance objectives. I need hardly mention that virtually every management or professional magazine and journal today is full of articles and papers about productivity.

But you might wonder a little, as I do, what all this is really about. To me, it means a return to sweeping the floor and keeping the place clean. It is taking us back to industrial engineering, back to time-and-motion studies, back to process charts and work simplification—all those great tools of the 1950s.

My question is whether such a preoccupation with productivity really is good. Naturally, the first answer has to be, "Yes." Productivity can't be bad, can it? Surely, you want to get every bit of it possible.

But, on the other hand, if focusing on productivity is all you do, and if this narrow focus is the way you try to run your facilities, then you are treating production as a kind of productivity machine. I think this is narrow, one-sided, and obsessive. We often talk about the "British disease," so I think it is fair to talk about the "productivity disease" our corporations seem to have contracted.

The obsession with productivity creates a culture of its own, characterized by personal pressures, cutting, scrimping, and saving at the margins. It produces a heavy, no-space feeling in most companies. It creates a working environment that drives away some of the best and most able of our young people. Try to get young people—other than highly technical people—to work in factories. It is tough going. I encounter those attitudes constantly.

In all honesty, we must get out on the table some concerns about the present generation of production managers who dominate factories. They are too detail oriented, too short-term oriented; they fuss and fuss about productivity.

Of course, much of this behavior is understandable. You cannot ship the car if it is missing the right-front wheel. The details are important.

But too many production people are cut off from strategic, competitive, and marketing issues. For whatever reason, they live in their own worlds.

The paradox is that professional management started in the factory yet the factory is now the least well-managed of any corporate function. The truth is that for a long time production managers were de-emphasized in the corporate environment. Look what happened when we left them in isolation, badly selected, badly trained, and badly supervised. They became a kind of lost generation, holding a narrow—almost religious—preoccupation with traditional productivity. And the result was that productivity went down and down and down, and so did quality and housekeeping.

There is now a new breed of production people coming along, I am glad to report. Those comers I interviewed are not plodding slowly along the old, straight, seniority-based career paths that production people have had to travel. They are coming up from quite a variety of different corporate career paths and different environments.

They are former computer programmers; they have managed experimental human-resource programs; they are systems engineers and design engineers. A lot of them are also coming through the new staff functions in computerized materials, requirements planning, quality control, and so forth. Some are experienced project managers and program managers, and I even ran into a couple of people from the sales department.

These people are agents of change; they are aggresive. They are showing new skills in team building and project management. They are leaders in organizational learning, and they love and encourage new attitudes.

The new breed is not conventional—no longer the good infantry soldiers whom I grew up with in the factory. Nor are they likely to be particularly loyal to your company. They know they have something they can merchandise in a lot of different places. They lack humility, almost to the point of arrogance; they delegate a great deal; they are very trusting of other people; and they don't necessarily have the rigor and follow-up discipline they should. But they are very interested in ideas and changes and new technology; in fact, they are gung-ho for change.

These people are not in power yet. But in five or ten years they certainly will be, with results that could be tremendously exciting.

I must be careful not to suggest that there is no human innovation going on in factories already. There is, for example, a major corporate re-emphasis on quality.

Although much of this goes back to the old techniques of statistical quality control, there is also a new thing I've never really seen before. In some companies, people are saying, "Look, to get good product quality, we have to have good tooling quality, good product-design quality, good engineering quality, good workmanship quality, good management quality, and so forth." For these companies, product quality has become the catchword—or, if you will, the preacher's theme—to lift the entire company up to new levels of achievement.

Another important area of activity is the increased emphasis some companies are placing on human relations. I remember in my army career as a buck private that if I had a good corporal—and usually I didn't—things always seemed to work out all right. Today we have companies like General Motors, who are doing a superb job of re-emphasizing good, basic human skills for supervisors. But this is still far too limited and narrowly focused in many firms.

There are over 200 documented human-resource management experiments going on right now and probably 2,000 that aren't documented: unsupervised work groups, job-restructuring, job-enrichment, and so forth. The interesting thing is that they are experiments and are labelled as experiments. There are very few that are applied to an entire facility. However, they usually fail because the old culture takes over after vigorous new management put them in place. The pioneers then move off, and the people who take their places drift back to the old ways. We need to do better.

In the old days, we thought of the factory as a place where you transformed materials. It was a physical environment where people performed with their hands or with machines. Now, only about one-eighth of the people in the factory are directly involved with changing materials. The other seven are handling and processing information.

The factory is going to be a very different place when we finally come to understand and appreciate this fact. While there are risks, there can be even greater strategic advantages in pre-empting your competition by placing a whole new emphasis on production. This emphasis is fast becoming the best game in town, and my only unhappiness is that there are as yet so few real converts to this point of view.

There are companies—such as General Electric, TRW, and Hewlett-Packard—who now see manufacturing in terms of strategy rather than just an operating system. They are trying to put in place a new philosophy that focuses on the manufacturing structure and process as a strategic weapon, rather than just trying to manage it in narrow terms of cost and efficiency.

The basic notion of manufacturing strategy should be that a plant or manufacturing production operation—just like an airplane or a boat—can only do certain things well. Therefore, we should design it for what it is going to do well, not design it to be everything to all people. If we make that mistake, we will end up with a plant that, metaphorically speaking, neither sails well nor flies properly.

This brings me to the new manufacturing technology. How is it coming? I am talking here about computer-aided design (CAD), computer-aided manufacturing (CAM), robotics, flexible machining centers, and integrated computerized manufacturing systems.

There is a lot of talk, a lot of literature, and a lot of apparent activity out there in the form of new technology—but very disappointing progress. Things are moving very slowly.

However, that shouldn't surprise us, really. The automobile took about 15 or 20 years before it really got going and drove all over us. Yet it is interesting to see why the new manufacturing technology is slow to take off.

The costs, uncertainties, and risks inherent in these new, complicated, totally integrated, microprocessor-based systems are very substantial. They seem to be changing so quickly. In other words, why should any organization want to go first? The capital budgeting system in most companies forces people to justify this huge expenditure on the basis of savings—and these new systems don't produce savings. They really don't. What they do produce is the strategic ability to move quickly in the competitive marketplace.

Even so, most companies have a tough time bringing these new systems into play. Aside from capital budget problems, reward and promotion systems in most companies do not encourage these types of investments. What ambitious, successful plant manager—one who has been promoted or moved every three or four years—is going to propose to the company a very big investment that he or she knows darn well isn't going to pay off for five, six, or seven years? Added to this is the knowledge that there could be seven years of misery and struggle to get the bugs worked out. This explains why very few people at the level of plant manager or even manufacturing vice-president are backing the new systems.

The Copeland Company produces a large share of the world's refrigeration compressors. The president felt the whole industry was increasingly vulnerable to foreign competition due to lack of investment in modern facilities. The competition was getting tougher, and all through the company there were old, worn-out plants.

He decided to invest in a whole new manufacturing set-up, and he bet $40 million dollars which was a very large risk. He has increased market share; even some of the established firms are moving out of it. It takes a bold, strategic move to bring off such results.

The great advantages of the new production technology are flexibility for product change; flexibility for product proliferation; flexibility for moving with changes in technology; faster delivery; and better and more consistent quality. These are not cost savings. But these things can change your whole impact on a market.

Very few companies are doing it. John Deere perhaps is one of the companies I visited that is doing an outstanding job. Apparently top management just said, "Well, we've got to do it. If we're there first, it's going to give us a big advantage."

It is this kind of thinking that's needed. When you contemplate competing with the Japanese, you don't ask yourself if five or ten percent gain at the margin, which you get through productivity, is really going to beat them. Nor is that five or ten percent we get back from sweeping the floor going to beat the Japanese, either. We are going to have to beat them by competing on the basis of better quality, faster turnaround times, and new technology.

Instead of limiting themselves to an old-fashioned productivity focus, some firms have been much more innovative. In the "rust bowl" territory of companies in the grip of severely noncompetitive costs, a manufacturing strategy that produces better than competitive quality, or delivery, or new product development cycles has been successful in overcoming industrial discouragement and malaise. This is the territory of the next chapter.

CHAPTER 16

Reinventing the Factory: A Manufacturing Strategy Response to Industrial Malaise

The key issue in manufacturing corporations in the Western world is how to respond to the problem of loss of competitive strength and industrial vitality. Western industry has lost market shares, millions of factory jobs, and its head start in equipment and process technology (EPT). Equally serious has been industry's failure to attract the best of our younger people and adequate reinvestment in new capital equipment as well. Without new people and new EPTs we have a state of industrial malaise that continues to erode.

With the present set of difficulties surrounding manufacturing one would expect a strong sense of urgency to adapt modern technology as a cure for eroding competitive positions and slow productivity. We have many obvious motives for trying to adopt new technology.

But, in the face of what appear to be exciting new technologies and opportunities all the way from flexible machining centers to computer-aided manufacturing and computer-aided design, the availability of these new equipment process technologies far outrun their adaptation and the realization of their potentials. On balance, the progress we are making is slow, hesitant, and, indeed, very spotty.

It leads to a strange paradox. While the factory is different from what it was 20 years ago, with working environments generally improved, computer terminals all around, and a few islands of automation, for the most part one sees much old equipment, a very slow rate of change, a modest evolution, and the same old problems: for instance, cost, quality, delivery, and work-force problems.

History suggests that economics will create change and technology will create change, but where is it? The factory of the future is still out there in the future. Is technology to be the white knight that stops our industrial decline? Is there a possibility of a real "shoe string catch," a turn-around that solves the problems of our sick industries? So far the answer is no—it is not happening.

If a technological revolution isn't what's happening, what is? Surely American managers with their tradition of activity and energetic response to problems will not sit and watch their manufacturing enterprises die on the vine. The answer to that is a firm "no." That is not what is happening.

What is happening instead is extraordinary and patently impressive. In my experience, I have never seen anything like it in terms of its energy, its scope, its intensity, and its hopes. I see U.S. industry right now at its traditional best. We have the tradition of getting ourselves three touchdowns behind, but winning in the fourth quarter.

Examine what is happening: Top management is rediscovering the factory. Corporate management is newly interested in the factory as it hasn't been in the last 25 years. It's perfectly obvious to them now, they have to be. Company after company is returning to basics. Industrial engineering standards are being brought out and dusted off. Operations are being tightened. Managers are scrutinizing every operation for signs of inefficiency and low productivity. They are refocusing on the basics of quality, redefining what quality involves and requires. Production managers are being given courses, lectures, and all kinds of training on those subjects. Companies are setting up productivity czars, productivity committees, corporate productivity groups, corporate technology laboratories, and corporate technology directors. Top managers are touring the country and speaking about the urgency of productivity, going before Congress, speaking to anyone and everyone who will listen. Business magazines are full of these issues and concerns.

The energetic, frenetic projects are taking many companies into addressing problems they've put off for years, such as their problems in all-purpose white elephant plants. Now they are trying to straighten them out, trying to create turnarounds. Management is attempting to involve more workers. Companies are approving some capital appropriations that they wouldn't have even thought about four or five years ago. There are closings of plants considered hopeless and moves South. We see some new greenfield plants. Managers of manufacturing are being admitted to meetings of their peers. At many companies now is the first time that manufacturing people have been invited to participate in a management development program.

What does all this really amount to? How do we interpret all this churning, this energetic and purposeful kind of activity? Will it save the day? Is it revitalization?

There is certainly a vitality that we haven't seen in years. Is it "reindustrialization"? I don't know what that means, but what is happening is certainly a reaffirmation of an old faith and a long-standing ideology. For it clearly is reemphasizing the importance of productive facilities and the development of effective management. But will it save the day? I don't think so.

In the auto industry today, for example, we see U.S. production management at its zealous best. We abhor waste, inefficiency, and laxness, and many foreign countries have learned that point of view from us. But what it amounts to is nothing more than reverting to successful tactics of the past. They are back to basics and good industrial engineering. It's productivity, efficiency, and cutting corners. But will the modest productivity gain that renewed focus on productivity save a thousand or fifteen hundred dollars per automobile?

The old game plan, the paradigm of industrial management, is productivity, working on the numbers, and industrial engineering basics: straight-line flows, controls, setting standards, standardizing, and mass production. But one thing we've learned recently is that the Japanese borrowed that game plan from us a long time ago, and they are not better at it than we are. So we must ask this question: Will the old game plan work as well as it used to? I don't think it will. So far, beyond the usual post-recession surge, there has been no significant long-range gain in productivity; we're still losing ground in industry after industry.

So what is to be done? First, we need to learn from the past five years that the single-minded pursuit of productivity is not working. It hasn't been working for 20 years and it doesn't work now. We have a productivity paradox.

Criticizing productivity is like saying that apple pie and meat and potatoes are no good or efficiency is no good. How could productivity be no good? Can we stop worrying about being cost effective? Improving productivity, of course, is absolutely necessary. But productivity is turning out to be something like happiness or fun—the more we pursue it directly, the more elusive it becomes. We need to begin to wonder whether it may be the wrong goal. It is a means to an end. It is a great byproduct; it is great to have it happen, but, as a principal objective, it has caused and continues to cause increasing trouble.

Why is productivity proving to be so elusive? A minor but continuing problem is that its definition is unclear. Many tend to think about it first in terms of direct labor. But when indirect labor is added and analysts include overhead to other costs in the equation and finally end up with sales per employee, the data are too gross to help much. There are statistics that show that some companies with the largest sales per employee don't have the best bottom lines. What about the amount of capital employed when you're thinking about productivity? And how do you balance your investment in capital with your major focus on productivity?

Probably more important than problems with definitions and accounting is that productivity says "squeeze, cut, scrimp, work at the margin, don't spend any more than you have to, don't invest—work harder and smarter." Furthermore, a focus on productivity is a focus on cost and efficiency instead of on competitive position or on building the manufacturing resource to be a competitive weapon.

The biggest and most important reason that productivity has been a wrong goal and has led firms into trouble is simply that it is working at a marginal, modest, and nonstrategic objective. Studies of major competitive improvements in manufacturing over five-to-eight year periods in a variety of companies demonstrate that the major improvements in performance have not derived from "productivity". Earlier I called it the 20-40-40 formula: 20% of the gain derives from changes in productivity, 40% results from changes in technology, and 40% from major changes in manufacturing strategy, in essence, structural changes in how manufacturing is set up, organized, and managed.

Instead of focusing management efforts on strategy and structure, the obsession with productivity has diverted and is now still diverting many top managements and manufacturing managements from the enormous potentials of improved, competitive performance in analyzing manufacturing structure and effecting structural change. The multiplier decisions are those having to do with capacity, with make or buy, with major choices of equipment and processes, with the number of plants, the size of plants, the location of plants, major production control systems, human resources and work resource management systems, as well as quality control systems and organization. There are too many tragic situations in which fine, intelligent, and hard-working managers are working 50–70 hours a week and getting nowhere because the problems are structural in nature and beyond short-term solutions. In essence, if the problems are structural, no amount of work at the margin, nor productivity and efficiency programs will return the firm to competitive superiority.

We have a productivity mind-set. We have a numbers mentality that may be one of the biggest single barriers to the introduction of new technology. It has been a significant cause of the present deterioration and malaise in Western industry. It accounts in large part for the rationale by which top managment cut off manufacturing from issues of finance and marketing and competitive strategy, and manufacturing managers allowed it to happen. For if manufacturing is merely a productivity game, it can be delegated to a low organizational level and handled by technologists and efficiency experts.

As always, much of our problem is due to our way of thinking about it. Our concepts and understandings have led us down useless paths. And continuing productivity-focused efforts bring forth the same noncompetitive results. But what about the 40% in technology and the 40% in manufacturing strategy and structure? Why are we moving so slowly on these fronts?

Many high barriers stand in the way of introduction of new technology. They divide into six groups: (1) problems with the new technologies themselves; (2) inappropriate/inadequate systems for capital allocations; (3) limitations of the vendors of the new technology; (4) personnel and labor problems in perceiving the new technology; (5) internal resistance and risk aversion on the part of manufacturing managers; and (6) lack of a manufacturing strategy.

First, let us discuss technology itself. Many of these new technologies are quite revolutionary. Few managers can predict accurately what factories will be like 10 or 15 years after adopting these new highly computerized and mechanized technologies. And the payoffs are not only subtle, they are also delayed. The delays are caused by years of problems, debugging, training, and evolving new systems. Anyone who anticipates fully successful payoffs within five or six years is probably overly optimistic. And the payoffs will not always be in cost savings. They are more apt to be in strategic advantage, such as faster new product introductions, ability to produce a broader product line, and superior product reliability. The bugs, the break-ins, and the problems signal a struggle of nightmarish years to get any of these things working. But, if we think we can wait until the technology is frozen and let someone else go first, we face the dilemma of losing competitive positioning. Meanwhile, the capital costs of new EPTs are skyrocketing. With such substantial risks and capital costs the few companies moving ahead are acting either in desperation or with sheer faith in the CEO.

Second, the capital budgeting systems in most of our companies have a one-year horizon, and high hurdle rates have made new investment difficult. The capital budgeting systems are fine for handling new capacity and new products. They require a high/short payback on cost-saving investments. But managers have a hard time selling a new competitive weapon that should be great in five to seven years but must be started now.

The financial skills in our large corporations produce apparently precise pro formas, but that same mind-set demands good return. So we keep on turning down new technology based on financial considerations. Some firms have turned down new EPTs one by one, year by year, and then have woken up to find themselves nearly out of business. We need new ways of conceptualizing and evaluating these new technology investments that deal with more than the cost and productivity dimensions. Few capital budgeting systems handle the strategic dimension.

Third, vendors—most of these new technologies consist of hardware and software of many pieces and ingredients. The systems are disaggregated, and no one vendor offers a whole system. There's no turnkey operation as there is in the chemical and utility industries. Most vendors supply components and lack any total, coordinated systems that they could install and guarantee. The vendors are cautious in what they offer. Our machine tool industry, for example, has acted on the assumption that in a cyclical industry companies should seek to have a one-year to two-year backlog and not lose money in the down years. With that philosophy it has lost market share year after year. Few vendors aggressively try to offer more complete factory systems with the service and assurance that it will work.

Fourth, the human resource dimension of new EPT introduction has been that of a cautious reserve toward new technology, not only because of the productivity backlash, but also because of a century of thinking that technology is the enemy. Workers fear not only the loss of jobs but also the impact of new technology on their working environments. Furthermore, we have shortages everywhere of excellent technicians, maintenance people, service people, supervisors, and trained knowledge workers. Looking ahead, we see that the new technology will require a better selection, a new kind of supervision, more training, and more responsibility for more capital. These factors are causing managements to go slow and workers and unions to be cautious.

The fifth factor impeding new technology is internal resistance and risk aversion by manufacturing managers. They are realistic in predicting the problems, pressures, and the difficulties that they will meet in trying to obtain new EPT appropriations through management. They would have to ask for large amounts of capital, often in a sick industry or when depreciation cash flows fail to provide funds needed for the new EPT. They must make some big promises about this nice new computerized technology that will make a great contribution, when they know well that it will be a struggle for five years, and even if it works superbly it is difficult now to predict and promise the specific favorable consequences five years hence.

Thus, few manufacturing managers are taking the personal career risks to ask for dollars for new technology in new facilities. The problem is made worse by the fact that many manufacturing managers are "chewed up" by sophisticated financial people who know the market, the business, and the strategic situation. The majority of manufacturing managers have been, until recently, cut off from the top corporate councils for 25 years. There are career risks and the rewards are very modest, while the risks are very large. So what can we expect? Manufacturing managers act as good soldiers. They have the infantry mentality and that is the way, unfortunately, they often are treated.

These five roadblocks are all set up by the lack of a manufacturing strategy. Without a long-term manufacturing strategy, it is impossible to make plans for a new, expensive, yet risky, EPT that won't pay off for years financially and offers only a strategic long-term advantage. A manufacturing strategy would not only protect production managers, but, in the process of developing it and getting it approved, manufacturing executives would also think through and make plans for a long-term sequence of building the production function to be a competitive weapon.

A manufacturing strategy is derived from corporate competitive strategy. It describes in explicit terms just what it is that manufacturing must do exceptionally well in the face of precisely defined obstacles and difficulties to play a proactive part in the corporate strategy. From such a statement of task, each element of manufacturing policy and structure can be designed.

The new EPTs offer a new era to manufacturing executives as they move from an operating posture to developing a strategic weapon. For not only is failure to move into and take advantage of the new technologies more competitively serious than ever before, but, in addition, the new microprocessor-based technologies offer totally new opportunities for companies to compete. This is because the new microprocessor technology's main advantage is an ability to be faster and more flexible on new product development, offering marketing new possibilities in successful product variations.

Single-minded obsession with productivity continues to keep many manufacturing managers down in the plant, and they fail to perceive new technology as a formidable, potentially competitive weapon. But without a process of manufacturing strategy development they lack the essential tool that could help them to break out of their confined and thereby conservative and cautious roles.

Is a new breed of manufacturing managers who will save the day coming along? We need some new set of skills, concepts, competencies, and attitudes in manufacturing. Are such men and women working up the organization via the normal process? In most of the dozen companies studied in 1982, such a new breed is developing. They are "new" in that they think about manufacturing in long-term, competitive terms and are taking high risks and providing broad conceptual and specific personal leadership for rebuilding their manufacturing structures. To be elaborated in Chapter 20, the differences between the "old" and "new" are relevant to the problem of barriers to new technology. In terms of career paths, the old breed has moved up slowly and in a relatively straight line, staying within production, with a relatively narrow rather than a broad variety of experiences. They have a rather slower path up the ladder of promotion.

The new ones are coming from an astounding mixture and variety of assignments and responsibilities; many come from engineering, from sales, and from manufacturing; some from finance; many have been project managers, program managers, or have led human-resource or computer-based information system innovations. They are coming from a much richer variety of experience than in the past.

In terms of breadth, the old ones have a depth of competency in the old tools of productivity. They are strong in industrial engineering, processes, methods, and labor relations. The new ones are apt to be a little weak in those areas, but they are stronger in terms of finance, accounting, and creative budgeting. And they are much stronger in terms of marketing, as well as program and project management, and they quickly grasp the concepts of manufacturing strategy. One surprising fact is that "new" and "old" are not always divided by age. At some firms, the new breed include people in their fifties and sixties.

In attitudes, the old ones are the infantry—they're patient, dutiful, and responsible. They keep appointments on time, they do everything on time. They have a strong sense of corporate loyalty; they have great respect for their bosses. The new ones are impatient and frequently over-confident. They often believe they are better than they really are. They're in a hurry, but they are good at delegating and team building. They are somewhat loose and laid back; they delegate in ways that would scare many old managers, for they don't follow up with the same type of rigor. But they are outstanding at inducing people to cooperate together and in coordinating new projects. They border on being disrespectful to the company and the industry and their colleagues, while they are very loyal to their functions, and to their own careers and self-esteem.

In skills, the old type can expedite, follow up, and tend to focus on cost and delivery. The new ones can handle more ambiguity, change, discontinuity, and uncertainty. Nothing bugs them very much. They don't expect things to be the same tomorrow. And they seem to be good at new technology development.

In executive styles, the old ones have much shorter fuses; they're more autocratic. At the same time, they're loyal team players; they support their peers and sustain their colleagues. The new ones have longer fuses with subordinates; they seem to be much more patient. They're more collegial and they excel at team problem solving.

There is great variety among companies as to how they handle the development and strengthening of this new breed. By and large, most personnel management and human resources programs worry a great deal about employees at lower levels, while neglecting where managers are coming from, and how to develop managers with a broader diversity of competencies.

Despite the seriousness of the situation in the early 1980s and the still negative trend in competitive strength in many industries, there is reason for optimism. Although there are substantial problems ahead, industrial history is full of examples that demonstrate the fundamental lesson that technology totally affects economics. History shows managers as prisoners of technology. For two hundred years society and technology have been seen as colliding rather than in partnership.

Exactly the opposite is now beginning to occur. By some good fortune, technology and society are now lined up right, in a way we've seldom seen before. There are many indications that the new technology is good for society. In the old technology machines substituted for people, starting with the steam engine. It resulted in standardization, in long runs, and it was good for process industries and mass production. We surrounded workers with staff, indirect labor, and controls. We ended up with monotony, boredom, and specialization.

The new technology is entirely different. It requires a whole new role for workers and a whole new set of management skills. In the handful of plants that have moved boldly into the new EPTs, we see workers doing much of their own scheduling, their own inspection, and their own production planning and inventory control. They make decisions with information at their fingertips. High school graduates with some training and with great pride are using on-site process computers. This is producing autonomy and involvement. And for the organization's competitive struggle it is producing an opportunity for flexibility, shorter runs, and more product variety.

The new technology will frequently provide a devastating competitive advantage for companies that learn it first. As one company in an industry finds new ways of producing and can supply new products quickly, it can be more flexible and adaptable, and it can move faster in markets; the effect will domino right through that industry. And those who don't go first must then play "catch up." But to get in on the ground floor requires a long-term manufacturing plan.

Since the Industrial Revolution, the name of the game in the factory has been productivity. For what was a factory other than a set of facilities for mass production? The corporate objectives were productivity, efficiency, and return on investment. The technologies were power and steam, electricity, and mechanical advantage. How did we manage it? We managed it with industrial engineering, efficiency experts, standards, controls, schedules, discipline, and short-range operations. The attempt to obtain low-cost, standardized merchandise dehumanized factories. As a result, employees had to give up many rights and to subject themselves to an organization. This created the backlash, the dullsville, and the preoccupation with the numbers—in short, the road we've been going down in the last 20 years.

What is a more productive way of thinking about the factory? Can we think of it as a competitive resource? Can we see a factory as a place where innovative people can produce outstanding products and meet market needs? And can we do this as the factory grows much more capital intensive? This requires concepts that are contradictory to the old notions. It requires more strategy and genuine long-range planning.

The factory as an institution has let us down. It has let us down because we let it down. We kept on seeing it as an efficiency machine, which it was in 1800. We managed it by and for productivity and profit. The irony is that we lost our productivity and our profit.

Now we have the technology and the ideas for reinventing the factory as an institution. If we can see it and manage it as a place for innovative and independent people to produce great products and have full lives, and if we use technology as a primary resource rather than the last decision we make, we'll reinvent the factory. If we are to do it, it must be done from the inside out, starting with a competitive long-range manufacturing strategy. Only by reinventing the factory can we see it emerge as a successful institution in Western society.

The final chapter in the sequence on innovative and aggressive manufacturing strategies deals, in particular, with putting the new manufacturing technologies described earlier to work to create strategic advantage. The new technologies are daring, expensive, and risky, but their potentials for transforming the sluggish old factory institution into a formidable, fast-moving competitive weapon are many. The next Chapter says: Get Physical!

CHAPTER 17

Getting Physical: New Strategic Leverage from Operations

An emerging wave of competitively aggressive moves originating in the operations function is a striking new phenomenon of the 1980s. These moves are creating an arsenal of strategic weapons that are essentially physical. While the weapons are numerous, their common feature is that they are derived from better deployment and management of physical assets.

The strategic resources developed include: outstanding quality of product or service, substantial reductions of delivery lead times, the ability to offer customer specials in small quantities at low prices, and a competence to develop new products in previously undreamed-of short development cycles. Such resources unleash a body barrage to the competition, while providing a unique strategic leverage to their possessors.

THREE RESPONSES

Three examples from the business literature of 1982 illustrate what is beginning to happen as innovative companies start to "get physical" by employing operations technology and production facilities to create strategic leverage.

As competition grew tougher, first in its traditional automotive markets, and subsequently in the electronics and defense industry divisions, TRW has taken the following actions:

- Appointed vice-presidents of productivity, quality, technical resources, manufacturing, and material to act as catalyzers for stimulating the sharing of ideas and technology across ninety independent divisions.
- Stimulated the establishment of productivity committees and projects in seventy of the divisions and, in so doing, redefining and broadening the formerly narrow focus of productivity on direct labor to include all human resources, energy, and material.
- Initiated a new corporatewide thrust on quality, emphasizing savings in total quality costs, reinstituting statistical quality control, and developing new ways of measuring quality.
- Invested in an across-the-board management development effort from the top down to educate management in the manufacturing strategy approach to production management.
- Begun to study performance measurement systems and management incentives to improve the problem of a short-term-oriented and narrow corporate culture created by conventional autonomous divisional management with substantial independence and annual bottom-line profit and loss responsibility. This culture is seen by top management to conflict with the need for a strategic viewpoint in operations, which would encourage the sharing of technology across the divisions, making capital investment decisions in facilities, and developing operations technology aimed at long-term competitive advantage rather than short-term profit.

General Electric, under the leadership of its new chairman, Jack Welch, is pioneering to bring about changes in its management reward systems, so as to measure performance, make promotions, and pay bonuses on large-term, qualitative (rather than merely quantitative) measures of contribution to the business. This is resulting in GE "getting physical" with radical new innovations in equipment and process technology, which are authorized more for their influence on corporate learning than normal return on investment criteria. GE, too, has been investing in management development for manufacturing directors and division managers, which focuses on acquiring manufacturing strategy concepts and skills rather than those conventional industrial management techniques aimed only at improving factory productivity.

A third leader is Deere & Co., which has invested heavily in radical new equipment and process technology, not primarily to save on manufacturing cost, but to improve quality, reliability, customer service and response, while reducing inventories and lead times. These facilities are crammed with new manufacturing technology—computer-aided design and computer-aided manufacturing, flexible machining centers, and dozens of computer terminals, which allow high-school educated employees to interact with production control and vastly raise the level of employee participation in daily decisions.

When this energetic wave of current activity in operations management is contrasted with the much maligned and discredited production function of the 1970s, what is going on is nearly astonishing. In the 1970s, the loss of competitive position of U.S. business to international competitors was generally blamed on high manufacturing costs, shoddy quality, and sluggish service levels. The discouraged state of industrial management was called our "industrial malaise." The prescription was "reindustrialization" and "revitalization." Operations managers were criticized as being backward—operating plants in the same manner for four decades oblivious to the dynamic changes going on in other professional areas of management, such as in modern budgeting, cost control, marketing finance, and corporate strategic management.

Much of this criticism was undoubtedly warranted. Surely part of the miserable competitive performance of much of U.S. industry must be laid to inadequacy in the concepts and practices of the operations function. Of course, extenuating circumstances are legion: the organizational treatment that cut off and isolated operations management from top corporate councils; the heavy-handed, short-term-oriented domination of financial concepts and decision rules; the phenomena of shorter product life cycles and creeping product line proliferation, to name several. But to take the argument a step further, why did operations managers let their influence decline and find themselves helplessly "outgunned" by other functions, to the clear detriment of the fortunes of the corporation? There was some sort of futility in the power of their concepts and the thrust of their performance—that much can be said in retrospect.

But this makes all the more remarkable the current outpouring of powerful and creative initiatives from the operations function. It was apparently nearly bankrupt of ideas and energies only a few years ago. What is it that seems to be taking place and why is it happening? We turn first to offer some response to these questions and, subsequently, to an analysis from current research as to the differences in approaches now being taken by more and less successful companies in making their operations a competitive weapon.

WHAT IS TAKING PLACE

To the examples cited above could be added many others:

- The engine manufacturer who moved products from a crowded, old plant, with literally hundreds of products for myriad markets, to set up two new focused factories. The old facility was then divided into two plants within a plant, each to serve a different market with two distinctly different products. The newfound competitive advantages from these facilities are attracting new customers, worldwide, and have so preempted the market that several competitors have dropped out.

- The big 3 in the auto industry are each reorganizing so as to accomplish major model changes in much less time than the noncompetitive five years now required.
- The flood of companies that have developed quality improvement programs because of customer competition and market and/or Japanese or foreign competition, only to find major improvements in cost, delivery, productivity and morale the result, as well as better quality [5].

What is going on under the surface of all this new attention to physical performance which is moving corporations away from purely financial, sales and growth measures? First of all, it is abundantly clear that there is a new burst of vitality and energy from the operations function. Driven by the clear facts of noncompetitive quality, service, costs, and delivery, many top managements have turned back to the apparent source of these problems—the operations function—with front-and-center attention to what is now recognized as a key "heart" source of the firm's health. These companies now appear to see that no amount of marketing, advertising, or financial manipulation can make a company healthy if its physical products, facilities, technologies, and people are not of competitive quality.

This new attention from the top has, of course, had many secondary effects. It is providing new opportunities for operations people to contribute, receive recognition, and gain excitement. It rewards the promise of new strategic resources with investment in new facilities and new technology. It permits and even encourages taking risks that would have been denied without hesitation five years ago. It signals to young managers that operations is where the action is. It signifies that, as in football, when the game gets tough it usually gets physical, and the winner wins more by having the better basic physical assets than by any strategy or game plan. The latter are merely concepts, while the game must be won out on the field. It says, "back to basics!"

But that analogy, while fun to pursue, is too superficial to explain all that is going on in today's astonishing turnaround in operations management. It is not just top management being forced back to basics and fundamentals. This does not explain why these new activities in operations are conceptually new, nor why they are, in fact, causing the abandonment of much of the old conventional wisdom of production management. "Productivity" is no longer the name of the game as it has been since Taylor formulated the principles of scientific management. For example, TRW learned in one division that poor delivery lead times were hurting market share much more than high costs, and they restructured manufacturing policies to focus on a new, overriding, single manufacturing task, that of becoming not low-cost producer but low-lead-time producer.

Equally significant is the new concept of quality as an organizing paradigm. Frank Leonard and Earl Sasser [5] introduced the idea that when outstanding physical quality becomes a central, dominant goal of an operations organization, the side effects on other performance criteria are always favorable, including not only cost but also quality of work life, quality of human resources, and quality of management [6]. So the old "cost versus quality" trade-off is being challenged with a totally new dynamic.

Similarly, some long-standing patterns and premises involved in the management of technology and equipment and process election now appear to be invalid. For example, the pattern of giving priority in capital budgeting to investing in product research over process and equipment technology development, both in time and money, is not standing up to the onrush of new manufacturing technology and to the Japanese challenge. Auto makers have been proven to be the captives of their own process technology, which is so capital intensive and product specialized that four-year plant turnarounds are required for major engine and model product changes [1].

The result in some firms is a new surge of research and development expenditure that for the first time is based on a recognition of the strategic implications—for either competitive advantage or disaster—of equipment and process technology (EPT). This is a reversal in practice and thinking that defies conventional corporate practice, which places EPT last in R&D and defines the manufacturing engineer's role as secondary and servile. For example, design engineers will design the product (to sell) and manufacturing engineers then figure out how to make it as cheaply as possible.

Bela Gold [3] suggests that another reversal in thinking is urgently needed:

In short, many industrial managements might well consider beginning their long range planning with a definition of technological improvement objectives and then redefining marketing strategies and financial requirements in accordance with resulting changes in technological capabilities. The reverse sequence which has long prevailed of limiting technological improvement efforts to what can be funded after first estimating financial availabilities and marketing potentials on the assumption of continuing inadequate technological progress no longer seems a viable approach.

Two other changes in technology management are also challenging conventional operations management wisdom. The first concept, which is perhaps turning out to be outmoded, is that proven by 200 years of industrial history and superbly described by Robert H. Hayes and Steven C. Wheelwright [4]: that as the normal product life cycle proceeds, the EPT moves inexorably from a one-of-a-kind shop to a job shop to dedicated equipment and, finally, to mass production technology. Computer-aided design and manufacturing (CAD/CAM) is ending that pattern and, in fact, its end was probably first signaled by the success of the first reliable NC machine. New microprocessor technology is bestowing processes with economic flexibility for a much wider range of order quantities than ever before.

The second change is equally fundamental. The old notion that people can and will adapt to machines is no longer acceptable. This outworn idea is now challenged by society in ethical terms. But, regardless of ethics, it simply doesn't work anymore. From the industrial revolution on, the concept was that a suitable person could be found for any job if the pay was right. We have now learned that each technology has its human consequences and if these are not anticipated and handled, the results, whether they be in quality, productivity, or alienation from the owner-investor-corporation, are ultimately noncompetitive.

CHANGES, RESULTS, AND IMPLICATIONS

The changes as companies discover the survival requirement of doing better in their physical operations are revealing not only new competitive leverage possibilities, but the necessity for wholly new ways of conceptualizing and managing the operations function of the business. Exhibit 17.1 shows a number of these changes going on in operations management, and suggests some of their first- and second-order results and implications.

Essentially these changes are being driven by the new industrial competition, which is not only more intense domestically but over the past decade has so quickly spread as to be global in nature [2]. The new industrial competition has generally forced down profits and placed pressure on growth, to the point that for many firms survival—not growth—has become, for the first time in decades, a real and frightening issue.

This new competition is, above all else, technological in nature. New products and shortened product life cycles result in a proliferation of product offerings and shortened production runs. New microprocessor-based equipment and process technologies are burgeoning: e.g., CAD/CAM, direct numerical control (DNC), computer centralized numerical control

EXHIBIT 17.1 Actions and Implications of Certain Changes in Industry

Ingredients in and Forces for Changes	First-Order Changes	Second-Order Results	Some Implications for Management
Increased Competition	More diverse performance criteria for production success	Emergence of EPT as strategic weapon	Competition via EPT, HRM, speed, flexibility, management of technological change, global production strategy
Domestic	Many management failures, plant closings, and corporate failures	Quality as an organizing paradigm	
Global	More global sourcing	Changes in capital budgeting	Curtailment of strictly financial decision rules and measures
Survival increasingly an issue (not growth)	More producer proliferation	Enlarged role of mfg. engnrs.	
New Technologies	Shorter production runs	More flexibility built into equipment	New vitality, focus, attention, importance on physical assets, resources, and corporate performance
Products	Shorter product life-cycles	Shortages of many skills	
Materials	Faster new-product development	Decline of conventional mass production techniques	Reeducation of workers, engineers, managers; new breed of managers
Organizational	Shorter product changeover cycles	New focus on program and project management	
Processes	Inadequacy of conventional functional organizations	New focus on teamwork, participation	
Equipment	Less dedicated equipment	New focus on HRM	
Information	Enlarged impact of quality	More joint union/mgt. efforts at collaboration	
Changed Sociology	New HRM/QWL experiments	Inadequacy of "productivity" as a single measure of performance	
Values	New generation of managers		
Motivations	Labor unions under pressure		
Expectations of employees and customers	Enlarged role of personnel department		

NOTE: In this exhibit no interrelationships are intended to be shown by items on the same horizontal level.

(CNC), robots, lasers, and flexible production centers. Human resource management experiments and concepts are fast emerging as well, under the pressure of rapidly changing values and expectations of employees, managers, and customers.

The result is not only the changes we have been discussing but a whole new emphasis on the physical side of the business. The driving need is to make the physical functioning of the business more flexible, faster to respond, and less a massive inertial impediment to accomplishing change. A key dilemma of operations managers has always been the long lead times and substantial capital investment demanded by physical facilities— plants, buildings, people, equipment, and technology—versus the need to change products, markets, customers, volumes, and focus of the operating system's particular competence. The accountants call these investments "fixed assets"—and that has always been the problem. Today they must be less fixed; they must change faster and be more flexible to survive in world competition.

The first-order result of these competitive pressures, of course, has been a wave of corporate and management failures. But, barring failure and assuming survival, operations managers have had to learn to cope with shorter product life cycles and the decline of mass production. We are having to develop new products faster and get them into production in half the time formerly required. To accomplish this, the operations challenge is now to learn to employ the new EPTs fast becoming available. Further, changes are essential in developing more responsive and flexible human resources. To this end industry is conducting hundreds of experiments in "quality of work life," nonsupervised work groups, and participative forms of employee management. We see unions under pressure just as are managers, and this is spawning many hopeful new forms of union-management collaboration.

Second-order results such as these new collaborative efforts and more democratic industrial organizations are potentially very significant. Another implication is certainly the emergence of equipment and process technology as a formidable strategic weapon. This is indeed a challenge to strategic management and conventional strategic planning processes. Manufacturing/operations managers can no longer be left out of that process. Their contributions to competitive break-throughs in quality, service, delivery, or cost can now be a starting point in strategy. Equally important, their contribution to marketing strength via the ability to produce more products, more quickly, in low volume, and economically can be a powerful way to compete.

And outstanding quality of product, process, service, work life, thinking, organization, and human resource is, in some companies, beginning to emerge as a way to think about, plan, develop, and manage the whole physical function of the business. This, along with the management of technological innovation and faster response to product and process change, is requiring a new focus on teamwork, project and program management, better listening, better communications, and a whole new spirit of vitality and movement in operations management.

The long-term implications for top management and operations management are probably far greater and more diverse, and surely more unpredictable, than this writer can foresee. At a minimum though, it is not hard to suggest at least these four implications:

- Successful competition will be based increasingly on an organization's ability to be more effective on a global scale with its physical resources, competing via aggressive operations and process technology, outstanding quality of human resources, products and services, and making major changes more quickly and easily in products, facilities, organization, and technology. Operations will be organized and staffed with the objective of excellence in learning, rather than in merely producing.
- Organizations will have to promote and develop a new focus that places strategic importance, attention, and vitality on their physical assets, including people and the managers of those functions.
- Now wanted: a "new breed" of operations managers. The "old breed's" skills were in achieving maximum productivity from a given, long-term set of fixed assets. The new breed will have to be broader in its ability to achieve more objectives than mere productivity, able to take part forcefully and effectively in top management councils, and extraordinarily flexible by today's standards to bring about change, handle ambiguity, accomplish rapid organizational learning, and secure superb communications and cooperation up, down, and sideways in the industrial organization. The reeducation of managers, engineers, and workers will become an increasingly urgent requirement.
- Finally, there will be a curtailment of the inadequate and disastrous strictly financial decision rules, controls, and measures by which much of Western business has been managed for the last quarter-century. These nonphysical, purely conceptual paradigms for both short-term and longer-term decisionmaking are now old-fashioned and outworn, for they have failed to deal either with the on-rush of modern technology or the new global competition and its demands for longer-term strategic decisionmaking and much more rapid change.

Let me conclude with several lessons that are emerging from the experiences of companies wrestling with these changes.

COPING AND NOT COPING

During the last two years I have visited a dozen leading industrial firms, focusing on their assimilation of new production technology. In this research sample a few companies are coping relatively well with these changes, but the majority are not. Not only is there just too much happening to handle it all effectively—new competitors, products, technologies, equipment, and people amidst a great deal of economic stress and adversity—but, even more important, the mental or conceptual outlook demanded is altogether different from that of the past.

The knowledge, skills, and attitudes that once made operations managers successful have changed. The single-minded preoccupation with productivity that propelled able and forceful operations managers to the top is too narrow a focus for today's criteria of success. "Efficiency" was their paradigm. By a process of "command and control," their attention was placed on getting the most production out of every worker and every dollar of investment. The old breed was good at this. To accomplish it they fought for stability and continuity of products, volume levels, facilities, work forces, and technology. The enemy more often than not was the marketing department, the volatile customer, and the never-satisfied labor union.

Operations managers were less successful, however, in dealing with top management and with marketing and finance executives. They could not argue with "the P and L," the balance sheet, earnings per share, the stock market, or with the irrefutable need for sales, earnings, and a capital-attracting return on investment. So they became isolated from the key business decisions and the key decision makers. Finance easily kept them captive and submissive with the business plan, budgets, capital budgeting, and monthly reports. Vulnerable to criticism because, in their preoccupation with productivity, they could always be (and were) faulted for declines in delivery, service, responsiveness, flexibility to volume and product change, and noncompetitive quality, they were often helpless putty in the hands of versatile multidimensioned top managers, and prisoners of their colleagues in finance. They had no weapons with which to counterattack. When they wanted funds for new and better equipment and processes, their only yardstick was supplied by their captors—the ROI yardstick. So their plants grew obsolete, and they gradually became obsolete themselves.

They became obsolete because they were unable to throw off the baggage of "efficiency" and "productivity" concepts, which dominated their instincts and their imaginations. Even now they struggle on for the privilege of isolating their production islands with stability—freezes on products, volumes, and technology—citing the Japanese as having those buffers from reality.

How are those operations managers who are coping and leading the emerging wave of competitive initiatives from operations doing it? They are taking the initiative: finding out what the business needs from a strategic analysis, learning what new technology can offer in the way of competitive advantages, and selling their ideas to top management on the basis of strategic survival and long-term gains in market shares, rather than submitting to old-fashioned and inappropriate capital budgeting measures. They have earned partnership in the top management of those businesses by understanding and using such concepts.

They have been restructuring their physical assets so as to build in more flexibility for product change and volume variations. They manage decisively but with more participation, less use of authority, and the ongoing involvement of the stakeholders in the organization. They constantly communicate objectives, criteria for success, performance results, and problems for the organization to solve. They organize for effective technological innovation. In the companies that are coping well, physical operations are no longer perceived as an "efficiency machine," but as a potentially vital, aggressive corporate strategic resource.

The only drawback to accomplishing this is a major one. It is the dearth of manufacturing managers who think in broad, strategic terms, can hold their own with top-level financial and marketing executives and manage technological and social change. This is a big order, for to get to the top the manager must first of all be a proven accomplisher and then or simultaneously acquire conceptual and strategic skills. The next two chapters focus on these two sectors of managerial skills, first the art of being an accomplishing manager.

REFERENCES

1. Abernathy, W , *The Productivity Dilemma: Roadblock to Innovation in the Automobile Industry* (Baltimore: Johns Hopkins University Press, 1978).
2. Abernathy, W., Clark, K., and Kantrow, A., "The New Industrial Competition," *Harvard Business Review*, Sept./Oct., 1981.
3. Gold, B., "Rediscovering the Technological Foundations of Industrial Competitiveness," *OMEGA*, pp. 503–504.

4. Hayes, R.H., and Wheelwright, S.C., "The Dynamics of the Process-Product Life Cycles," *Harvard Business Review,* March/April 1979.
5. Leonard, F.S., and Sasser, W.E., "The Incline of Quality," *Harvard Business Review,* Sept./Oct., 1982.
6. Peters, T.J., and Waterman, Jr., R.M., *In Search of Excellence: Lessons from America's Best Run Companies* (New York: Harper & Row, 1982).

WANTED: A NEW BREED OF MANUFACTURING MANAGER

R esearch in the past few years demonstrates the powerful competitive advantages that can be created by successful manufacturing strategy. And the strategic resources, which imaginative deployment of new manufacturing technologies brings to bear, are dramatic in their potential.

Yet, progress in changing the institution called "manufacturing" is disappointingly slow. Case-by-case analyses demonstrate beyond much doubt the not surprising conclusion: the bottleneck is the manager.

Competing by using manufacturing strategy and by successfully introducing new manufacturing technology demands a wholecloth change in the skills, attitudes, and mindsets of manufacturing managers. The focus on old and limited industrial management techniques and the preoccupation with "productivity" are seriously limiting progress. We need a "new breed," and there is evidence that such individuals are now emerging via a Darwinian evolutionary process.

CHAPTER 18

The Accomplishing Manager

OPERATING SKILLS OF THE MANAGER

W hy is it that after expending much managerial energy and time in discussion or planning, often nothing happens? Why do managers who appear crisp, logical, and determined at the conference table frequently accomplish little or nothing when they return to their offices? Why do certain managers work effectively both within and outside their organizations and produce a string of significant accomplishments in a short time?

Thirty-one managers were studied as a basis for this chapter. These managers were typically working in manufacturing industries. Large and small firms and top-, middle-, and lower-level managers were almost equally represented. While the sample is small, our analysis of the case histories involving the 31 managers suggests a possibly surprising conclusion: Managers who consistently accomplish are notably inconsistent in their manner of attacking problems. They constantly change their focus, their priorities, their behavior patterns with superiors and subordinates, and their own "executive styles."* Managers who consistently accomplish little are usually predictably constant in what they concentrate on and how they go at their work. Consistency, if our findings are correct, is the hobgoblin of small and inconsistent accomplishment.

In this chapter our subject is the operating skills of the manager, the process of getting work done, changes made, and implementing rather than formulating policy. Our concern is that at least as many management

---

*By *executive style* we mean the mix of relationships, approaches in giving orders, communications, follow-up, delegation, pace, and risktaking that characterizes an executive's mode of managing.

Written with Professor W. Earl Sasser, Harvard Business School.

careers seem to be damaged by weak operating skills as by a lack of competence in the realm of strategy and policy making.

Beginning with some fundamental causes for poor accomplishment that emerged from our analysis of the most frequent themes in failure observed in the managers studied, we then trace some of the key dilemmas involved in the operating side of managing and present some ideas for resolving these dilemmas. These ideas center on the development of a constantly shifting and adaptive personal approach to problems in operating management.

FREQUENT THEMES OF FAILURE OF LOW ACCOMPLISHERS

Inadequate Involvement at the Critical Level of Detail

Well-educated, younger managers more often failed to be involved adequately at the detail level than less educated, "self-made" managers. The cause may perhaps be the widespread acceptance of commonly accepted notions such as the following: "A manager must stay out of detail"; "a manager must learn to delegate"; and "a manager must never get involved in day-to-day, short-term firefighting." These deceptively simple notions hurt several careers in our study and even, in our observation, devastated several enterprises. In-depth knowledge at the critical level of detail provides the manager with the facts as well as the confidence to come to a correct decision, stick to it without compromise, and effectively achieve its implementation.

On the other hand, attention to details without a strategy or plan or direction led several of our subjects into a morass of floundering and a subsequent struggle for a sense of control. When things are not going well and the pressure is on, the operating manager is often afraid to delegate much, tends to draw problems into personal control, becomes increasingly engrossed, and may finally be overwhelmed by the workload generated. This vicious cycle is a common syndrome most readers have probably observed. It was especially prevalent among older managers who have worked themselves up through the organization. They were apparently comfortable with what they knew best and they stuck with it, investing themselves with energy into nearly every problem that entered their span of observation.

Losing the Handle on Priorities

With the telephone constantly ringing, a never-ending series of meetings and conferences, and the flurries of a constant exchange of memos and paperwork, the operating manager can easily work day after day at a feverish pace and feel a comforting sense of accomplishments. However, for quite a few of the managers studied, results of the past six months of the year revealed that nothing major had been accomplished, even in the face of looming or existing problems; in some instances, the situation for which they were responsible had deteriorated.

Indecision

Determining when to take action can also be difficult. We studied one manager who took a year too long to get costs under control. Although his primary assignment was to "reduce costs," he spent most of that year asking his people to give him advice and attempting to gain their whole-hearted participation and support in recommending changes. Because the time available for reducing costs was short, he simply could not afford to take a long time to pull the improvements up through his organization or to let his ideas "trickle down." His division lost the next big contract for cost reasons and had to be closed down.

Failure of Boldness, Nerve, and Self-Confidence

This failure was observed in a number of the case studies. The theme is illustrated by a situation in which a young MBA assigned to a decentralized division could see after several months that the reason the division was losing money was a poor labor contract that made the company noncompetitive with foreign imports. Because the union was unwilling to renegotiate the contract, only a bold move leading to a major confrontation could correct the situation. The MBA recognized rightly that his boss, a middle-aged plant manager, would probably never precipitate this move. Afterward, it seemed apparent that the young man had been placed there by the management in the hope that his trained analytical skill and personality would force the issue. When he failed to do this because he was unwilling to make that bold and personally risky move, he was ultimately sidelined.

Failure to Admonish or Replace Ineffective Subordinates

Some managers who considered themselves excellent at developing subordinates took pride in attempting to "turn around" people to change their behavior radically. They were also reluctant to fire or replace an individual, always hoping that performance would soon improve. Some offered mild hints and suggestions for improvement; others ignored a bad situation in the apparent hope that the individual would be able to learn on his or her own. We commonly observed beliefs that "the best managers are those whose people are happy" and "happiness" came from encouragement and praise, and consistent demands for better performance were "bad for morale." With this conventional "wisdom" often came the simultaneous toleration of ineffective subordinates.

Not Seeking Advice or Help

Several failures could be attributed to a kind of "managerial arrogance," the inability of the manager to recognize or admit that help was needed. A director of manufacturing kept insisting to his superior vice-president that he and his group could and would soon straighten out a set of new product problems that were bottlenecking all output at 50% of plan. The vice-president was held at arm's length from personal involvement in a situation in which he was eager to help. His participation would not only have been useful but would have also secured his involvement and probably defused his subsequent attack on the director of manufacturing, which resulted in the latter's firing.

Similarly, we observed failures of managers who were unable to seek advice from knowledgeable, experienced subordinates. They seemed to feel that this might be an admission of weakness and that they must always show themselves to be equal to their own problems. The result was a waste of know-how and, perhaps worse, a negative and critical set of subordinates.

Failure to Analyze

Accepting established "rules of thumb" without question or analysis was surprisingly frequent, even among highly trained managers. In most organizations informal rules ease decision making, and guides such as "carry two weeks inventory," "no overtime," "promote from within," or "keep direct labor costs at 19¢" become conventional wisdom. Rules such as these may have made sense at some time but often no longer had economic or strategic rationale. Unquestioning adherence to existing ways of doing things was surprisingly prevalent even among managers formally trained to analyze. The common tendency observed was to do a great deal of analysis in the first few months of a new job but to "wing it" after that.

Managing One's Own Emotions, Pressures, and Needs

Some managers failed because they felt compelled to "take command," to make a showing with a decision, and to deal with situations that probably would have been better ignored or pushed "upstairs." Compulsive needs to be the boss and exert leadership through immediate action were not infrequent in our case studies. There were several situations in our cases when no decision and a delay would have been wiser than moving aggressively ahead.

Blind Spots

Blind spots were frequent among the executives studied. Some managers acted as if they were unaware of their own weaknesses. As they described experiences, they did not appear to realize that they lacked a certain skill or body of knowledge. For example, a manager in a hardware manufacturing firm did a fine job in improving the sales force and developing effective sales strategy. He was moved into marketing and obtained good results in introducing new products. He was promoted to executive vice-president. There he failed. His failure can be traced to his lack of realization that he did not understand production and manufacturing operations well enough to manage his subordinates. They were able to mislead him.

His blind spot was a realization that implementation, follow-up, and close attention to detail are critical in manufacturing and that his executive style was to focus solely on strategy and conceptual matters.

CONCLUSIONS FROM PATTERNS OF LOW ACCOMPLISHERS

Themes in failure are so numerous and so contradictory that they may seem frightening. They are! They explain why so many managers fail in the operating sector of their jobs. Managers get involved in too much or too little detail. They are too cautious or too bold. They are too critical or too accepting. They are too tough or too supportive. They delegate too much or too infrequently. They plan and analyze and procrastinate, or they blindly plunge ahead day after day without arithmetic, "homework," analysis, or plan. They are excessively aware of their weaknesses and damaging compulsive tendencies or they have blind spots.

In fact, at any level in the organization, the operating sector of managing is enormously difficult. When analyzed, managing is downright "scary," and it is amazing that any mortal succeeds for long. No single approach to these trade offs seems to work consistently. You are "damned if you do and damned if you don't." The best formula seems to be "it all depends"!

To find a more useful approach we found ourselves looking at these themes of failure quite differently. They appear at first to offer contradiction—for example, the level of detail versus the level of generalization. The managers studied got into trouble at both ends of this spectrum. But the key to the paradox is that no manager observed failed because of performing at the level of detail at the wrong time and at the level of generalization at another time when it was equally inappropriate. On the contrary, each manager who had a problem had it consistently at one end of the scale or the other, but never at both. Each manager tended to develop a set style or approach, and when that manager erred, it was always in the same particular direction.

What went wrong for the low accomplishers was that the situation changed and the manager did not. Most managers had developed a certain set of habits, premises, and behaviors such that their "executive style" had become repetitive and altogether predictable. Serious failure occurred when some major elements of the situation changed quickly and the managers charged on with their usual assumptions, behaviors, and styles.

The less dramatic, but more prevalent problems are those of the average or below-average accomplishers. Consistency is their downfall, for the case research shows a general consistency of executive style for each manager and a tendency to persist in using a set style and a limited number of tools, techniques, and approaches to perceiving problems based on a small assortment of managerial premises, which they use over and over again.

Each outstanding implementor had several different executive styles and was thereby inconsistent in personal executive style. A successful executive style turned out to be a "nonstyle." Successful implementators have many styles. They are regularly inconsistent.

The paradox is revealing. The high accomplishers get into fine detail in one situation yet stay at the strategic level in another. They delegate a lot one time or a little the next time. They are close and supportive one day and remote and demanding another. They communicate verbally with some colleagues and in writing with others, varying this pattern as well. They analyze some problems in great depth for months while they move with seeming abruptness and intuition on others. They talk a great deal or suddenly are apt listeners.

For the low accomplishers, consistency was the shadow of their failures. Apparently as bright, energetic, and mature as the high accomplishers, they sounded analytical and persuasive, but their results were hollow. Meanwhile, their styles were persistent and predictable. The consistent manager had a consistent executive style, one set of practices and "rules of thumb" hard learned from experience, usually a "philosophy of management," and a group of personal central tendencies affecting his or her action as a manager. The consistent manager had one executive style.

The consistency, which causes managers to fail, is not so surprising, since one cardinal imperative of life as a manager is the necessity to perceive differences from one situation to another and between people, circumstances, physical/technological realities, motives, assumptions, and antecedents. The manager analyzes to discern differences that can entirely change a situation.

The problem is that situations change, but the ordinary executive often does not perceive it and fails to adopt an appropriate approach. The approach that has worked out so well often will not work on what seems to be the same problem. Why? Because one or two critical ingredients changed. Meanwhile, the harried manager is under pressure to simplify the decision-making process by extracting from experience some generalizations for the next time that kind of problem is faced.

The more experienced the manager, the greater the likelihood that she or he will have adopted one, consistent approach to decision making, delegation, communication, and relationships. The missing quality is being unable to detect an incorrect approach. The executive could not learn about his or her own style. The very style a manager organizes to simplify life may keep that manager blind.

Our study suggests that consistency, which arises from habit, premises about technology and people or organizations, psychological pressures for simplicity and mental-emotional comfort, and the adoption of one executive style, tends to lead to mediocrity or failures in operating management. An apparently small difference in any one factor changes the requirement for success. When the requirement changes, so must executive style and the appropriateness of certain tools and techniques for management and implementation, priorities, and timing.

Basic elements of personal behavior are apparently rather well fixed from childhood. How a manager can modify his or her rather basic psychological "givens"—motives, self-concepts, and cognitive styles—is beyond the scope of this article, but the fact is that some managers are able to modify their styles and modes of managing better than others. Our observation of successful operating managers includes men and women who seem to have always been versatile—inconsistent—and others who have apparently learned from experience to loosen their prior rigidities and adopt a more situationally adjusted mode of managing. In the balance of this chapter we offer some prescriptive concepts learned from the managers whose accomplishments were well above average and in some cases outstanding.

THE HIGH ACCOMPLISHERS

The high accomplishers were consistent, but in a different way. They were persistent in analysis and self-discipline, which permitted them to be inconsistent in their own executive styles. Consistency was no problem for these people. We observed the following approaches, concepts, or techniques that they used.

Analysis

The high accomplishers were, above all, analyzers. They analyzed each situation. The most common cause of operating failure among the low-accomplishment managers was their unwillingness to do this. Careful analysis reveals the facts, cause-and-effect relationships, and strategic realities. Careful analysis leads to an approach in operating management that is freshly tuned to the situation. Managers do it in MBA and advanced management programs; it is done in management training courses and seminars; it is done under pressure when a superior demands it. Good analysis produces power and credibility that cannot be turned aside easily. It leads to practical, realistic solutions, and, most important, develops personal confidence in the manager that he or she knows what is going on.

Most operating managers "wing it" 99% of the time. There seems to be little time to think things through. We rely on the lessons of past success. Curiously, most of the failures we observed were those of previously successful managers. What had always worked before was precisely what caused the failure. A consistent approach is the recipe for disaster. Operating skills can never be considered set; they must always be renewed, reconsidered, developed.

Analysis benefits from concepts and frameworks. We observed the following practices and concepts of the high performers that seemed to be useful in their processes of performing a situational analysis of what to do and how to do it.

An Operating Strategy

A strategy is necessary for the operating manager to develop and hold a sense of direction, purpose, and objectives. But a strategy is more than a choice of objectives; it involves recognizing what will be difficult and making an assessment of the favorable and unfavorable factors involved in the situation and of strengths and weaknesses.

An operating strategy can seldom be long lasting; it needs reanalysis every three to six months. It includes a way to deal with key elements of the situation such as determining the needs, wishes, and expectations of the boss and the boss's boss. It clearly establishes objectives and sets priorities. It includes development of policies and plans that marshall alternatives, opportunities, and resources.

Awareness of Classical Themes and Dilemmas

The high accomplishers appeared to be aware that their problems and dilemmas were not unique. Indeed, this research shows that certain situations repeat themselves and that nearly every operating manager faces at one time or another a common set of problems. Understanding that there are common themes and dilemmas is an insight shared by most high accomplishing managers. They seemed to develop competent judgment and an element of maturity that enabled them to lift themselves beyond the bounds of their habitual responses and handle each situation appropriately.

For example, the first four to eight weeks on a new job is a situation faced by every manager. This time period is both critical and hazardous. The manager must size up the situation and subordinates at the same time that the manager is being sized up by them. They are especially sensitive to every signal that may indicate what it will be like to work for this new boss. What is done in those first few days and weeks is multiplied in its significance by those watching, involved, and concerned, both "upstairs" and "downstairs."

The new operating manager faces a further dilemma in that whatever standards of performance are set or not set for subordinates at the start tend to become precedents for the future. It is more difficult to criticize a poor practice after seeming to tolerate it for a month or two. But early criticism or demands for change are risky at best, for the new manager could be wrong, make a mistake, be unaware of valid reasons for the superficially apparent poor practice. The problem faced is how to avoid establishing unfortunate relations and precedents, tolerating low standards, or making foolish moves in the beginning when in-depth understanding of the situation is low.

Another set of classical issues or dilemmas for operating managers at every organizational level centers around information needs. The operating manager needs, but is often cut off from, information about objectives, strategies, and priorities held by superiors. The manager must know the superior's expectations for the manager's organization. The dilemma, however, is that frequently this information is not available at the lower level because it is not communicated from "upstairs" levels' purposely or carelessly. Sometimes it is not available, of course, because the executives at high levels have no plans and have not made their expectations explicit. The operating manager is often in the dark about not only what is expected but also what should *not* be done. In these circumstances several of the managers studied made moves that to their surprise immediately brought down upon themselves the wrath of their superiors.

Other dilemmas of the operating manager are equally inevitable. The operating manager must often deal with difficult employees, employees whose values or motives differ from the manager, or who have serious problems in morale, hold negative reactions to the organization, or unrealistic expectations. Dealing upstairs may be equally difficult. The example of one manager studied is typical.

How do I deal with a boss who, while brilliant and held in esteem at high levels in the industry, won't sit down long enough to plan objectives and strategy or even read his mail. He says, "Don't write it, tell it." But when you talk with him, he's easily distracted. When you're discussing one problem, his mind jumps to another and he usually doesn't listen well. When you are trying to reason with him, he extends your argument to an absurd extreme, argues rhetorically with unrealistic "what ifs' " or makes totally unreasonable "principles" out of your points. He makes sudden, impulsive, and sometimes angry decisions based on little data and mostly intuition. In making these hasty, long-postponed decisions, however, he often fails to consider their inevitable second-order implications. He doesn't keep me informed and seldom levels with me about what's on his mind or concerns him. We never set clear objectives or goals. He forgets from one time to the next what we've talked about or decided. Sometimes he tells me the same thing two or three times. We have few staff meetings when we can discuss our problems and plan together. When we do meet, we ramble around and reach few clear decisions unless he suddenly and sometimes angrily lays down the law. He is successful and technically competent, but as a boss he's a disaster. All I get is specific criticisms or vague praise. He has no idea really, in any depth, of what I do.

This operating manager cannot be content merely to "blow off steam" and criticize his boss. He must learn somehow to find out what the organization and the boss need from him; he must assist the boss in the boss's own way to do some planning; he must learn to get through to him. He cannot blame things on the "disastrous boss," for he will usually be the loser if the relationship is poor and he's kept in an information vacuum. He is the one who will be criticized when things aren't perfect, when expectations which are vague, are not met. The management of the relationship upstairs is often a necessary responsibility incumbent upon the subordinate. "It's his neck"; he must make it work.

Other typical issues and dilemmas may also be listed:

- How to stir up a sleepy, frozen, stagnant organization.
- When and how to question higher-level policies; running "the system" versus changing it; fighting city hall.
- How to handle "no-win" situations.
- Whether to seek consensus, wait for it to emerge, or go ahead and make a decision.

- How to identify, manage, and make use of power, "clout," pressure points in the organization.
- How to overcome bureaucratic resistance, red tape, and inertia.

Variety of Operating Tools and Techniques

Lower accomplishers seemed to be unaware of the enormous array of techniques available to managers for implementing policy and bringing about change. They used a few techniques repeatedly. The high accomplishers were frequently masterful in the introduction of techniques that proved effective.

The range of operating problems is so great that one habitual set of responses or choice of tools and alternatives is entirely inadequate. The understanding that there is a vast array of tools and alternatives and that discriminating choices must be made appeared to be another part of the development of judgment of high accomplishers.

Our cases of operating problems showed the list of tools and techniques to be impressively large. Exhibit 18.1 is a list of a 39-item arsenal of action-oriented tools and techniques from which the operating manager can choose to introduce change and bring about improvements.

Despite the existence of this powerhouse of tools and techniques, it was surprising how many managers felt baffled and frustrated about how little they could do in a situation. "I feel boxed in and helpless," one said. "The people and procedures and precedents are so firmly set up and frozen in place. Change is resisted by everybody around here. I can't seem to get any change whatsoever accomplished."

The frequency of this response among low accomplishers in the face of the great number of open options needs explanation. Our interviews suggest some reasons for this operating myopia, which reminds one of a machinist or carpenter with a wall full of mounted tools before his eyes but who, scratching his head in discouragement, mutters to himself, "I don't know how to go at this job." Some managers were unaware of the tools and approaches and unfamiliar with their usage. When managers were too close to their problems, they lost perspective and, mentally locking out positive and constructive possibilities, tended to become either conservative or unimaginative.

The discouraged manager believed that nothing would work, anyway. Arrogant managers believed that the few techniques or tools they were using or had used in the past were the proper and best ones to use again. They used these familiar approaches whether or not analysis of the situation would have indicated that another approach would be better. At other times there was either a failure of energy or the situation had begun

Exhibit 18.1   Some Action-Oriented Tools and Techniques Available to the Operating Manager

Structural
1. Formal organization
2. Change EPT methods, processes
3. Physical moves, relocations
4. Expanded resources, invest
5. Procedures, systems, routines
6. Job content(s)
7. Job assignments
8. Lend, borrow, exchange personnel
9. Project, task organization
10. Long-range planning exercises
11. Consultants, outside advisors

Employee Management and Development
1. Reward system
2. Training, courses, management development, coaching
3. Performance evaluations
4. Incentives
5. Informal assignments
6. Problem-solving meetings
7. Short-range planning exercises
8. Encourage/initiate competition
9. Replace managers
10. Increase participation in decision making

Communication
1. Short-range goals
2. Clear change in tone, atmosphere, system, norms, direction
3. Management by objectives: set objectives, get precise plan to achieve, set up precise measurement/controls
4. Timing: postpone/delay/speed up
5. Written announcements
6. Meetings
7. Ceremony, speeches
8. Conflict resolution
9. Get commitment

Controls
1. Standards, norms, limits, specifications
2. Due dates/schedules/timing
3. Measurement system regarding output, individual performance, subordinates
4. Regular reporting sessions
5. Ask for report, plans, process, results

Evaluation, Redesign
1. Evaluation of performance of unit, individuals, systems
2. Analysis of falldowns
3. Redesign to overcome organizational weaknesses
4. Redesign to buttress/support own personal weaknesses

to tailspin to the point that the manager was unable to pull together the time and organization to mount a carefully planned attack on the problem. A manager may lack self-confidence, boldness, and nerve. A manager may be afraid to take the initiative and try some bold approach if visibility is high and failure would be costly.

Changes in Executive Style to Fit Operating Situations

The dilemma of the operating managers studied was that each person tended toward the gradual adaption of one executive style (Exhibit 18.2), while different situations called for different managerial activities and tactics. Our research suggests that for each different situation there is a particular executive style that would be most effective.

This was an enigma for most of the managers. It is a curious yet reasonable fact that nearly all managers tend to settle into a fairly rigid or limited executive style. Each low-accomplishment manager studied had a certain profile when his or her regular practices were marked on the range of the 16 attributes listed in Exhibit 18.2. Managers tend toward a

Exhibit 18.2   Some Attributes of an Executive Style

Attributes	Range/Continuum	
Analytical patterns	Intuitive ⟷	Analytical
Cognitive style	Inductive ⟷	Deductive, use of generalizations
Decision making	Authoritative ⟷	Consultative
Decision-making speed	Fast, quick ⟷	Studied, worried
Delegation	Little ⟷	Much
Explicit "rules of thumb"	Few ⟷	Many
Type of follow-up	Loose, little ⟷	Much, rigorous
Communication	Informal, verbal ⟷	Formal, written
Personal relationships	Supportive ⟷	Demanding, challenging
Pressure, pace	Relaxed ⟷	Rigorous, energetic
Availability	Easily available ⟷	Remote
Boldness, audacity	Bold, risk taker ⟷	Cautious, risk aversive
Focus on time dimension	Seldom ⟷	Continuous
Openness to persuasion	Flexible ⟷	Dogged, persistent, single-minded
Work with subordinates	One on one ⟷	In a group
Work with superior	Wants support ⟷	Works alone

"set," because each manager proceeds from a given set of mental and physical capacities, a given amount of technical/managerial/industry training from which he or she has absorbed a finite set of knowledge or understandings, a fairly well-fixed hierarchy of motives inherent in personality and personal history, an implicit set of premises about people, a particular habitual and usually comfortable mode of relating to others, and a set of beliefs and assumptions about managing and management built from personal experience, rewards and punishment, success and failure.

In contrast, the high accomplishers seemed to tune into the fact that the demands upon a manager vary enormously from one situation and one period of time to another. The analogy of a college or university is relevant: In one period of time the institution may need a president who is strong in building a faculty. In another time the need may be for fundraising, extending relationships with the legislature and student groups, supervising the construction of new facilities, or developing financial control. Similarly, in business the needs change from the management of growth, new products, cost control, improved lead times, mergers, cash management, and so on. Each focus cannot be equally important. At any given time there exists indirectly or explicitly a key *operating task* that must be a success, which requires focus and a top priority and demands a unique executive style.

Yet typically, over a period of months and years, one manager must be competent at a variety of key operating tasks. In baseball, when a particular quality of pitching is called for, the manager brings in a certain relief pitcher. In business management this step is a last resort. In a number of the situations we studied the manager was finally replaced when his or her executive style finally proved to be inadequate for handling a certain kind of problem. In each case the manager did not realize the need for a change in style, or, if he did realize it, he was unable to accomplish such a change. Considerable flexibility was a hallmark of the high accomplishers.

This is a big order. It says, "Be different. Don't always manage the same way." Yet only a few managers studied were able to accomplish this kind of self-control and discipline. Those who did acted intuitively for the most part and often prior experience influenced them to realize that different behavior was called for in a particular new situation: "I've got to be tougher, more decisive, faster paced, delegate more than usual." Successful retooling and refocus of executive style appeared to be the most important change that might have turned failures to successes in the situations we studied.

Why this step is seldom carried out is due perhaps in part to these prevailing attitudes: "You must be natural and do your thing in your own natural way." "A successful manager would be foolish to tinker with his or her style." "A good manager can manage anything and any situation." Our analysis suggests that these notions are largely myths and that careful, honest experimentation with executive style is a tool of vast potential, seldom used.

How can a manager evaluate whether an executive style is appropriate for a given situation? The checklist in Exhibit 18.2 can be used to yield both a profile of the pro-forma executive style for a specific situation and a profile of the manager's present executive style. Examining the differences between the pro-forma and actual profiles should suggest the appropriate changes in the executive's style.

Analysis, self-discipline, sensitivity, intellect, and physical stamina are well-known requirements of the expert manager. To this list of super-human demands we now add personal liability for careful tuning of one's executive style. Constant reexamination of one's own habits and assumptions is perhaps one of the most difficult of all demands on the person who seeks to be a great manager.

The final concern that emerged from our studies of operating managers was the widespread tendency toward stagnation. The consistency of style and attack that led to inappropriate executive style factors and blinded, myopic selection of operating management tools and techniques was born out of stagnation.

A high percentage of our subjects, old and young, had slipped into a kind of lethargy where one day and one experience led to another; time slid smoothly by; they became mature and integrated, rigid in their styles, and slowly, seemly inexorably, had become a member of the grey army of low accomplishers. Their problems surfaced only in our studies. They showed no realization that they had ceased being diligent.

Many managers settle into executive life and immediately begin to stagnate in their habits. Faced with a dramatic new situation, they may do some analysis, but ordinarily they "wing it."

A pattern of stagnation among active executives is a striking phenomenon. The very reason for employing executives is to provide organizations with a mechanism for making changes as situations and circumstances change. Bombarded as managers are by a continuous flow of change by corporate and economic events, normal human indolence and mental lethargy represent not only a pragmatic paradox but even a moral one. One answer seems clear: The promise of personal reward is not enough to refuel this state of intellectual energy, which we found frequently dissipated. Needed is a state of mind that nature itself does not seem to evolve or fortify. As in the law of entropy, things run downhill.

SUMMARY: LESSONS FROM THE HIGH-LEVEL ACCOMPLISHERS

The high level accomplishers were characterized by the following:

They employed the practice of analysis with great effect. They used analytical tools and practice with such discipline and consistency that their establishment of objectives, strategies, plans and priorities were sound and distinctly tuned to the situation. At the same time, they developed controls and information systems so that they had a flow of data that uncovered details and operational problems on which they should spend their time.

From regular analysis on both the strategic and tactical levels, they decided how to allocate their time and focus their energies. They used analysis to give their work direction and so avoided the common trap of being consistent—and consistently getting into too much or too little detail. They thoughtfully tuned their style to be appropriate to each situation.

They succeeded in motivating subordinates and satisfying superiors. The words *motivating* and *satisfying* are critical. In examining all interactions between an executive and a subordinate—leading, instructing, coaching, communicating, listening, demanding, delegating, reporting, supporting, and motivating—the key to high operating accomplishment was shown to be motivated subordinates.

Similarly, the satisfaction of the manager's superior is vital to the manager's bottom line performance. How to be a good subordinate is a part of the operating art that was frequently neglected. Managing the relationship "upstairs" was as or more vital then managing "downstairs."

They managed themselves. They understood their internal pressures and needs and their central tendencies in executive style; they disciplined themselves to control and modify drives toward anger, action, delay, or domination, which would have been counterproductive; they were able to modify their styles according to the needs of the situation; they were sufficiently disciplined to do the analysis necessary to provide long- and short-term directional guidance for themselves. They avoided stagnation in mental and physical diligence.

They focused on one most important task at a time. We call this concept "the operating task." It is the task that is especially difficult, but absolutely critical at a given time to the achievement of one's objectives. Among all the tasks that could be accomplished, there is usually one task that makes or breaks the situation in the short run, and it must precede all others. For example:

A new production manager found himself in charge of installing a new coveyor system for furniture finishing. The equipment had been approved by his boss and was scheduled to start up in 10 days. A quick assessment of the equipment, however, suggested that there were going to be many start-up problems, and he doubted whether the equipment would actually work out nearly as well as anticipated. The operating manager's industrial engineer was enthusiastic about the new equipment. However, the superintendent stated that it would not work.

If he backed off, the new manager faced a disappointed boss. If he went ahead, he would probably "be hung" with the inevitable high costs and low production ahead. What was the operating task he faced?

He decided to do nothing and let the chips fall where they may. When the equipment did not work out well, his next four months were nearly disastrous. He "caught hell" from all sides.

What was his operating task during the first week? It could be to get the organization together to make a decision and full plans for what to do about the new equipment. Without such an operating task to set focus, strategy, and priorities, the low-level accomplishers often milled about from problem to problem.

CONCLUSION

These four concepts are perhaps a startlingly simple approach to what it takes to be a successful operating manager. A formula becomes clear from the experiences of our research subjects: Analyze, motivate subordinates and mind the "upstairs" relationship, understand and discipline oneself to avoid consistency, and the result could be to become one of the rare managers who accomplishes a great deal.

We step back from this work with a sense of wonder and admiration for that small fraction of managers—the high-level accomplishers—whose persistence in analysis and self-discipline permits them to be inconsistent in their own executive styles. The great managers we studied were permanently turned on—sensitive, diligent, analytical. The observer sees no stagnation, no lethargy, but a person excited by challenge. The life of the accomplishing manager is exciting. That persistent state of mind is the key to the accomplishing manager.

As the accomplishing manager moves up in the organization, she or he needs to develop conceptual and strategic skills. It is the theme of the next chapter that a lack of production managers with these skills is limiting progress toward the "factory of the future" and more importantly, toward major wholesale change in the factory as a Western institution, which is needed to restore our competitive edge.

CHAPTER 19

Wanted: Managers for the Factory of the Future

After two centuries of providing ever higher standards of living to Western civilization, the remarkable institution called the factory is now drifting toward failure. Its success in pouring out low-cost, high-volume production of manufactured products has produced economic benefits for every society that has invested in it. Today, however, many of our factories have become liabilities instead of assets.

Our factories are failing us primarily because they are increasingly noncompetitive. Productivity has seriously slowed down its heretofore inexorable climb. The output is often shoddy. New product introduction takes longer than in factory systems sited in several other societies. It is failing us too because it is an unhappy institution: its employee-members often speak of it as a jungle, stressful in its demands, tedious and repetitious in its job content, full of territorial and jurisdictional conflicts, governed via authoritarian processes of command and control, and unhealthy—often even dangerous—in its demands on the humans it employs.

The factory has been implicitly condemned as an unattractive institution by the millions of our young who, voting with their feet, turn down factory jobs if other means of earning a livelihood are possible. And to the high-potential men and women entering the job market from graduate schools of business administration, manufacturing management positions have ranked for 25 years near the bottom of alternative career paths.

Even its strongest advocates admit that in spite of its usual outstanding economics, the factory has never been a placid, contented institution. Its performance has been marked from the beginning by strife and discord between employees and managers, workers and owners.[1] From the early factories in England to the frequently violent, bloody battles of the 1930s and 1940s, unions of frustrated workers have bitterly contested "the rights of management to manage,'' sometimes even sabotaging the very machinery that provided their jobs. Factory jobs have been tolerated at best, hated at worst, and accepted only as a last resort for earning a living—a bad job accepted for a good wage. And from the late 1960s on, the changing sociology of expectations and demands for a higher quality of work life have served to increase employee discontent.[2]

These are not the marks of a successful social institution but of an institution showing signs of stress and obsolescence. Particularly sobering is its apparent inability to change itself. The auto and steel industries, for example, are victims of their own massive investments in the wrong equipment and process technologies (EPTs). Their dinosaurian mass production systems have been unable to change products flexibly and quickly enough to meet international competition in the late 1970s.

In a curious irony the factory, first spawned by the industrial revolution—a revolution of new mass production technology—is now being strangled by the very same kind of EPT, mass production, that made it so uniquely productive when it burst onto the scene 200 years ago. Today our mass production is a strategic millstone, dangerously inflexible in its ability to change products and output levels, while offering distasteful, monotonous jobs for a high proportion of employees.

So what is the future of the institution? Surely it will continue in some form, for the world's population wants ever more manufactured goods. Consumer demand, raw materials, EPTs, and energy are generally available, and in some societies people still seem to want to work in factories. Somewhere the factory will go on; but what is its future for Western society? Our interest naturally focuses on Western society and the U.S. factory. Our questions include: Will we reindustrialize? Will life in the factory become more attractive and rewarding? Can we regain, in some industries at least, a substantial competitive edge?

Now enters the factory of the future,[3] the ever elusive dream always just ahead, talked about since the early days of automation and robots in the 1950s. Since the "factory of the future" has many meanings, let me simply so label the constellation of new, highly mechanized, automatic, hands-off, low-labor content, self-correcting, self-controlling EPTs we have seen just ahead for 30 years and now are actually introducing. What will be the impact of this new technology on the future of the factory? Will it make it a more successful institution? A happier one?

In this chapter I will take the position that the answer is becoming clear enough to be beyond much debate: the new manufacturing technologies are so different in kind from what was available in the past that their effects—when the investments are made and fully implemented—will be sweeping. They will above all allow our factory systems to be more flexible and responsive to the new industrial competition[4]—competition based largely on ever more rapid changes in product and process technology—and create largely different and improved human jobs and working environments.

Let me just go back to the hook slipped into the last paragraph—"when invested in and implemented." For just when this will come about is not so clear. The technology looks highly promising, but we have to invest in it and manage its implementation. How are these stages progressing? What have we learned so far? What is the role of managers or managements in bringing the factory of the future into being?

Some data bearing on these questions have emerged from my research in 12 major manufacturing firms in 1981–82. The article will review these findings, offering the conclusion that the new technology is indeed hopeful in its promise but is being delayed by present industrial managers—those key players who must be the movers and shakers in any industrial change scenario.

Managers, it will be argued, are the chief agents holding back these promising moves into new manufacturing technology. The roadblock is of course neither organized nor explicitly intentional. There is no conspiracy. Industrial managers are impeding change because of conventional, short-term modes of corporate decision making,[5] combined with the underlying premises and managerial characteristics of a professional breed of manager, nurtured and hardened by a 200-year history of self-reinforcement. In particular it appears that thinking patterns centered around that good called productivity may in fact be the most pervasive roadblock of all.

The article concludes with some encouraging evidence that a more effective paradigm of industrial objectives and decision making may now be emerging, driven in part by a new breed of industrial manager who appears to be emerging by a Darwinian process from the present scene of crisis and failure.

THE NEW MANUFACTURING TECHNOLOGY: PROGRESS AND PROBLEMS

In 1981–82 I visited a dozen large American manufacturing firms in a variety of industries asking the following questions: (1) What is the extent to which your firm has employed the new manufacturing technologies? (2) What has influenced the extent of the penetration and the effectiveness of these new EPTs in your facilities? (3) May I interview managers considered by top management as "best, high potential 'comers' who will probably be running major facilities in five to seven years?"

Some Initial Research Findings

From these visits, interviews, questions, and subsequent analysis of data have developed the following preliminary research findings, expressed in necessarily sketchy and cursory assertions, as follows.

The new technology for sale is emerging thick and fast. It is being driven primarily by electronics and computer firms but also by industrial equipment firms, all of whom see large, even gigantic markets ahead. Foreign suppliers, especially in equipment, are playing a major role. U.S. machine toolmakers produce high-quality equipment but are risk aversive and fail to offer more than small chunks of a total system's needs. They tend to base their business planning on the objective of surviving in low periods and growing modestly in good times, and hence are not very aggressive.

The potential impact of the new technology is enormous. Its present penetration and impact, however, is very modest in all but the already largely mechanized process industries. It is moving slowly for many interrelated reasons. Some of the reasons include the fact that the technology is new and little understood, yet much feared, by potential users. A typical problem is that the new equipment does not work well for two to five years, and "those years are hell" for operations management. It is generally looked upon with skepticism by organized labor. Workers have mixed experiences in adjusting to it. Sometimes it is stressful to be in charge of so much expensive machinery, but often it makes the actual job far more interesting. The new technology substantially changes the jobs of supervisors and middle management, shifting the focus from watchdog and disciplinarian to planning, training, and communicating.

The new technology also shifts management power within companies, conferring the power of knowledge and capability upon the system's designers, coordinators, and troubleshooters. Conventional line managers experience a loss of influence. It is difficult to measure results of the new manufacturing technology because accounting methods and processes are lagging behind manufacturing technology by at least 25 years, but it is very clear that the major benefits are not in cost savings. The major benefits do not come about until virtually the whole factory is reequipped and all systems are changed over. Islands of automation offer only modest benefits, but vendors sell only islands or chunks. The technology and process equipment are fragmented across a churning new industry. No vendor, like a Bechtel or a Turner in power plants and chemical plants, offers a whole turnkey system with guaranteed results. This is what is needed but no one can do it yet.

No one can do it yet because the technology is so immature and the investment and risks are seen as out of this world. Few companies want to go first. "Let the competition bloody their noses," is the normal stance. But the normal stance is also, "let us experiment a little," "let us buy a few robots," "let us have staff people so as to be sure to keep up with the state of the art." So there are many corporate staff people muddling around in this. They go to conferences and talk to each other and plead for money and experimentation, all with much frustration.

Division managers are not buying, however. They are sensible people, and they simply compare projected capital invested to what they have now; knowing that the technology will not work for two to five years and, if they perform well and stay out of trouble, they will be promoted and gone by then, they conclude that they would be foolish to be the ones to go all out for a whole new production system now. Further, company capital budgeting systems are good at handling expansions or cost savings or bottlenecks, but they are not good at investing in uncertainty and nebulous, though promising, payoffs that are difficult to quantify.[6] Few companies—in spite of Abernathy, Clark, Hays, Leonard, Sasser, Skinner, and Wheelright[7] and their pleas and formulae for developing a manufacturing strategy—do have a manufacturing strategy. As one manufacturing vice-president put it, "So how can you plan for new technology with a four to five year payoff if you still plan only a year at a time?"

The research also confirms what is supposedly generally known, that manufacturing managers are typically conservative, risk-aversive people who prefer sequential to parallel uncertainties, with a low tolerance for ambiguity, and a strong distaste for any prospect of wholesale changes. Their paradigm is productivity and efficiency, and that mind-set accounts for many of the problems and sluggishness of change in manufacturing.

But there may be a new breed coming on fast, characterized by nonlinear and variegated career paths. Featuring information technology competences, team project leadership, thriving on change and ambiguity, nearly disrespectful of their elders, they are not as stubbornly loyal to their companies as were their predecessors. Their style contains a strong but sometimes unrealistic measure of self-confidence. They will be coming into substantial power in five to ten years, but few have it now.

The new manufacturing technologies will be powerful and influential, probably far more than most corporate executives realize. They are based on the microprocessor and ever cheaper computing and memory power. They will cause the replacement of much traditional labor. Their biggest advantage may be to create an order of magnitude increase in flexibility for product variation. They can economically produce very short runs. They will be self-correcting and improve quality and reliability. They will replace human variability with machine consistency.

Their biggest impact, however, will probably be strategic: to make manufacturing more readily a competitive weapon because of their speed in new product introduction, customer specials, short runs, and superior quality.

The impact of the new technologies will be particularly powerful in their effects on working environments and human resource management. Many jobs will be less physical, monotonous, dirty, and dangerous. More jobs will require more knowledge and judgment. More jobs will focus more on keeping the system going and less on production output in units. Workers will have more autonomy, freedom, information, and discretion. Supervisors may become more coordinators, implementers, and sources of knowledge and expertise, and less the disciplinarian, counter, and cost watcher. The corporate name of the game will be more than ever human resource management, with corporate performance in recruiting, selection, training and development, and communications becoming critical, as the emphasis shifts to managing more capital-intensive and knowledge-dependent production systems.

While progress is still slow, this is after all the normal pace and pattern of major technological change. The power of the technologies, the coming of the new breed, and the phenomenon of one company in an industry gaining a major strategic, competitive advantage over the rest and thus setting off a grass fire that sweeps through the industry—all imply that in a five- to fifteen-year period profound and dramatic changes will occur in many production factories and service operations. Theses changes will enormously alter and indeed reinvent this old and slow-moving institution, the factory.

Industrial Managers and Their Leadership

What is going on in this once great factory institution seems paradoxical. Why is the factory's social and leadership infrastructure holding back the very changes that might be its economic salvation? While the factory is apparently slowly dying in the Western world, its leadership seems unable to make the decisions, take the risks and invest the capital to reequip itself and survive.

So the question is, Why not? From the viewpoint of the observer outside the system, it appears to be illogical and shortsighted behavior; but to the actors on the scene their risk-aversive, business-as-usual response is not so illogical. They are reacting rationally in accordance with the reward/punishment characteristics of their corporation's management systems; they must play by the rules of prevailing corporate capital budgeting and financial management systems. Their experience has taught them that anything that can go wrong will go wrong, and that any overlooked detail can stop the production line. When that happens they are criticized; so they behave as they have been conditioned and constrained. Their motto is "productivity now."

The net result of this set of conditions and responses is that the very technology that might help manufacturing companies recover competitive position and gain strategic advantage is being adopted extremely slowly. The few situations, among the companies studied, in which firms have moved ahead faster have featured one or both of the following: (1) top management has had a clear, long-range vision of the advantages and indeed necessity of investing in advanced manufacturing technology, and has said, "Do it"; and/or (2) manufacturing executives have been so aggressive, broad in their vision, successful, secure, and influential at top levels that they have forcefully urged the investment and prevailed in being allowed to lead their organizations into the learning process.

The evidence is that it takes one or the other—or both—kinds of executive to move away from the let-someone-else-go-first syndrome that prevails. Further, the evidence is clear that if top management forces the new experimental technologies on less than enthusiastic and able production managers, the learning process is inevitably more painful, expensive, and drawn out in time than when the production people are eager, ready, and proactive in their attitudes toward the new EPTs. This may appear only too obvious to the researcher, but the problem is that these management phenomena form a major roadblock holding back the industrial catch-up so badly needed in U.S. industry.

The weakness in production management that manifests itself in a cautious, careful, and narrow focus in relation to investments in the new manufacturing technology is not a new phenomenon. It has been evident in case studies of production management over the past 30 years. The production management field is characterized by slow progress and modest changes when compared to the rate of change in financial management, marketing, control systems, information systems, strategic planning, and human resource management. In each of these sectors of administrative science, progress in the past 20 years has been remarkable. We have seen the emergence of such concepts and techniques as present-value analysis, scientific market research and analysis, corporate budgeting and control systems, and totally new approaches in information system design and handling. Over 200 documented, experimental approaches in human resource management have been developed, including nonsupervised work groups, totally new work restructuring and compensation systems, and most recently human resource strategic planning concepts and practices.

Advances in conceptual management in production must be considered modest. The much publicized materials requirements planning (MRP) is little more than simply a computerized process of ordering needed materials, which is what has been done for 40 years, only by slow and cumbersome hand methods. Statistical quality control was invented in the decade before World War II and then used less in the 1970s than in the 1950s; we have added the advantages of project and program management learned from aerospace industries in the 1950s and 1960s. Operations research has offered the use of mathematical models for scheduling and inventory management but has had a disappointingly small impact in practice. One new management concept and practice area has been that of manufacturing strategy, first conceptualized by John G. McLean in 1950,[8] and even that concept has been adopted very slowly.

The ironic fact is that while scientific management began in the factory, factory management has been outrun by every other functional area of management since the halcyon days of Frederick Taylor, Lilian Gilbreth, and efficiency experts in time-and-motion study. Using a product or technology analogy, the field has been mature for a long time. Its rate of change and its members' rate of new learning has been relatively flat.

It is necessary to speculate on the reasons for the maturing of the field of production management by the end of World War II, its subsequently slow rate of change, and its present role in impeding progress toward the ever elusive factory of the future. We seem to have a generation of men— there are a few women but not many—who, compared to their counterparts in finance, marketing, control, and human resource management, appear to be cautious, reactive, and occasionally unimaginative. They are seldom promoted to top management. They are often criticized by top managers as being too narrow to see and understand the whole business, and as having an excessively tactical rather than a strategic point of view; they are functionally oriented rather than able to integrate well across other functions of the business. They are often seen by human resource managers as authoritative, dominating, and mechanistic in their personal management styles. In practice they emphasize details of costs, schedules, efficiency, logistics, set-up and running times, and productivity. Driven simultaneously by cost, time, delivery, and quality objectives that represent unrecognized trade-offs,[11] their factories are often unfocused[12] and anachronistic. When push comes to shove, as it has in the 1980s, the ingrained instinctive response is as always[9] to return to the productivity paradigm.

These managers are the mud-slogging soldiers of our industrial time. They are heroes in the sense that they dig in, do the nasty, detailed, day-by-day planning, expediting, and follow-through necessary to get out the production and keep cost variances down. They are under relentless pressure from above on conflicting performance yardsticks and face strident social and often union-driven pressure from below to keep discontented, often unhappy people working productively. They are a product of those pressures and their heritage. Their survival instincts create a kind of technological imperative that is a powerful influence. It is small wonder, therefore, that they behave as they do.

WANTED: A NEW BREED OF MANAGERS

What kind of managers and managements are needed to become positive rather than negative factors in bringing the factory of the future effectively to bear on our industrial problems? The research described before leads the analyst to the following prescriptive characteristics for the men and women who will be needed.

1. Knowledge will include comfort-level knowledge of mechanical, electronic, and management science technology, and all business functions—production, marketing, finance, control, and personnel.
2. Skills will include system design—logistical, information, human systems, planning, coordination; project management and team building; interpersonal communications, handling large groups, and labor relations; general management, for example, integration of business and technical functions—in contrast to specialized technical skills.
3. Attitudes will be positive toward change, restless unless making progress in change, and will reflect security in professional life.
4. Cognitive/thinking style will involve the ability to conceptualize combined with the ability to work from specifics in a systematic and analytical rather than purely intuitive pattern.
5. Premises/assumptions will be that the objections of a manufacturing system are multidimensional. Rather than always focusing the production system primarily on cost and efficiency, the manager must set objectives based on the strategic needs of the corporation. These objectives will include criteria concerning the following, specifically establishing both priorities among and specific trade-offs between:

- Cost-efficiency-productivity.
- Customer response time, i.e., delivery lead times.
- Reliability of delivery promises.
- Quality of product.
- Investment in equipment and inventory.
- Flexibility for product changes.
- Flexibility for volume changes.

This is admittedly a pie-in-the-sky description of the "compleat manager", who will bring the factory of the future into being. A contrasting description of the typical present-day manager also emerged from this set of research interviews. This is a composite picture that no one manager would completely fulfill, admittedly overdrawn to make the point:

1. Knowledge includes specialized, technical expertise generally limited to the existing product and EPT, and it is usually heavily weighted toward one, either professional or functional, sector of production, such as production control, inventory control, or manufacturing engineering.
2. Skills include strengths in handling and dealing with large numbers of people, in expediting meeting schedules, and in cost control, with weaknesses in finance, marketing, and business strategy.
3. Attitudes reflect the assumption that management has a right to manage, and that I must keep control, using the authority conferred by the organization chart.
4. Cognitive/thinking style will focus in on specifics and details, using intuitive analysis based on experience.
5. Premises/assumptions are that the manager's job is to command and control, and that productivity is the most important, overriding criterion for manufacturing success.

The contrast between the people presently in power and what appears to be needed is striking. The limitations of many production managers can be traced in part to three principal sources: (1) the industrial revolution and its legacies; (2) Frederick Taylor and the principles of scientific management; and (3) the influences of the industrial engineering profession.

The industrial revolution substituted steam and water power, combined with new, mechanically-based machinery, for human power and craft skills. Its theme was the mass production of cheap goods. Its workers received wages that were extremely attractive. Its owners' returns on capital invested at risk depended on the phenomenon of heretofore undreamed-of efficiency. For the owners and managers the success of the operation depended primarily upon the achievement of efficiency.

A century later Frederick Taylor showed production managers that by planning, measuring, and systematic organizing, large increases in efficiency could be obtained. He was the pioneer industrial engineer and was followed by a long procession of superb analytical industrial engineers and efficiency experts. Their expertise was in detailed analysis of human and logistical movements, the establishment of stopwatch standards, time-and-motion studies, and ultimately whole books of predetermined standards based on human physiology, which resulted in accounting standards and variance controls. It built year by year into a profession and established a pattern of thinking, the paradigm called productivity.

Its thinking dominates the scene even today. To be productive demands a systematic mental focus on details, time, schedules, dimensions, and minute operations. But being productive this week and this month is nearly impossible if destabilizing changes are being introduced. Production managers seek the maximum of continuity of schedules, products, and processes. Productivity is a good that is hard to dispute. For years the more productive departments, factories, companies, industries, and countries tended to win out in competition. The problem today is that competition is based not only on productivity but on quality and delivery and flexibility as well. The achievement of quality and flexibility of volume and product in Western society depends upon a firm's ability to attract and hold outstanding people in its production operations.

The vicious circle is apparent. Thinking based on productivity dominates the industrial scene and drives out more practical and realistic premises that might include the multidimensional parameters needed; it holds back investment in and successful implementation of the promise of new manufacturing technology; it discourages the selection and development of men and women who might think of the factory in broad and more flexible alternatives, handle change and ambiguity, solve problems without resort to authority, and attract and develop more of their own kind. In the language of cognitive styles the four-way matrix in Exhibit 19.1 suggests some dimensions of the contrast between what generally predominates today and what appears to be needed for the factory of the future.

The Emerging Production Manager—A New Breed?

During the course of the research described earlier, I interviewed many comers, typically younger managers emerging as high-potential people who were expected by their firm's top managers to "be running the place" in five to seven years. The interviews reviewed the manager's education, training, and career path; open-ended questions also explored the man-

Exhibit 19.1 Cognitive Styles

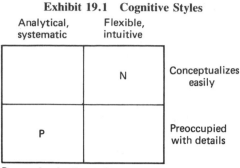

P = predominating today
N = needed for the factory of the future

ager's premises and attitudes concerning executive practices, problem solving, introducing changes, and managing people.

The data* suggest that it may be possible that the managers needed are in fact emerging via the competitive processes of self-selection, survival, and promotion. The sufficiency of their numbers and the rate by which they will emerge is of course still open to question; but their qualities and potential for growth and meeting the challenges appear impressive.

Instead of coming up through the conventional career paths—relatively few but long-duration positions in first-line supervision, production and industrial engineering, or production staff departments—these men and women are apt to have had a greater variety of career paths. They have come from such work experience as research, design engineering, accounting, sales, marketing, or personnel. They often have had computer programming experience, been in charge of human resource experiments, installed small sections of newly automated equipment or experience with new plant planning and operations or program/project management.

Their positions are apt to have been of shorter duration than their predecessors'. Their skills feature the abilities to form up and lead effective teams for problem solving, systems design, and experimental manufacturing systems. They are apparently rapid learners and tend to surround themselves with others who adapt quickly. They seem to thrive on change, uncertainty, and ambiguity and indeed become easily bored with routine production. They delegate easily and in fact rather loosely, relying more on trust and less on formal controls and reports. Their casual styles, somewhat surprisingly perhaps, seem to be acceptable and even refreshing to union stewards and business agents. They seem less loyal to their employers than to their professions, and might be termed "universal production system designers and managers."

*This data is reviewed in more detail in the next chapter.

The emergence of this new breed of production managers is not surprising as a response to economic and technological needs. What is unexpected is their success in what might have been predicted to be an alien environment. For these new breed managers are of course being selected and promoted by their older superiors, who represent an earlier and now declining elite. The old are developing the young not in their own image but in the new skills, premises, and attitudes that appear necessary and functional for today. It is as if the older generations recognize that what is needed now is not more of what they, the older generation, have had to offer, but something new.

CONCLUSION

Recommendations from this research into the management implications of our slow progress in investing in and implementing new manufacturing technology fall into two categories: recommendations (1) to corporate managements and (2) to thoughtful citizens and students of the industrial scene.

To managements, the scenario of slow progress due to managerial behavior molded by outdated business practices in capital budgeting, technological assessments, and management reward systems might ring out a warning bell of alarm. Sophisticated managers and students of administration have seen this same syndrome many times before, as have students of governmental and social systems. The decision makers become prisoners of their own systems of governance. This is what is happening in industry today. Industry needs to attack its own confining management infrastructure systems, and when these mechanisms are effectively overhauled, better decisions made with a boldness and daring appropriate to the times can be expected to begin remaking the factory.

The human resource system for attracting, developing, and nurturing a wholly new breed of production managers needs particular attention. An able new breed is developing, largely by selection of the fittest, but this process could be speeded up enormously by more deliberate, purposeful management development.

To the thoughtful observer outside of industry and corporate responsibility the implications are equally substantial. What is going on now, albeit slowly, is the reinvention of this old institution, the factory. Its direction suggests that life for people in future factories may be quite different from the bitter experiences of its past unhappy history. It suggests too that there are already exciting jobs in the factory for the able of our young, and great opportunities for young managers who seek careers in which they can make a contribution and work with people, rather than dealing with second-order abstractions. It may be true now that in contrast to 200 years of mass production, the new microprocessor-based equipment and process technologies are positive engines of change moving industry toward the human uses of human beings in industry.

The limiting ingredient to a more rapid development of the new factory is no longer the technology or its economics; it is the manager and management systems. Thoughtful, responsible, broad-gauged, innovative and daring—these are the managers needed now for a new future for the factory.

In the next and last chapter we pose the question: How did manufacturing leadership evolve into its present state? The issue is that we seem to need a "new breed," but if it is a new breed, what's the old breed, what is wrong with it, and how did it get that way?

So we must turn first to history. The next chapter goes back to early American industry and traces the evolution of manufacturing leadership through about 100 years, up to today. Then, to better understand today's mixed picture, the new breed of "comers" is compared to the incumbents, presently in charge in American industry. From these comparisons across several dozen attributes of skills and abilities, the chapter concludes with a look at the question: Is natural evolution developing the kind of quality of manufacturing managers we need in U.S. industry?

NOTES

1. Andrew Ure, "The Philosophy of Manufacturers" (1835), in *The Philosophy of Manufacturers,* ed. Michael Brewster Folsom and Steven D. Lubar (Cambridge, MA: MIT Press, 1982), p. 365.
2. Wickham Skinner, "The Anachronistic Factory," *Harvard Business Review,* Jan.–Feb. 1971.
3. "The Factory of the Future: Always in the Future?" in *Towards the Factory of the Future,* ed. L. Kops (New York: American Society of Mechanical Engineers, 1980).
4. W. Abernathy, K. Clark, and A. Kantrow, "The New Industrial Competition," *Harvard Business Review,* Sept.–Oct. 1981.
5. Robert Hayes and William Abernathy, "Managing Our Way to Economic Decline," *Harvard Business Review,* July–Aug. 1980.
6. Bela Gold, "CAM Sets New Roles for Production," *Harvard Business Review,* Nov.–Dec. 1982.

7. William Abernathy, *The Productivity Dilemma* (Cambridge, MA: MIT Press, 1982); Abernathy, Clark, and Kantrow, "New Industrial Competition"; Hayes and Abernathy, "Managing Our Way"; Frank S. Leonard and W. Earl Sasser, "The Incline of Quality," *Harvard Business Review,* Sept.–Oct. 1982; Steven C. Wheelwright, "Integration of Manufacturing Strategy and Business Strategy," in *Manufacturing Trends in the 1980s* (New York: Booz, Allen, and Hamilton, 1981).

8. *Advanced Production Problems* (Homewood, IL: Irwin,1952).

9. Alfred D. Chandler, Jr., *The Visible Hand* (Cambridge, MA: Harvard University Press, 1977).

CHAPTER 20

The Taming of Lions: How Manufacturing Leadership Evolved 1780–1984

R ecent competitive events remind us with great force of the necessity for excellence in manufacturing. Starting from a position of American dominance of many industries in the fifties, we look back now on two decades of declines in world market share. This steady deterioration raises questions about that former dominance and our vaunted manufacturing leadership.

Was our former high level of manufacturing performance due to our proficiency in the management of manufacturing rather than the fact of limited competition? And are the inefficiencies and fundamental structural problems[1] that have surfaced during these two troubled decades new, or have they been there all along, hidden by easy success? Such a lengthy decline suggests a problem of "mind-set," of mistaken premises or implicit objectives that are no longer appropriate and useful.

The central thesis of this chapter is that we have a management problem in American manufacturing today that is due to a "mind-set," rooted in the history of production management, which is now dysfunctional. In its

Acknowledgments: This chapter has benefited from the generous efforts and thoughtful comments of many colleagues, particularly Alice Amsden, Alfred Chandler, Jr., E. Raymond Corey, Robert Hayes, Alan Kantrow, George Lodge, and W. Earl Sasser, of the Harvard Business School, Anne Firor Scott of Duke University, and Virginia C. Welles, whose able work as research associate is much appreciated.

first 160 years American manufacturing leadership developed skills, techniques, concepts, and patterns of thinking—a paradigm for a profession that appeared enormously successful. Now many conditions have changed. Worldwide industrial competition and changing technology are among the many factors that have rewritten the rulebook and changed the game.[2] There are new rules. Meanwhile, we think about the factory institution and make manufacturing decisions in much the same way as 60 years ago. Our premises and perceptions and even our objectives do not always fit reality. The resulting "wrong thinking" caused us to fall into trouble and still keeps us there. The question today is not whether but how the manufacturing management profession must change its ways of thinking.

But what are its "ways of thinking"? How and in what patterns did they develop? Analysis of American industrial history suggests five traditional characteristics of American manufacturing leadership that are now holding back industrial performance. These characteristic tendencies are as follows:

1. To accept that the performance of the factory and its management is principally measured by financial yardsticks (such as cost reduction, return on investment, and efficiency).
2. To accept a secondary role in the firm as custodians of fixed assets.
3. To perceive the keys to managerial success to be achieving maximum production and minimum cost by excellence in controlling and coordinating, while stabilizing the factory in every way possible against external changes.
4. To perceive the work force as an annoying, potentially destabilizing, and frequently pernicious factor of production to be handled by simultaneously delegating work-force management to first-level supervision and minimizing the involvement and preoccupation of top-level management.[3]
5. As a consequence of these four tendencies, to seek the maximum degree of process mechanization and high volume-mass production-continuous flow processes permitted by production economics.

These characteristics are rooted in history and they persist today. They are the way the profession evolved during the nineteenth century. Such managerial behavior was reinforced and rewarded with successful careers, and it contributed to American industry's 180-year climb to a peak of industrial success about 1960.

But after 1960 these premises appear to have been dysfunctional. The new industrial competition has proved to be technology based, with processes, products, and information systems changing with accelerating rapidity, requiring a different, more flexible, and proactive kind of manufacturing management. To compete in 1984 it appears that the thinking and premises of American manufacturing leadership may have to be almost diametrically opposed to the five characteristics developed in history. The following characteristic concepts seem to be needed now:

1. To see the factory as a competitive resource rather than as a financial investment.
2. To carry out a primary role in the corporation as the architect and builder of new manufacturing systems structured to provide competitive and strategic advantage, rather than to act as custodian and housekeeper.
3. To emphasize as key skills those of managing technological and product change and building flexible, learning organizations, rather than acting as coordinator and stabilizer.
4. To become involved with and gain the support and commitment of the work force, rather than to consider labor as a cost and a disturbing element to be managed well down the organization.
5. To seek the maximum of flexibility for product and volume change by choosing technology appropriate for the competitive market, rather than to seek only maximum mechanization and the use of mass production processes.

In this chapter I will first trace the antecedents of the outmoded characteristics from our industrial history (Part I). In Part II, I will describe how they have continued as a dominant paradigm and have been increasingly ineffective in the past 20 years. In Part III, I will describe ongoing field research based on interviews with 46 "fast-track comers," directed toward the following question: Will the next generation of manufacturing managers, developed under adversity and new, more demanding competitive conditions, have the same or different characteristics? Part IV focuses on conclusions.

We conclude that, although we see many encouraging signs about these "comers," the picture is not altogether optimistic. For the hand of history is heavy and, while the next generation appears to think more broadly and to demonstrate more of a general management focus in skills and outlook, most of them still function as "custodians" and "housekeepers" rather than as determined "architects." Though the competitive world is changing its demands, a profession steeped in the values and traditions of a century apparently cannot make such basic changes in one, short generation.

More optimistically, the history of manufacturing leadership shows that basic changes in management focus and characteristics were brought about by major developments in technology and markets, the transition requiring about 20 to 30 years, the equivalent of two or three generations of top manufacturing leadership. Today we are already being impacted by the very ingredients history seems to require for change: new economics, in the form of severe competition, and major innovations in process technology.[4,5] In many industries technology offers the greatest changes in a century,[6] such as microprocessor-based computer-aided design and manufacturing (CAD/CAM), robotics, computer-integrated manufacturing (CIM), and flexible machining centers. Taken together, these revolutionary factors may be powerful enough eventually to sweep away worn-out paradigms of manufacturing leadership and bring on something new. But this will be discussed at the end of the chapter; first, a look at American industrial history and the derivations of today's manufacturing leadership.

PART I: THE EVOLUTION OF MANUFACTURING MANAGEMENT

Five periods of industrial history stand out in the development of dominant characteristics of manufacturing management:

1780–1850   Manufacturing leaders as technological capitalists.
1850–1890   Manufacturing leaders as architects of mass production.
1890–1920   Manufacturing management moves down in the organization.
1920–1960   Manufacturing management refines its skills in controlling and stabilizing.
1960–1980   Shaking the foundations of industrial management.

The Manufacturing Leader as Technological Capitalist—1750–1850

New technology first allowed production to begin to shift from the traditional enterprise of low-volume artisan shops to capital-intensive use of machinery. The harnessing of water and steam energy to power machinery was combined with new machines and equipment using recently engineered mechanisms for power transmission and mechanization of hand-performed operations. Shafting, gears, bearings, and ingenious mechanical movements added the ability to eliminate many manual operations. The shift was limited as well as triggered by technological factors, because there were as yet inadequate means of transporting coal, of producing strong and nonbrittle metals, and, equally detrimental, limited means of communication and only slow, small-scale transportation—all factors that kept markets small and local and power supplied by people, animals, or flow of water. As a result, the industrial "revolution" was slow in developing in all but textile production,[7] some metalworking and machine-making facilities, and modest agricultural processing plants such as grain mills.

In America the first water-powered mill was developed by a partnership between a Samuel Slater and four Brown Brothers, the former being a skilled mechanic and the latter, wealthy merchants.[8] The first integrated textile mill was built by Francis Cabot Lowell, "an able self-taught engineer" as well as a merchant, and he "recognized the primary of technological problems."[9] These operations built up to unprecedented scale and degree of integration.

While the management of the large, integrated textile mills was something that had never been done before, it was still basically not complex.[10] Because of equipment constraints and lack of flexibility, each mill had a relatively small range of product. The equipment was essentially balanced and integrated around that product range.[11]

The main tasks of management—after the mill was engineered and built, with power shafting and belting installed and machinery purchased and set up by a technologically oriented and mechanically assisted top management—were delegated to the "overseers," one on each floor. Overseers reported to the owner's "agent" who more or less singlehandedly (and often from a distance) ran the mill. Profits were calculated twice a year; accounting was by the mercantile system with no product costing. The agent's specialized knowledge and competence were also essentially technical. He or she focused on the machinery and equipment and performed the calculations needed for setting up spinning ratios and cloth balances.[12]

As this early factory period moved along in time, large increases in productivity came about as technological changes took place in spinning, metalworking machinery improved, and continuous processes were developed for the milling of grains.

In metalworking and parts and assembly industries, such as rifle-making, a major innovation late in the period[13] was the shift from individual parts and unique products to making interchangeable parts and products that could be readily repaired later by substituting new parts. This "American factory system" required fixtures and gauges and more complex measuring and inspection equipment and procedures. It also required a standard method of manufacture and, therefore, worker discipline and supervisory surveillance.[14] At the Springfield Armory, for example, where guaranteed markets based on annual production contracts allowed large batches to be made and, hence, standardized, the use of the interchangeable parts philosophy induced standardization of processes, specialized jobs (making a few parts rather than a whole or major assembly of the rifle), and, finally, the beginning of detailed accounts to provide management with cost information.[15]

The management of manufacturing was relatively simple and performed by the owner's "agent." After the system was started by the technologically competent owners, they were much less involved. The most demanding aspect of plant operation was technological, centering on the engineering of the plant, the mechanics of machinery operation, and instructing overseers on each floor. The overseer took entire responsibility for every aspect of the employee and employment arrangements. Even the agent was often remote.

From the outset an unmistakable characteristic of the early factory period was worker resistance and unrest, the formation of unions, and occasional sabotage.[16] This seems surprising at first, since there were many advantages of the factory system to employees. The pay and working conditions were far superior to farm and physical labor. Furthermore, the work was light and easy compared to tasks not performed by a machine powered by coal or water. The hours were long but not at all unusual for those times. There were opportunities for advancement and, for some, the challenge of machinery. The tasks of coordinating materials and products were simple, but for all there was the opportunity for normal pleasurable social interaction, as well as the support and warmth of friendly and cooperative associations at work.[17]

For some, of course, this was enough. Satisfying economic, physical, and social needs, the factory was a good place to spend one's working life. For apparently many others, however, the factory was an alien environment for a human being.[18] It required strict self-discipline to get to work on time; the work was performed in accordance with prescribed methods; starting and stopping work was not a matter of personal choice but was ordered by a preemptory bell or whistle; the pace, often driven by machine and overseer, could feel relentless.[19] There was an overseer on each floor who had total authority to hire, fire, discipline, and use physical punishment if he chose. The factory may have been warm and dry and even relatively clean, but it was usually noisy, and frequently the belt-driven machinery was dangerous. Although the work might not have been easy, it was often monotonous. The transition to industrial society "entailed a severe restructuring of working habits—new disciplines, new incentives, and a new human nature upon which these incentives could bite effectively."[20]

In 1887 Arnold Toynbee wrote of the early factories in England:

When huge factories were established there could no longer be a close tie between the master and his men; the workman hated his employer and the employer looked on his workmen simply as hands. From 1800 to 1843 their mutual relations, as was admitted by both parties, were as bad as they could be. There could be no union, said employees, between classes whose interests were so different. . . . Trade-unions, too, have done much to sever what was left of the old ties. Workmen are obliged, in self-defense, to act in bodies. [p. 132]

Between the individual workman and the capitalist who employed hundreds of hands a wide gulf opened. The workman . . . became the living tool of whom the employer knew less than he did of his steam engine. The breach was admitted by the employer who declared it to be impossible. "It is as impossible," said one, "to effect a union between the high and low classes of society as to mix oil and water. There can be no union between employer and employed because it is the interest of the employer to get as much work as he can done for the smallest sum possible." [p. 206]

So there was "the labor problem"[21] from the very beginning. People did not easily adjust to factory life. "Subordination is the very essence of the factory system."[22] Those who were willing to take factory jobs tended, therefore, to be from the lower rungs of society. Each wave of farm and other immigrants ultimately provided the labor source for the insatiably growing factory system. These workers usually had the least education, were not acculturated to the United States, and often spoke little or no English. But they were cheap and they were willing to work. Management had no reason or need to associate with them and for more than a century this area of management was simply delegated and ignored.

Worker assignments, discipline, and compensations were handled by the overseers, while families and relatives often worked together. Even a support system was frequently inadequate to cushion the shock of a restricted, constrained life in the factory. As a result, from the beginning of industrial society, there were strikes, unions, and occasional violence and sabotage. "Thus gloomily amid tumult, fear and suffering was the modern factory system introduced" wrote R. W. C. Taylor concerning the resistance of workers to the factory.[23]

In sum, the early factory period saw a genuine revolution in how products were made and how large numbers of workers worked. Its concepts and its factories began to change Western civilization. Its leadership came from technologically competent entrepreneurs, investing in new labor-saving equipment to gain an economic return. Aside from ownership and mechanics it required little management and only the simplest management hierarchy.[24] Nevertheless, the seeds of mass production—capital invested in equipment and process technology, the use of a central power source, the producing of standardized products, the use of interchangeable parts and repetitive operations,[25] a few isolated experiments in accounting as a control mechanism, and the employment of large numbers of workers on machine-controlled jobs—had been sown.[26] But the owners were not much involved with the workers. In 1881, looking back at the short history of the factory system, R. W. C. Taylor wrote:

The captain of industry has not played that splendid part in industry which was assigned to him operatives were dependent on him for present support and future progress. He has been content with the far more vulgar one of a more or less successful trader.[27]

A big revolution had occurred—on a small scale—and a real industrial revolution awaited further key technological breakthroughs in power, transportation, communication, and equipment and process technologies.

Manufacturing Leadership as Architects of Mass Production—1840–1890

The real industrial revolution, which took place during the next 40 years, was one of the most massive, powerful, and rapid changes in economic history. What took place was not only nearly total change in how most products were made but also a large scale-up in industrial employment, in industrial output, and a total revolution in the sophistication, penetration, and contribution of equipment and process technology.

What made all this possible was what Chandler called "the end of technological constraints,"[28] in particular the limitations of water power. Because of newly dug canals (and, subsequently, railroads) in the United States, coal could now be transported in bulk to sites where raw materials could also be gathered, closer to sources of employees and markets. With coal and new developments in iron and steel metallurgy, machinery progress accelerated, including great improvements in the efficiency, safety, and versatility of steam power. All these factors led to new locations for plants; in addition, when they were accompanied by scientific and engineering progress in heat-using industries, such as chemicals, chinaware, metals production, glass, rubber, paper, sugar, and distilleries, industrial growth was rapid. The American factory system expanded from the notion of interchangeable parts to high-volume, continuous processes of identical products called mass production.

The revolution was fueled not only by the ending of technological constraints but also by increases in population and markets and by vast increases in the speed of production. Its manufacturing leadership was provided from the top down by owner-investor-capitalists who were technologically competent, because the new processes required bold investments in processes that were untried on massive scales. The manufacturing manager had to be closely enough involved in the design and structuring of manufacturing on unprecedented scales to assure himself that it would work and produce sufficiently low costs and high volumes. During the 40 years after 1850 mass production with such leadership found its way into the processing of liquids, such as sugar, beer, and whiskey, and next into the continuous processing of agricultural products, such as wheat and other grains. In metalmaking and metalworking mass production came later, held back by the need for advances in metallurgy, a science more sophisticated than that required for most liquids and agricultural products processing.[29]

Increases in speed of production and volumes of production, attended by lower prices, more uniform quality, and population growth, resulted in much larger productive units. Through economies of scale an increase in plant size often permitted more fully integrated facilities. Single plants began to include more of the processing stages from raw material to finished product.

For these reasons after about 1880 the task of management of manufacturing began to involve plant design and system economics while still delegating work-force management to powerful overseers or foremen. Bigger, integrated plants required coordination skills and techniques to balance and match inputs and outputs at various levels and stages of production. This coordination had to be handled by foremen for there was no one else to do it. (Technicians, clerks, and staff specialists were unknown until the late nineteenth-century factory.) As "undisputed rulers,"[30] foremen had complete charge of their departments, often, in fact, acting as contractors to the owner. They bought materials and supplies, hired workers, and produced the product at a contract price. With such command and control when the plants were one-product and single-unit production facilities, coordination-type management tasks in manufacturing could be handled by the foremen in spite of the increasing size.

There were no personnel officers, and virtually none of what would today be called "staff." Even material handling was usually performed by production workers. The foremen and production workers set up, maintained, and changed over the machinery with occasional specialized help from a "master mechanic" as needed.

The foreman had a virtual empire. They hired, fired, assigned jobs, exerted discipline, established individual wages, trained, promoted, and often procured the necessary materials. "The foremen's authority derived from the fact that technical skills were the key to power."[31]

In the mechanical industries this 40-year period saw rapid technological advances early on but then a leveling out. In textiles the major technical advances in carding, spinning, and weaving were largely accomplished by the 1850s.[32] In other mechanical industries this rate of technological advance also slowed after earlier breakthroughs. In other industries, such as cigarette making, matches, and food processing, new process technologies developed and allowed for more continuous processing.[33] This in turn simplified the tasks of management. Similarly, in chemical process industries, such as soap, dyes, rubber, and basic chemicals, new processes allowed substantial improvement in both product quality and product variety. In these process-type industries there was an especially close collaboration between top management and production-process developers, and great technological innovation thus resulted.

Mass production had largely arrived by 1890; the American factory system was well established. While management of factories remained both relatively technical and simple, manufacturing leadership remained at the top with owner-investors playing a substantial role in the technological and economic concepts underlying the operation.[34] Since competitive advantage was created by investment of capital in mass-production equipment and processes, this was the critical decision. Afterwards, running the plant hard, driving foremen for output and they, in turn, the workers made the formula successful. Since workers were usually immigrants with little education who were accustomed to hard work and considered themselves fortunate to have the job, foremen handled everything down in the plant from worker discipline to coordination. But, as Abernathy and Corcoran stated, ''the standard of excellence that emerged in American industry during the nineteenth century owed much to the fact that there existed a broad class of 'industrial entrepreneurs'—men who made continuous efforts to develop and refine process equipment internally, and to exploit outside sources in unrelated industries.''[35]

Manufacturing Management Moves Down in the Organization— 1890–1920

By the decade 1880–1890, the American factory system was flourishing. New industrial technologies, the railroad, the telegraph, coal-steam power, large-scale immigration, and expanding markets had provided the impetus for this remarkable system. But the next 40 years saw it multiply tenfold in output, employment, and complexity.

The history of manufacturing management until 1890 saw leadership held at the top of the organization by top officers usually involved in key choices of equipment and process technology. Of course, the factory, equipment, and workers all had to be "managed." But the economics and the equipment and facilities were engineered, designed, and constructed by technical people working with top officers heavily involved, while delegating work-force management to the foremen. The foremen had to keep the materials moving on the floor between operations so as to keep expensive machines producing. But this was not very complicated as long as the firm had few plants and few products.

After 1880–1890, however, the growth of corporations, sales volumes, and multiunit, multiproduct enterprise led to the need for systematic controls, and this evolved into "scientific management." The new complexity came about through more of the same growth in markets that forced expansion of facilities and multiple plant sites, and through improved process technologies that increased productive capacities and speeds of output. But a great deal more happened as well. There was growth within companies. There was a profusion of new products, new industries, and new modes of power, construction, transportation, and communication. Business and industry exploded in size, variety, complexity, and diversity.[36]

Companies such as Du Pont, General Electric, Westinghouse, and dozens of others, began to expand product lines, cross over into new industries, market nationally rather than regionally, and manufacture in more than one location.[37] New products proliferated; many, such as electric motors, lights, and the telephone, were based on the use of electricity. In the early 1880s electric lights began to be used in the factories. Ten years later electric motors were applied for the first time to run individual machines. Gone was the necessity for power mechanically transferred through shafts and belts from a central point all over a factory. Moreover, the use of reinforced concrete in construction allowed buildings to be higher and larger with wider spacing between columns. Factories could now be bigger, and with size came additional economics of scale, savings in purchasing and transportation by making more and buying less, and centralizing and integrating entire manufacturing systems under one roof or in one large complex.

With all these growth-inducing factors came "model factories," such as those set up by Westinghouse in 1895, National Cash Register in 1896, Allis in 1902, United Shoe Machinery in 1904, plants of a size that had never been built before. These plants became a much more complex challenge to manage. Gone were the days of only small plants, producing a few products for only regional markets. But the modern multiunit, multiproduct industrial enterprise produced a whole new set of tasks for management.

As a result, the "foreman's empire" and the "contracting system" that delegated decisions to first-line supervision were simply overpowered when product varieties and volumes proliferated, and schedules changed under conditions of rapid growth.[38] The increased uncertainty and instability that derive from multiunit enterprises with departments trans-shipping to each other across the web of supply points inherent in integrated production systems produced complex coordination demands that were unprecedented.

As technologies allowed for faster production and innovations in telephone and telegraph communication reduced the long delays previously involved in placing orders and changing schedules, industrial management had to devise entirely new forms of organization and concepts and techniques with which to handle mounting problems of coordination and complexity.[39] Clerks and expediters, accountants, schedulers, method and procedures planners, and purchasing departments were added and became necessary overhead. And as many employees had to specialize more and the facts of growth and size raised issues of employee equity (especially around compensation), the first personnel officers were established. The foreman's empire began to decline as their range of clear-cut, accountable authority was eroded by these new managerial functionaries.[40]

Of course all this overhead creation did not take place without considerable internal controversy. It was sheer cost, and accountants called it "burden" with some justification. It was justified partly by necessity, for without coordination and control the wrong things were produced at the wrong time in the wrong amount. Thus delays, scrap, rework, and excessive lead time and inventories were the result. Men like Frederick Taylor tried to prove that a dollar spent for staff people would save two dollars in direct labor. Middle managers were needed. Four staff departments began to be common: (1) the personnel department; (2) plant facilities and equipment planning; (3) materials control; and (4) methods and procedures department.[41] Indeed, all of management had to become more systematic to make the system work at all.

In this way, this period saw the rise and development of the first systematic efforts to plan, coordinate, and control manufacturing. The foreman declined in influence since he was increasingly directed by staff departments concerning whom he could employ, how much they were to be paid, what work was to be done each week or day, detailed priorities for production, the methods and processes to be used, the product specifications to be met, the costs that were acceptable, and in-process inventories allowable.[42]

Size, volume, speed, variety, and integration brought about such control and coordination problems. But management techniques and methods and systems for handling these problems were nonexistent before 1890. Into this vacuum entered the pioneers of industrial engineering—Taylor, Gilbreth, Cooke, Barth, and others. They were not only reformers who endeavored to bring system and planning to chaotic factories but they were also creators of totally new management concepts. As Nelson explains, there was no management literature before 1880.[43] These men began to write it in the 1890s.[44]

Taylor and his followers founded the school of "scientific management." It was probably more "systematic" than "scientific." Its principal notion was that any operation involving people and/or materials could be made more efficient by analysis of a breakdown of the operation into its components, measuring those components, and diagnosing where waste occurred and could be eliminated. A great burst of energy and activity followed Taylor and his disciples' early work. By the time of his death in 1915, a new profession had been created—the industrial engineer.

Industrial engineering introduced a totally new viewpoint about manufacturing: Factories must be not only engineered and staffed, but also managed. Until 1890 management of industry took place at only two levels: at top management and on the plant floor. The top management allocated capital to equipment and processes they usually had engineered personally or closely monitored. The plant operation was entirely delegated to first-line supervision who controlled the workers and pushed out the production. Swiftly in the 30-year period from 1890 to 1920 a new management function, demanded by the physical realities of growth, size, and complexity, led to development of the production department and a production manager whose responsibility it was to tie together and coordinate all the elements of manufacturing into a working, functioning, and economically efficient system. That was a whole new idea, and it was in place by 1920. It added the functions of planning, analysis, operation, improvements, coordination, control, and personnel management, bringing the function elaboration and a conceptual base. It shifted nearly all the scope and power of manufacturing management from the president-foremen team to a middle level in the organization.

This was the first major drastic change in the prior smooth evolution of manufacturing management. It shattered a century-old pattern of technological innovation and investment decisions involving management at the top and the heretofore total, comfortable delegation of work-force management and daily production problems to be handled at the bottom. Henceforth, the "production department" was to do both functions.

First, the foreman's power demise: In the 1890–1920 period, the impact of the worker on efficiency and productivity was realized; thus their jobs were engineered, simplified, standardized, and thereby controlled without the prior total dependence on supervision. The foreman's authority and scope was reduced in other aspects as well by the coming of scientific management. No longer was the foreman solely in charge of the department, since planners took over scheduling, expediting, dispatching, materials handling, inspectors for quality control, while method engineers developed the engineered methods and process techniques, specifying the tooling and equipment to be used for each step in the process. The foreman's job has never been the same since 1920 because their scope and authority were drastically reduced over three decades by clerks and staff.

More serious to the foreman and production management as a whole, the job became ambiguous in its authority, responsibility, and accountability. What was she or he really responsible for now? Productivity? No, not without methods and process control and scheduling latitude. Morale and worker commitment and competency? No, not without the authority to define job content. Schedule completion? Only partially, for the dispatching and expediting staff took over the responsibility for setting priorities and told the foreman what to run first. With this ambiguity, the foreman's empire had fallen.

The new allocation of manufacturing leadership began to develop a whole new bureaucracy—the production department. Until 1890 corporate management *was* manufacturing management. Industrial entrepreneurs were technologist-capitalist-investors. They invested in new equipment and processes based on technology and economics they knew intimately. The DuPonts, the founders of Brown and Sharpe, Andrew Carnegie and Alexander Lyman Holley for the steel industry, and George Pullman—all were men who created mass-production process-type industries through combining technological and entrepreneurial innovations. Manufacturing leadership was technological leadership and that created the business concept and competitive advantage. The rest of management could be delegated to the plant floor.

The new bureaucracy of the production department created only to handle complicated coordination problems soon became the custodians of the entire manufacturing investment. Held responsible for the production function of the firm, it was their job to make it work and to answer for the financial investment in fixed assets with adequate returns.

It soon became an economic model. For if the production manager was to be granted funds for new production equipment, he had to assure the owners of a good economic return on investment. He typically was custodian of 70–85% of a firm's assets. The name of the game was "efficiency" for profit, year by year. The process of management, of course, became more bureaucratic with size and complexity. Coordination and control and stabilization of the productive unit became of increasing concern, for changes upset the smooth flows that were key to efficiency, volume, and profitable operations.

This revolutionary period also saw two other major developments. One was the explosion of the automobile industry early in the century. It grew so quickly that by 1908 Ford built a superbly modern auto plant at Highland Park and in 1913 began to produce using a new technique—the moving assembly line. The auto industry spawned dozens of subsidiary industries; its products revolutionized transportation and further created markets and the need for more geographically decentralized multiunit enterprises serving the nation.

A second powerful factor was the massive impact on industrial development furnished by the first world war. The "great war" provided step-function impetus to industrial production, and induced the initiation of many new technologies, processes, products, and markets. By 1920 modern industry as we know it today—with immense productive facilities, multiunit, multiproduct, line and staff management, paperwork planning, scheduling, accounting, and controlling—was a flourishing reality. And it was managed by a new and flourishing bureaucracy of staff specialists with a grown sense of becoming a group of professions, under a rubric called production management. Manufacturing leadership had been moved down in the organization.

Manufacturing Management Refines Its Skills in Controlling and Stabilizing—1920–1960

The 40 years following World War I saw further growth in the American industrial system with attendant geometrical increases in the scope and complexity of production management problems of controlling and stabilizing. As a consequence, it also spurred a spontaneous eruption in the form of the dynamic creation of management tools and techniques that built on the early efforts of "systematic management" and "scientific management" but led into vast new arenas of management, spawning an entirely new era of professional management.

Marred by serious labor problems and held back in the 1930s by economic depression, these four decades nevertheless have become in retrospect a kind of golden age for American industrial managers and their body of knowledge. By 1960 the dominance of U.S. industry in many world markets was supreme.

Employment grew 109% from 1920 to 1960, manufacturing output by a factor of three, productivity at an average rate of 3%, and market share of U.S. manufactured goods consumed reached 97%. The logistics and supply for the biggest war in history were carried out with astonishing success. U.S. companies continued the tradition begun in the 1880s to produce abroad, in particular in Europe, and more than 2,000 U.S. factories were established outside of the United States. American products and manufacturing proficiency resulted in worldwide domination of giant industries: automobiles, trucks, construction equipment, office equipment and business machines, household appliances, industrial machinery and equipment, textile machinery, shoe machinery, communications equipment, pharmaceuticals, personal consumer goods, electrical machinery and equipment, power plants and generators, and more.

In top management councils, manufacturing executives played key roles. They were responsible for contributing to the P&L statement the difference between sales and costs of goods sold, the cash flow vital for R&D, engineering, and marketing and sales. As a source of corporate presidents, the production department was the largest of any functional group.[45]

It was in production as a body of knowledge and a discipline that the energetic power of this era is most clear. The flow of new ideas and techniques and the honing of older ones suggest an extraordinary vitality and motivation of the managers, engineers, and academics who worked on the management tools to support the American industrial machine.

The scope and volume of this outpouring of managerial science and technology is impressive. Beginning where Taylor and his followers had left off in the field of time study and improving work methods, a great deal more was accomplished in refining time-study techniques, including the use of microfilming and the setting of standards for wages and control purposes. This led to the development and extensive use of predetermined standards that could be built up from data banks of standard motions and operations. Standards came to be nearly universal in use, frequently for incentive wage rates but even more typically for what came to be known as *measured day-work*. In the early 1950s, Alan Mogenson pioneered in making widespread the knowledge and practical techniques for "work simplification," a technique that managers and workers could use to analyze and improve their jobs.

The focus of much of the industrial engineering work in this period continued where it had started—on the direct labor worker. Meanwhile, however, with all the staff/burden/overhead expense, concerns arose regarding how to control indirect labor. A new technique "work sampling," based on statistics, became a useful tool for analyzing the efficiency of such workers as materials handlers, tool and die workers, and inspectors.

A flood of other new concepts and techniques came into being as responses to the complexity and coordination problems of size and multiunits that had been increasing since the century began. The first was simply a projection of schedules of parts needed using lead times and bills of materials to create parts and materials requirements and, after deducting inventories, to result in shop orders. This was, in effect, a computerless form of modern MRP (Materials Requirements Planning) with the calculation done by the business machines of the 1920s and 1930s.

The eternal dilemma of how much to produce was apparently "solved" by the Economic Order Quantity (EOQ) formula, which balanced inventory carrying costs with setup costs to minimize total costs. More refinements in Production Planning and Control (PPC) came along fast in the 1940s and 1950s, including the use of probabilistic statistics with improved forecasting methods. The concept of the "learning curve" emerged from aircraft build-ups in World War II and predicted the improvements in cost that tend to accompany the accumulation of production experience.

The war and pressures for unheard-of volumes of production in new products and high technology brought into being many other techniques in production control and project planning. These included PERT (Project Evaluation and Review Technique) and CPM (Critical Path Method), techniques extremely useful in construction, new product development, and other project-like production tasks. The Line of Balance technique was another effective technique developed for controling major production build-ups and taking action to prevent shortages when sufficient time for overcoming the problem was still available.

Success to the production manager meant profit, and that meant "coordination" above all else. Management's most difficult job in the volume explosion of 1920–1960 was principally that of coordinating sales, customers' requirements, and the factors of capital, engineering, equipment, materials, and labor resources required. Its objectives were the utmost in efficiency, or *productivity* as it is now called. It is a difficult function, indeed an impossible one. Manufacturing managers are constantly pressed to produce a good return on capital invested and achieve ever better productivity. But the worst enemy of efficiency and profit is change. And every factor of production is subject to change. Products, sales rates, engineering product design, specifications, materials needed—all change in kind, rate, and quantity. Scientific managements attempt to measure, predict, schedule, rationalize, and control all these elements.

The great burst of management concepts and techniques during the decades from 1920 to 1960 were directed toward closer and better control of all these nasty fluctuating variables. Thus the basic nature of the profession of production management from its start in 1890 has been the attempt to stabilize, systematize, simplify, and control every ingredient.[46]

Many other new techniques for control and reduction of uncertainty came out of a new science that developed between 1947 and 1960: "Operations Research" (OR). OR came into being to help handle the increasingly complex problems of forecasting, coordinating, and controlling large manufacturing operations with an ever-growing product mix, geographical decentralization, shorter product life-cycles, internationally located facilities, and considerable vertical integration. OR is simply the application of mathematics and modeling combined with computer science to production management. It found its usefulness in job shop scheduling, inventory management, logistics, quality control, work sampling, MRP, and linear programming. It used modeling and simulation techniques to predict and minimize queues and inventories, improve quality, shorten lead times, and plan optimal capacity levels under conditions of uncertainty.

The period was also featured by modest step-by-step improvements in equipment and process technologies. While the word "automation" became popular, there was little of it accomplished outside of the process industries. But there were gradual process improvements that were driven in wartime by electronics and servo-mechanisms. As such, they came on the scene after the war and accelerated in the late 1950s with the first stages of "automation," with servo-controlled feedback loops, advanced instrumentation, transfer machines (which transferred parts from one machine to another), allowing continuous operations free from the need of machine operators.

Process industries, such as chemicals, paper, glass, and rubber, benefited early from electronic automatic process controls that started to remove much of the manual "art" and human guesswork from industrial processes. The parts-making and assembly industries were more difficult to mechanize. But linked machines using transfer mechanisms and semi-automatic mechanisms, such as in electroplating, paint spraying, and welding, began to be used in functional departments in these industries, mechanizing where repetition made it possible.

The numerically controlled machine tool (NC) was a major breakthrough in the parts-making/assembly industries. Operated first by punched cards and later by computer control, these machines increased precision and quality output, allowed for short runs via automatic tool changing and minimal fixturing, and reduced lead times by combining in one "machining center" operations previously requiring parts moved to several machine departments. Since their costs were astronomical by comparison to standard machine tools and they eliminated old skills and demanded many new ones, their penetration, despite their enormous advantages, was slow.[47] The NC took 30 years to become the dominant technology in metalworking.

This buoyant 40 years in industry was marred by a long depression and a more or less continuous rumbling of labor unrest. The depression was a positive factor in one sense, namely, that it promoted industrial efficiency. Depression engendered price cutting, furthered the importance of effective industrial engineering, cost reduction, productivity improvements, and aggressive industrial management. Production executives were corporate kings for much of this 40-year period, for ten years when survival depended on becoming a low-cost producer, and for five years of wartime production, and for three years of unfilled demand that followed the war. Manufacturing leaders were in the "cat-bird seat" in corporate management.

But the labor situation was another story. In this otherwise golden age of industrial management, while new administrative concepts, tools, and techniques were mushrooming yearly, there boiled to the surface strident discontent. There was tragic physical violence and a series of battles over the unionization of millions of noncraft workers. The rising power of organized labor featured these four decades as the percentage of unionized workers rose from 6.8% in 1930 to 23.6% in 1960.[48] In nearly every industry strikes at contract time were common and the union strategy of isolating a company as a target, shutting them down with a strike, winning a favorable settlement, and using it as a pattern for the rest of the industry drove up wages far faster than productivity.

But even plush, popular wage and benefit settlements seldom seemed to lead to contented and committed workers. The problem was impossible to ignore. The realization that workers were usually not committed to their employer and the company's growth and prosperity, that morale was frequently poor, that adversarial relationships benefited neither party, that employees pegged production and withheld ideas and full-out enthusiasm—all became more clear.

A positive feature of this otherwise discordant period of industrial history was continuous efforts on many fronts to improve labor relations. For example, in this period grievance procedures were much improved, along with better pensions and health insurance, safety and accident prevention procedures, workers' compensation, and the emergence of a more professional industrial relations and personnel department.

Academics began to try to understand human relations better. Elton Mayo and Fritz Roethlisberger researched these issues. The famous Hawthorne experiments demonstrated that working conditions may be important but social expectations and personal feelings are even more so. Worker counseling, foreman training, human relations training for managers, sensitivity training, worker participation plans, profit-sharing, gainsharing plans (such as the Scanlon Plan) were given time, money, and hope. Experiments of many types were tried in the late 1950s, often featuring such heresy as nonsupervised work groups and off-plant sessions with third parties to surface feelings and promote better understanding. Whether this wave of experiments in new human resource management concepts worked is less the question than the fact that for the first time long-smoldering serious labor prolems were seen in terms other than adversarial or paternal. Corporate managers and academics had finally begun to invest in experimentation in radically new solutions.

In total, 1920–1960 was a period of progress primarily focused on improving controls and coordination mechanisms but with modest technological accomplishments as well. Manufacturing managers were riding high but at least in some quarters they also finally began to face their heritage of employee disaffection and to support isolated but determinedly optimistic efforts to improve industrial society. At the end of President Eisenhower's second term, American industry had grown to a position of overtowering financial, technological, and managerial strength. It looked unbeatable.

Shaking the Foundations of Industrial Wisdom—1960–1980

During the next 20 years the American self-concept of industrial leadership was severely shaken, first by a growing inability to compete in the steel and auto industries and the resulting flood of imports, then by similar catastrophes in dozens of other industries led by the electrical machinery, machine tools, textile equipment, and consumer electronics industries.

By 1980 there were many indications that nationwide confidence in manufacturing leadership had largely collapsed. The business periodicals ran countless articles on our "industrial malaise," "the loss of the work ethic," and the need for "reindustrialization."[49] Industrial analysts and managers returned from Japan to report that we were outthought and outclassed in every area of production management.[50] The turnabout in results was only outleveraged by the total cave-in pride of U.S. industrial might, matched in some instances with scathing criticism of the people who had managed "our way to industrial decline."[51,52]

From Japan, Germany, Switzerland, Korea, Singapore, and Taiwan came shiploads of imports of goods, many of which formerly would have been labelled "made in U.S.A." Worse, the Japanese and many other foreign managements were seen as beating us not just with cheaper labor— that would have been easy to understand—but also with better worker effort and cooperation. They had better management systems for scheduling and production control, made better use of both old and new process technologies, had infinitely better quality systems, procedures, and attitudes, better internal management communications and group problem-solving, better financial controls, a massive outpouring of suggestions and ideas from employees, and more committed and better trained workers.[53] They had made imaginative use of the computer, excellent application of operations research techniques, disciplined preventive maintenance systems, outstanding employee benefits and job security, unbelievably low work-in-process inventories, consistent support and cooperation from vendors, and so on.

They had beaten us, it seemed, at every single one of our vaunted industrial management techniques. Either they took what we had and did it better, as in statistical quality control and the use of engineered standards, or they took what we had and threw it out, as in our traditional heavy use of work-in-process inventories for buffering variable rates of production between operations (versus Japanese "just in-time," KanBan systems).[54] In either case, it was devastating to any lingering beliefs that American manufacturing management know-how was still an outstanding competitive weapon on the world scene.

Quite the contrary, the results suggested that 200 years of the evolution of manufacturing management knowledge and wisdom had led us to something that only seemed to work quite well. For when competitive pressures finally came along, it was revealed to be not very good at all. How could we have so deluded ourselves? It seemed so good. It made our workers the world's most productive people. It helped to produce the world's best living standards and the richest consumer economy. Yet in 20 years we came to realize that, by comparison, maybe it was only "Grade B," not the most productive, and in many industries competitively deficient.

Was something wrong with manufacturing leadership's thinking that not only made our manufacturing systems Grade B, but also blinded them to that fact? Certainly the prior lack of international competition made for complacency. Being number one carries its penalty along with its rewards. In fairness to the production managers of 1900–1960, they had been pressured for volume and growth in all but 10 of those years and had been extremely successful. Furthermore, history shows that since 1900 they have been placed in a secondary role in the corporate scheme, with contradictory and nearly insurmountable, paradoxical objectives, creating dilemmas that catapulted them from "catbird seat" to a certain oblivion.

IMPACTS FROM HISTORY

This history suggests that leadership of American manufacturing which was provided at the top of the corporation for nearly a century, was steadily delegated to a lower level beginning around the late 1890s. There are two periods, therefore, in which the management responsibilities for manufacturing were handled distinctly differently.

Prior to the turn of the century the technically competent industrial-entrepreneur developed the economic and technological concepts, procured the equipment and facilities, supervised its installation and startup, and delegated the work-force management to overseers or foremen. There was no production staff. After 1900 the requirements of size and product, process, and physical complexities brought about the creation of a production department and production management with specialized staff groups and responsibilities.

The characteristics of modern production management and its managers were much more influenced by twentieth century industrial history than by what went on before, except for one major exception—the labor problem. That problem, as stated earlier, has always been delegated to establish the greatest distance between management leadership and the source of annoying disturbances—the worker. After 1900 the delegation was even more complete, because the foreman's power had been decimated in every respect including authority over the worker which was now ambiguously shared with personnel and labor relations departments. Thus in one respect it was delegated to no single accountable manager, but into a vacuum.

The delegation of manufacturing leadership in the twentieth century to the new production department resulted in a type of bureaucratization of the function and its relationship with top management. For example:

- Growing specialization and professionalization of staff experts.
- The extraordinary and energetic innovation of imaginative and creative control and coordination techniques.
- An implicit contract between top management and production managers that read something like the following:

Top Management Demands	Production Management Responses
We entrust dollars of fixed assets to you.	We accept that custody.
You must earn a good return on that investment for the investors of that capital.	We accept that reality.
You will be measured on that return.	We must keep volume high and costs low.
To receive more assets you must project a good financial return.	We must be careful not to choose equipment that does not work out well.
You must deliver the right product at the right time, and these will change.	Of course we must ensure delivery, but product and schedule changes always hurt.
Your job is to coordinate the whole works, that is why we pay you well.	Our only hope is to coordinate, stabilize, placate workers, satisfy customers.
Productivity is what counts in the end. Mass production and automation has been the best way since the industrial revolution.	The fewer workers and coordination problems the better. That means mechanization—wherever we can justify it.

This contract is implicit in the nature of the production function, once it is necessarily delegated to the department level. It develops because of the following:

- Delegation requires performance evaluation.
- Production requires substantial assets.
- Investors must have adequate returns.
- For a given production system, in place, the return is enhanced by volume production, continuous steady output, mechanization, stability of products, technology, and volume reliability of the work force.
- But all these factors change and keep changing.
- Cost performance is important, but customers want quality and on-time reliable delivery, marketers want new products, engineers want design improvements, and treasurers want low investment in facilities and inventories.

These demands conflict. Their implicit trade-offs became the basis for a serious set of ongoing dilemmas for manufacturing managers. Were these the same dilemmas before 1900 when top management ran manufacturing? The problems were there, although to a lesser extent because businesses were smaller, more single-unit, single-product entities. But the problems did not create dilemmas because trade-offs are only a dilemma to a manager with a superior to whom she or he must answer for conflicting demands. Thus the act of delegation, which created the production department, also made for the dilemmas of trade offs and a virtually no-win set of responsibilities.

In this way history has planted the deep roots of present-day management thinking. Manufacturing managers are custodians of assets, and in this secondary role they must focus on productivity, control, coordination, and stabilization; they must also mechanize to the utmost to ensure simplicity and cost reduction. This scenario produces a Grade B industrial establishment.

It is frequently Grade B and competitively deficient because production managers on the defensive are forced to become careful and protective. They know only too well that production systems are complex and fragile and, like a freeway at rush hour when even one thing goes wrong, disasters ensue one after another. They become experts at control, stabilization, and industrial engineering techniques, in addition to making ample use of buffer inventories and concentrating on meeting weekly schedules. They are so vulnerable to criticism that they must focus on the short term, be systematic, detailed, and pedestrian in their thinking, and exert unceasing control over the work force.

One other element, which is just as serious in the scenario of production management, emerged after 1900 when top management delegated manufacturing dealership to a newly formed management department: in essence, technological innovation of processes was lost in nonaccountable bureaucracy.

Prior to 1900 top management—which built the first factories before 1850 and the mass production systems by 1890, and then moved into the modern complex industrial corporation—more often than not were technologically competent and often brilliantly so. As entrepreneurs building enterprises, those people seized on process innovation possibilities, and they developed or selected the latest in equipment and process technology. After 1900, however, who was to do it?

Not corporate heads, for after the turn of the century, top management typically focused more toward new complexities of finance and corporate structure. It was sales in the 1930s, marketing in the 1950s, financial maneuvers in the 1960s, and governmental and legal complexities in the 1970s. Technological innovation and the architecture of manufacturing systems were left to the new bureaucracy of production management.

There it has stayed and decayed—or at least has been frequently managed with an absence of the verve and daring of top managers in the nineteenth century. This fact, of course, should not be surprising. Docility in this function is a natural response to the realities of vulnerability to criticisms on conflicting criteria that are built into the job.

Technological innovation and system architectural change introduce the maximum of risk and the minimum of stability. Productivity enhancement may be the long-range objective, but it is apt to be the short-range victim. New equipment and major changes in system structure—such as new plants, locations, and improved infrastructures—all take years to work out and are personally risky ventures for any manager caught in the corporate bureaucracy. Thus the habitual response to technological innovation is apt to be—be careful. Get your boss and boss's boss involved. Don't try to be a hero. Let someone else go first.

Exhibit 20.1 attempts to portray the results of the massive organizational change in American industry at the turn of the century. Its significance is as follows:

1. Work-force management has never had top priority and since 1900 has been considered mostly a labor relations staff function.
2. The production manager's original role as a custodian held responsible for financial performance of hard-to-manage assets and meeting contradictory performance criteria grew in the twentieth century to be that of mainly coordinating and controling.
3. Equipment and process technology and system architecture were handled actively and aggressively before 1900 and not thereafter.

4. After 1900 the development and innovation of equipment and process technologies and the architecture of production systems were no longer principal concerns of top management, and typically they were not pursued aggressively by the production department. Hence, major system innovations were left dependent on the initiatives of vendors and the R&D departments.[55]

Exhibit 20.2 summarizes several impacts of these facts and constraints as they influenced the development of the role of the manufacturing manager through the years.

Under pressure as custodians of capital assets and needing to demonstrate productivity in their use, bedeviled by their often seemingly uncooperative and obstinate labor forces, with efficiency requiring stable long runs and resource stability, but with every resource essentially unstable and changing—production managers became masters of coordination and control. The game was one of minimizing changes and uncertainty, while maximizing control to achieve economic success. Nearly every manufacturing management concept or technique has had those objectives.[56,57]

In this way history and the realities of what production is all about have produced eight or ten generations of manufacturing leaders who see their roles as keeping a complex mix of people, machines, and materials working at full productivity. It is a coordinating, operating viewpoint, which produces extraordinarily competent skills in getting things done, adjusting, reacting, and rolling with the punches. Manufacturing managers are the infantry who fight in the trenches with the nasty facts and unpleasant realities of engineering and schedule changes. They are constantly vulnerable to criticism for failure to deliver, or poor quality or high costs, or excessive inventories, or taking too long to produce a new product. Their every instinct—since they must react and respond to change—is toward stabilization and protection of their system from the ravages of change. Operate it, but don't change it.

Internally, they use authority to control and direct whatever they can. Externally, they respect authority, keep their place, and are somewhat in awe of an outside world they cannot fully control, direct, or even communicate with. They are "lions" in the factory, but many are "pussycats" when they go up to the executive offices where they are regularly overpowered with the undeniable but unfamiliar logic of markets, customers, financial models, and grand issues of corporate strategy.

The impact of these patterns on the characteristics of manufacturing leadership and its thinking is shown in Exhibit 20.3. Manufacturing managers learned to adapt, survive, and succeed by accepting the financial performance requisites, mechanizing to the utmost, keeping labor at arm's

Exhibit 20.1 The Organizational Change at the End of the Century

	Manufacturing Responsibilities							
	Before 1900				After 1900			
Organizational Level	Labor	EPT*	System Structure	Coordination Control	Labor	EPT	System Structure	Coordination and Control
Top Management	U	F	F	U	U	U	U	U
Production Department			[Did not exist]		C	C	C	F
Plant Level— FLS**	F	U	U	F	C	U	U	C

Key   F = fully and actively pursued
        C = cautiously pursued or abdicated
        U = generally uninvolved
*Equipment and process technology.
**First-level supervision.

Exhibit 20.2   The Historical Process by Which Manufacturing Managers' Thinking Developed

Our Mission from Top Management Is	Therefore We Need	But We Operate in Much Uncertainty	So We Learned That Certain Practices Work Best	And We Developed Ten Good Success Rules
Meet customer needs	Low costs	Equipment does not always work	Maximum scale of pdn	1. Meet customer schedules.
Produce a good return on investment	Low investment	Off-quality pdn	Continuous process	2. Minimize costs.
	High efficiency	Costs change	Tool for volume	3. Maximize productivity.
		Schedules change	Freeze designs	4. Mechanize processes for volume, repetitive, mass continuous production, so as to have the fewest possible workers and least problems of coordination.
		Parts get lost or rejected	Standardize	
		Vendors miss deliveries	Good forecasts	
		Designs change	Measure	
		Specifications change	Stabilize schedules	
		Jobs change	Schedule and control every element	5. Control and direct the work force via industrial engineering,
		Too few/many workers	Control systems	
			Mature, proven technologies	

303

Exhibit 20.2 *(continued)*

Our Mission from Top Management Is	Therefore We Need	But We Operate in Much Uncertainty	So We Learned That Certain Practices Work Best	And We Developed Ten Good Success Rules
		Workers unhappy, not competent, not committed	Short job cycles Engineer processes Simplify jobs Delegate worker responsibility to FLS and Personnel Close inspection of pdn Ample buffer inventories	supervision, and the personnel department. 6. Focus on the short term, be systematic, detailed, precise, and accurate. 7. Follow the accounting and financial rules handed down by management. 8. Seek maximal simplicity, stability, and close managerial controls. 9. Minimize risks by minimizing changes. 10. Manage pressures for change from engineers, salespeople, and marketeers.

Exhibit 20.3 Typical Characteristics of Manufacturing Leadership

Skills	Instincts	Beliefs/Wisdom	Cognitive Style
Coordination	Self-protection	Hedge with inventories	Systematic
Operations control	Avoid change	Workers need much supervision	Detailed (rather than conceptual and intuitive)
Mass production processes	•products	Productivity via	Short-term orientation
Continuous processes	•processes	•volume equipment	Preoccupation with issues within our purview
High-volume tooling	•schedules	•repetition	*Executive Style:*
Orderly, detailed thinking	Control the environment	•large runs	•direct
Simplify	Keep workers at a distance	Distrust of impracticality of managers not in pdn	•outspoken
Standardize	Control/direct	Limit plant capacity	•short-term urgency
Rationalize	•process	Keep job content simple	•cautious
Troubleshooting in production	•logistics	Authority of management	•safe
	•workers	The big decisions are out of my control	•conservative
	Theory X/mechanistic	Our job is to respond	•protective
	Avoid ambiguity in organization and assignments	Economies of scale	•paternal
	Make the best of what you are given	Spread overheads	•use of authority
		Machines control better than people	•respectful of authority
		Accountability	

305

length, fighting for stability and steady schedules, and developing complex and ingenious mechanisms for coordination and control.

The end result of this historical process is a paradigm of thinking that conceptualizes the factory as a "productivity machine," the goal as a profit, labor as a troublesome cost, change as an expensive intrusion, and the mass production technology of volume production using mechanized equipment as the smoothest road to productivity. This is the "mind-set" that characterized American manufacturing management thinking at the peak of its success in 1960 and, as we shall see, is still affecting managers of production today.

PART II—MANUFACTURING LEADERSHIP IN THE 1980s

In the 1960s and 1970s manufacturing in the United States lost market share in many industries. When competition became severe and foreign competitors built products at less cost and higher quality, many manufacturing leaders did not seem to recognize that the problem was not caused only by low-cost foreign labor. Effective corrective action was not taken. Finally, not much before 1979–1980, the problem was recognized sufficiently to arouse an energetic and determined response. That recognition only came about after widespread analysis of Japanese manufacturing techniques that demonstrated some comparative inadequacies of American manufacturing management.[58,59,60,61,62]

The nature of the response is important. For the most part it took a form that focused on "productivity"—questioning why our productivity growth had declined and what could be done to get us back on the track again. Companies set up productivity committees, productivity czars and corporatewide productivity coordinators, and even productivity departments, laboratories, and centers. Three national productivity institutions were formed and dozens of articles about productivity and its various ingredients began to appear in business and economic journals.[63]

Within firms it was back to basics. Industrial engineering departments were restaffed and standards reset, jobs and layouts studied and improved, materials handling methods streamlined, and all forms of waste and inefficiency scrutinized. It was back to basics, too, in quality with the old tools of statistical quality control, process and control charts, and quality assurance dusted off and newly reinvigorated with the ceremonial blessings of top management. Companies were advised that "high investment is the result rather than the cause of productivity growth."[64] In other words, don't try to invest your way to productivity. Get back to basics first.

These responses were as vigorous and energetic as they were desperate. And they were nationwide and industrywide in their scope. It is too early to judge whether they have been effective. Some competitive erosion may have been stopped.[65] And, as always, a resurgence in the industrial sector automatically makes the government productivity data look better.[66,67] Nevertheless, it appears now that little has been accomplished to restore lost competitive edge.

It is clear that what U.S. industry has done is to revert to its customary and long-standing know-how in the crisis. Back to the old game plan! And the old game plan seems to be to try to maximize productivity through the use of industrial engineering concepts and techniques of coordination and control, just as it worked so well in the 40-year golden age that ran out in 1960.

The premise is that rationalization, standardization, high volume, stability, large-scale production, and strict coordination and controls will restore healthy industrial productivity and growth, which will in turn recreate the former competitive edge and bring about a genuine industrial renaissance.[68] This premise is very debatable.[69] It sounds like "business as usual." And: "We're sorry we got sloppy. We only got sloppy because management would not pay us the attention we should have had and used to have."

Clearly, we need better productivity. The question is how to obtain it and whether "productivity" is all we need.[70,71] A frontal attack on waste and inefficiency—standard productivity doctrine—is fine if it hasn't been done recently. But its potential results are modest in the face of 35¢ Korean labor, for example. Thus it seems doubtful that productivity medicine and basics and good disciplined control of details is a sufficient prescription.

Such a prescription does not deal with the fact that our capital equipment is typically old, that we have failed to invest boldly, experiment, or take advantage of the new manufacturing technology. Nor does it explain the fact that diffusion of that new technology is proceeding very slowly.[72] The productivity solution does not deal with the powerful changes in markets and technology as evidenced by shorter product life-cycles, more customer specials, shorter runs, an accelerated pace of technological innovations in products and processes, and the rapid growth in the cost of capital equipment. Nor does it, per se, deal with ongoing problems in the work force.

The curious, but not so surprising fact is that in crisis manufacturing management has reverted to its old paradigm. When it came into being production management's first role was that of exercising control and coordination essential for productivity. The choice of roles remains unchanged. It is an adaptive function. The job is to react to changes in technology, customer demand, product specifications, processes made available by engineers, costs, and materials. The objective was productivity—an economic measure derived from the concept that maximum output per person produces maximum return per machine, and a maximum return to owners pays back invested capital faster. The thinking is based on a financial model that sees manufacturing mangers as custodians of capital assets, and whose purpose it is to return capital to owners.

Thus in retrospect the failures of the years since 1960 are not difficult to understand. What hit was the competition from cheap labor combined with rapid technological change and previously unseen quality levels.[73,74] What was necessary to survive these new rules was rapid change in products, processes, cost mix, and the use of new technologies,[75] restructuring manufacturing to become a competitive weapon, and proactive strategic thinking with great imagination and innovation. But the production managers as careful, conservative coordinators, controllers, and commanders were unable to play by the new rules.

We needed aggressive leadership to take charge of massive overhaul and change. Instead, their instincts took them pell-mell back to productivity, efficiency, and a short-term adaptive, operations focus. Their instincts were 180 degrees out of phase with the new rules.[76] Their thinking and executive styles seemed unable to cope with the rapid overhauls necessary—particularly an inability to provide the ideas and convincing leadership top management needed to make large new investments in newly structured manufacturing systems, under duress and uncertainty.[77] Even their accounting tools no longer gave them control information so badly needed.[78,79] Rip van Winkle had awakened at last, only to find himself in a world in which what he had learned before he went to sleep was no longer of much use. It was a world in which his traditional responses could not cope.

PART III—THE NEXT GENERATION OF MANUFACTURING MANAGERS

The question for today is whether the harsh environment of the last 20-plus years is producing a new generation of manufacturing managers who will cope better. Is a "new breed" evolving under the duress of the new industrial competition, and now surviving by being the fittest and is thereby moving up into leadership? That new breed, it might be hypothesized, would be moving up because they are successful at bringing about change, introducing new products and technology, managing the work force with less use of authority, more participation, team building, and involvement. If this is true, we could expect to look forward soon to a major role change in manufacturing leadership, the first real shift since 1900.

A counter-theory would be that, no, the "comers" are apt to be molded in the images of their bosses, the present generation in power, and, hence, will not be very different, and have been promoted because they are similar to their superiors, and no new leadership is on the way. History moves but the movement is glacial.

To begin to learn what is actually going on, six large manufacturing companies in the electronics, metalworking, electrical equipment, auto and defense industries were invited to participate in a research project in which the companies identified promising future manufacturing managers, who were then interviewed by a researcher from the Harvard Business School. Sixty interviews were conducted, including 46 "fast-track" managers ("comers") and 14 executives presently in high-level manufacturing positions ("incumbents").[80]

Research Results

The "comers" were found to be as follows:

- More college educated.
- Broader in manufacturing skills and focus.
- More participative and interested in team building and collaboration.
- More zealous, driving and independent, and confident.
- More intuitive and conceptual.
- Moving faster than the incumbents had moved careerwise.
- Having had more staff experience than the incumbents.
- More highly educated in terms of formal education.
- More independent, less loyal.
- Much more critical of their superiors.
- Better balanced vis-à-vis workaholic tendencies.
- More achievement oriented.
- More perfectionistic than the nonperfectionistic incumbents.
- More comfortable at tolerating ambiguity.
- Critical of the company's lack of communication.
- More supportive of the company's direction.
- Equally (and positively) supportive of the company's "management style."
- Fewer engineering educated, with more MBAs and other nonengineering degrees.

Somewhat surprisingly, the comers were rather sure that in-depth technical knowledge was not necessary or important for them as managers.

It was disappointing that both comers and incumbents focused on the short term, and they both focused in general on departmental rather than on companywide or strategic issues.

Exhibit 20.4 shows the comers to be about 15 years younger than the incumbents. The comers had worked about 15 years, and the incumbents 28. But already the comers had worked for more companies on average than the incumbents. Each had held seven or eight jobs on the average, and the comers had 20% of their jobs outside of manufacturing, while the incumbents had only 10%. The comers had worked six years per company, and the incumbents sixteen. For the incumbents all the outside jobs had been in engineering, while some comers had worked in engineering, finance and accounting, marketing, and personnel.

Exhibit 20.5 shows that the bulk of time of both groups is spent on scheduling, delivery, and coordination. About 50% of the comers' time

Exhibit 20.4 Career Questionnaire Data*

	Comers (n = 46)	Incumbents (n = 14)
Age	37.8	53.3
Number of jobs	7.7	8.3
Different companies worked for	2.5	2.1
Years per company	6.2	16.0
Jobs held per company	3.1	4.0
Years per job	2.0	3.3
Line jobs in manufacturing	2.7	4.6
Staff jobs in manufacturing	3.6	3.0
Jobs outside manufacturing	1.4	0.8
Breakdown of Jobs Outside:		
Engineering	0.7	0.8
Marketing/sales	0.3	0
Finance/accounting	0.4	0
Years in manufacturing in line positions	5.7	15.8
Years outside manufacturing	3.2	1.1
Breakdown of Years Outside:		
Engineering	2.3	1.1
Marketing/sales	0.4	0
Finance/accounting	0.5	0

*Data expressed in averages.

Exhibit 20.5   Allocation of Time: Percentage Spent on Various Kinds of Decisions

	Control and Coordination	Maintenance and Impacts of Engineering Changes	Work Force	Other
Comers	47	30	16	7
Incumbents	38	36	20	6

is devoted to those traditional, largely short-term focused activities, and 39% of the incumbents'. The data suggest that, as the executive advances, he or she spends a little more time on work-force issues and equipment and process technology. In terms of time the incumbents were usually satisfied with their allocations; in addition, the comers showed a strong desire to spend more time on new products and technologies, whereas the incumbents indicated that they were satisfied to be spending their time as they were presently doing. Exhibit 20.6 compares the comers and incumbents on various factors. Note the consistency of the differences.

From these findings some hopeful indications emerge. The comers are broader, more outspoken, more zealous, more participative, like to be team builders, had more education but less engineering, and are more strategically oriented.[81] They were more critical of their superiors, better adjusted and at ease with the interviewer, and indicated more comfort with dealing with upper echelons of management. It begins to look as though the difficult experiences of U.S. industry in the last 25 years may be producing a "new breed."[82]

Before yielding to the temptation of predicting a turnaround led by a magnificent "new breed," we must introduce a number of warnings:

1. The sample size for this research is small, especially for the incumbents of whom there were only 14. While the inferences are very interesting and suggestive, a sample of this size does not *prove* very much.
2. There could be a bias from the interviewer—in essence, that she knew in advance whether the company had classified the subject as incumbent or comer and, therefore, may have been subtly or overtly influenced by this knowledge in rating the subject on the judgmental factors. Such a bias could probably have been discerned by the researcher in reading the interview summaries and checking the factor ratings, and no bias appeared to exist. Nevertheless, it remains a possibility.

Exhibit 20.6   Characteristics and Attributes of Comers and Incumbents

	Low (Few, Slow)	Medium	High (Many, First)

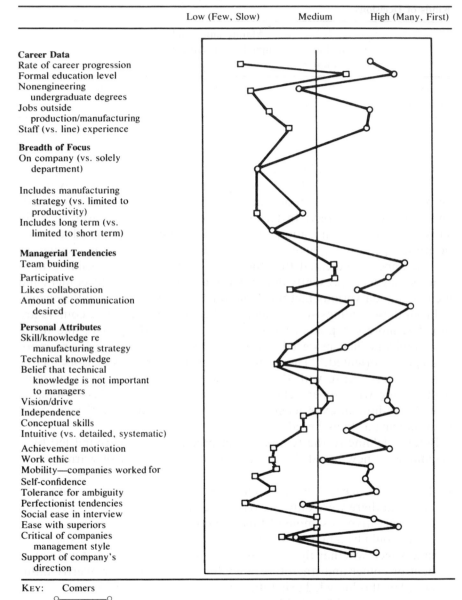

Career Data
Rate of career progression
Formal education level
Nonengineering
   undergraduate degrees
Jobs outside
   production/manufacturing
Staff (vs. line) experience

Breadth of Focus
On company (vs. solely
   department)

Includes manufacturing
   strategy (vs. limited to
   productivity)
Includes long term (vs.
   limited to short term)

Managerial Tendencies
Team buiding

Participative

Likes collaboration
Amount of communication
   desired

Personal Attributes
Skill/knowledge re
   manufacturing strategy
Technical knowledge
Belief that technical
   knowledge is not important
   to managers
Vision/drive
Independence
Conceptual skills
Intuitive (vs. detailed, systematic)

Achievement motivation
Work ethic
Mobility—companies worked for
Self-confidence
Tolerance for ambiguity
Perfectionist tendencies
Social ease in interview
Ease with superiors
Critical of companies
   management style
Support of company's
   direction

KEY: Comers
       o————————o
       Incumbents
       □————————□

312

3. The data may be influenced by the choice of companies and industries, the executives selecting the comers, and so forth.
4. Due to age differences between "comers" and "incumbents" and job-level differences, responsibility differences, and experience differences, it could perhaps be expected that the scores from comers and incumbents would naturally be different, and the contrasts found, therefore, would be less significant.
5. Similarly, it may be that time and the natural pressures of responsibility plus maturation and the inevitable leveling off of most executive careers may change the "comers" so that in 10 years they could look just like the "incumbents"!

One final set of impressions of the comers by the interviewer may be significant. She felt that they are chafing at the bureaucratic jungle in which they feel themselves to be caught.[83] They are highly critical of their superiors, concerned about how the whole corporation is being run, and nearly arrogant at times in their opinions of what is needed. They show consistent zeal and insistence for change, and they want their companies to be more open and communicative with all employees. Although most comers indicated that technical knowledge was not essential in their managerial roles, they believe that the adaptation and use of new technologies is essential for the future success of their manufacturing operations.

More educated and with more breadth in their education, the comers feel more mobile, more confident, and less willing to just wait for the next promotion. They feel less company loyalty, they move between jobs more often than the incumbents, and they move more often between companies. Despite their success and position as comers in their companies, they are restless and show impatience and even a tinge of anger at the "no-win" dilemmas many manufacturing managers feel are part of their jobs. They are being evaluated as are their superiors by the same melange of performance criteria in use for 80 years. They are still coordinators and their bottom line is still more often than not efficiency and productivity.

The comers seem to be a fast-track group, and they want to move even faster. But is it realistic to expect that they will grow to do what their elders, the incumbents, and several generations before them have not been able to do while still being measured and evaluated by the same yardsticks as before? Can they and will they be the ones to supply the manufacturing leadership to begin to restore the American competitive edge? Surely it will not come about readily unless management development practices and programs focus on the problem.

PART IV—CONCLUSION

Persistent Signals from Industrial History

History of the manufacturing institution features several dominant themes. The first concerns the relentless pursuit and actual accomplishment of ever-rising productivity to meet economic goals. The second is that of equally relentless protests and dissatisfactions of manufacturing workers. The third is that of the role and locus of manufacturing leadership: before 1900 as top-level technological entrepreneur, and after that as departmental coordinator, adaptor, and stabilizer. When the nineteenth century ended, the production department began, not as an initiator or shaper of production systems, but as custodians of assets. In contrast to their forefathers, they have been "housekeepers," often bureaucratic, and seldom "architects."

At the end of the 1960s American industrial leadership was considered the world's best. By 1980 we had to question this. Now we can see that except for exceptional companies[84] and certain industries, in many important respects manufacturing has not been really "led" for many decades.

Despite its success in 1940–1960, the burst of wartime and postwar production, there were a number of persistent signals of weakness. The system had seldom worked very well for the work force, at least in their opinions. Their generally negative feelings, lukewarm loyalty, and low commitment levels surfaced repeatedly for two centuries.[85] After 1900 the newly developed management concepts, techniques, and practices focused on operating the system rather than on structuring it. The production department was required to be short-term oriented and efficiency focused by demands for investment returns rather than being pluralistic in its objectives so as to be able to match its success criteria to meet strategic needs.

The techniques and concepts of industrial management show this single-minded quest for system, rationalization, simplicity, certainty, efficiency, and stability amid a constantly changing environment.[86] When the foremen's empires were not coping with scheduling, inventories, costs, and product changes, Taylor and his followers established the fundamental concepts and techniques of a body of knowledge for manufacturing management. Its precepts were straightforward and its thinking linear: measure, analyze, rationalize, command, and control. In the period from 1920–1960 these themes were carried out in depth and in infinite detail—from micromotion to predetermined standards to EOQ, MRP, and the giant, dream showplace plants of Appliance Park, Sparrows Point, and Lordstown.

Maximal production per-labor-hour and per-machine-hour was the logical, straightforward approach to the industrial engineer. Streamline, standardize, simplify. Go for long runs, few changeovers, stability in every possible dimension. Select processes from the mass production commodity, process-type technologies. Design jobs so as to be minimal in job content, maximize repetition, minimize learning, engineer every micromotion for minimal waste, tell the foremen and their workers how to perform their jobs, set standards to measure and control each person's daily output, pay good wages to attract the better workers, and keep them happy with money. We have dreamed an impossible dream of stable markets, giant plants, economies of scale, docile work forces, and mature technologies.

Paradoxically, these productivity premises led to failure in the 1960s and 1970s. Before that they led to self-satisfaction as long as markets grew, immigrants immigrated, and the United States had the only game in town.

But these inherent weaknesses were not so obvious during the twentieth century and not even in 1960. For the industrial manager, the servant of investors-owners, it was the only way to succeed. Success was measured by economics—profit and loss statements—and success was achieved by high volume, ever higher productivity, and consistent quality of product. And to do it with ever restless workers, salespeople who would not or could not forecast, new processes that never worked well at first—they turned instinctively to the same rules. The name of the game was "productivity," and it was best achieved by three rules:

1. Mass production processes to the maximum extent.
2. Rationalize, standardize, coordinate, simplify, and stabilize.
3. Direct and control subordinates and employees.

The paradigm was remarkably simple. It was essentially a financially based model of the basis of good industrial management. It was single-minded and nearly obsessive in its theme that the best factory was the most productive factory.

Even today, in 1985, it is natural to say, "Well, what's so wrong with that? Surely we can't have successful factories if they are less than optimally productive, can we?"

But there are new rules now, and "productivity" can no longer be the name of the game. In fact, it never should have been. It only worked in times of expanding markets and limited competition. It failed under international competitive pressures because treating the factory as a financial model, labor as a cost, change to be avoided, the proper leadership role as one of coordinating, and mass production/high volume/continuous processes as the ideal is inappropriate and insufficient in the 1980s. To succeed today the factory must now be not just an investment; it must also be a competitive resource. And labor can now be seen as a source of energy and imagination, as well as change to be taken advantage of, leadership as proactive and technologically competent, and processes flexible for a stream of product and volume changes. Why did the rules for success change?

It happened simply because the requirements for success have drastically altered the manufacturing manager's world and thereby the rules that determine who wins the race.[87] Some of the key rules that changed are as follows:

- There is more competition, internationally and domestically.
- Product life-cycles are shorter.
- Product volumes are apt to be smaller.
- Product variety is apt to be greater.
- New product development cycles are shortening.
- New product technologies are proliferating.
- New process technologies, especially microprocessor-based, are accelerating.
- Worker culture, demographics, and the sociology of work are vastly different than in 1960.[88]
- Government exerts more control and influence.
- Product quality, service, delivery, and reliability are generally increasing in importance.
- The mix of costs is shifting, with overheads, materials, and energy costs rising and direct labor declining.[89]

In the old rules, the factory model was essentially financial. The new rules demand a concept for the factory that is entirely different. First, it must now be an institution that can tolerate and handle pluralistic values and measures for its success. There are at least five investors now, many values to be created besides profits, and at least seven measures of success.[90]

The new rules require new players, or at least, players with different skills, attitudes, and beliefs. Manufacturing leadership, it appears, will be more successful if it can let go of its heritage of a unidimensional framework of productivity and standardization and see the factory as an instrument for competitive success, handling a continuous shifting of manufacturing tasks as they are presented by the changes in technology, the competitive situation, and the firm's competitive strategy. More often

A New Concept of the Factory as a Competitive Resource

Stakeholders		Institution		Values		Competitive Success Measures
Owners	INVEST	In the	WHICH	More quickly	WHICH	Cost/efficiency
Managers		Factory	MAY	More reliably	CREATE	Delivery
Employees			PRODUCE	Fine products	COMPETI-	cycles
Community				Profits	TIVE	Delivery reli-
Government				Meaningful	ADVAN-	ability
				careers	TAGE	Quality
				Satisfying		Minimal
				jobs		investment
				Community		Flexibility for
				health		volume
				National		change
				progress		Products
				Organizational		change
				learning		Technological
						change

than not managers will have to develop structures that can handle a great deal of product change and variety, technological innovation, and organizational learning.

Seen this way, what is needed is a new ideology, or, as George Lodge explains, a new "collection of ideas through which we translate values into action."[91] The old notions of a factory and the old rules of manufacturing leadership are worn out.

Before 1900, despite its weaknesses in effective management of workers, manufacturing leadership was well provided by top management. They were technological entrepreneurs, architects of productive systems, veritable lions of industry. But when they delegated their production responsibilities to a second-level department, the factory institution never recovered its vitality. The lion was tamed. Its management systems became protective, and generally neither very entrepreneurial nor strategic. Moreover, production managers since then have typically had little to do with initiating substantially new process technology—in contrast to their predecessors before 1900.

In contrast, a new, more useful, and effective paradigm perceives manufacturing as designers of production systems that include people and technology, organizing factories to manage a great deal of change and learning, and structuring manufacturing to perform as a strategic resource for the firm.

We now return briefly to the starting point presented in this chapter. We suggested the mechanisms and antecedents in history that have produced "how manufacturing leaders think," and we proposed that events beginning about 1960 have made anachronistic and ineffective most of the paradigms of industrial leadership that had evolved after 1900, sadly bringing about the taming of the lion of American industrial leadership.

The next question and the final one for this chapter: Will the next generation of manufacturing leadership, those men and women who will be our manufacturing leaders in the 1990s, evolve a new and more effective paradigm, an ideology for the factory, and concepts and techniques that will displace the mind-set, premises, and skills, which appear outmoded today?

The "comers" interviewed are promising in their broadened skills, energetic attitudes, wider knowledge, and zealous, independent spirits. But to restore competitive strength will require a degree of imaginative leadership and basically new concepts that we did not discern other than in a few rare instances. Do they see the factory in pluralistic, multidimensional, strategic, and stakeholder vision rather than in strictly economic terms? They are starting to see labor not as a cost but as a potential resource of powerful dimensions, and that is encouraging. But do they see the manager as not merely a coordinator and "housekeeper," but also as responsible for a creative architectural design of a formidable competitive resource, and of a factory that will attract the best of human resources in our society? Are they technologically competent and imbued with a powerful zeal to be industrial change agents? Are they educated and fully prepared to be effective in top executive councils—"lions," rather than "pussycats"?

The answer to these questions is a careful, no. We did not meet more than a handful of such people in our comers. Nor are the data on Exhibits 20.4–20.6 encouraging regarding technical knowledge, use of time, focus of time, company focus, and focus within management. The comers are different and show many good signs, but it is not clearly a new breed as yet, based on these data.

It appears that a change in the mind-set and the premises of any set of functional managers is a big order. It is much more a question of a major shift in ideology than a modest shift to add new skills or insights. Therefore, it is probably unrealistic to expect that a "new breed" could or would grow biologically from within the ongoing structure in only one or two generations, even under the adverse and demanding conditions of the last 20 years. Any new breed is systematically discouraged by the corporate bureaucracy of short-term reward structures and penalties for taking risks that fail. The intermediate value systems discourage, and the old values prevail.

The notion of a factory as a competitive resource and as a learning and growing and living working place, and of manufacturing leadership as architect rather than housekeeper is very different from that of twentieth century industrial history. But in the nineteenth century the owner-managers managed manufacturing, and they were architects of production systems and innovative process technologies. Will top management recover its lost involvement with technology and the factory and become again, "a visible hand" in manufacturing management? Will competitive demands for more new products and the advantages of new microprocessor-based technologies combine to vault manufacturing managers again into a leadership role?

Of course managers need not patiently wait for evolution to do the job. To summarize the recommendations made earlier, I have suggested that competitive advantages will be created by changing how the corporation perceives its factories, by modifying reward systems to focus less on productivity and more on process innovation and building manufacturing structures that develop strategic leverage, by conceiving of employees as a potential creative resource, and by changing practices in the selection and development of manufacturing leaders to attract the best talent in the corporation and so develop that needed new generation of managers.

History is on the side of the impatient today. Breaking old patterns and setting new ones in their place is a process that will be speeded along by the impacts of major new technologies, continued severe competition, and perhaps a different mode of aggressive process innovation to recover the nineteenth century pattern of top management as technological innovators.

But this will surely come to pass, and, indeed, it will probably come soon. For one lesson of this history is that while old ideologies and managerial habits are powerful and enduring, new economics and technology eventually have their way.

NOTES

1. Abernathy, 1977.
2. Abernathy, Clark, and Kantrow, 1981.
3. Clawson, 1980.
4. Toynbee, 1884.
5. Skinner, "Getting Physical," 1984.

6. "Never before have so many manufacturers had so many ways to do things better. New technologies are revolutionizing manufacturing. . . ." *DUNS,* February 1984. Twenty-six page-report on manufacturing technology.

7. Chandler, 1977, p. 57.

8. Chandler, 1983.

9. Douglas, 1971.

10. Chandler, 1983, p. 246.

11. Nelson, 1975, p. 18.

12. Chandler, 1983, pp. 68–72.

13. Chandler, 1983, p. 72.

14. Smith, 1977.

15. Chandler, 1983, p. 72.

16. Rosenbloom, 1984.

17. Ure, 1835, pp. 277–373.

18. Thompson, 1967.

19. Gutman, 1977, p. 14.

20. Nelson, 1975, p. 55.

21. F. W. Taylor, 1895 Frederick Taylor referred to "the Labor Problem" half a century later than Toynbee's reference.

22. R. W. C. Taylor, 1886, p. 441.

23. R. W. C. Taylor, 1886, p. 429.

24. Chandler, 1983, p. 14.

25. Rosenberg, 1969.

26. Fong, 1930.

27. R. W. C. Taylor, 1886, p. 438.

28. Chandler, 1983, p. 75.

29. Glover, 1936.

30. Nelson, 1975, p. 42.

31. Nelson, 1975, p. 47.

32. Chandler, 1983, p. 247.

33. Glover, 1936.

34. Hammond, 1941.

35. Abernathy and Corcoran, 1983, p. 158.

36. Chandler, 1983, p. 249.

37. Glover, 1936.

38. Chandler, 1983, p. 274.

39. Bernard, 1971.
40. Pollard, 1965.
41. Chandler, 1983, p. 277.
42. Wells, 1890.
43. Nelson, 1975, p. 40.
44. F. B. Taylor, 1895.
45. Hayes and Abernathy, 1980.
46. Adam, 1983.
47. Skinner, 1968.
48. Source: Department of Labor. Series D946-951.
49. *Business Week,* 1980.
50. Baranson, 1981, Marsland and Beer, 1983, Schonberger, 1982.
51. Hayes and Abernathy, 1980.
52. National Academy of Engineering, 1983.
53. Schonberger, 1982.
54. Hayes, 1981.
55. These comments apply better to the fabricate-and-assemble industries than to many process type industries, such as chemicals, where product and process innovations are developed simultaneously, with the principal responsibilities typically located outside the production department.
56. For example, the American factory system began early to use "buffer inventories" and "safety stocks" to cushion the impact of the uncertainties of the factors of production in order to ensure smooth flows and continuous operations. In contrast, the Japanese minimize inventories and seek to prevent changes from the outside, as well as maintenance, scrap, or other discontinuities from the inside.
57. Hayes, 1980.
58. Hayes, 1981.
59. Wheelwright, 1981.
60. Baranson, 1981.
61. Schonberger, 1982.
62. Marsland and Beer, 1983.
63. Deutsch, 1980.
64. Grayson, 1982.
65. *Fortune,* January 23, 1984.
66. *Business Week,* January 23, 1984.
67. Kearney, 1982.

68. Abernathy, Clark, and Kantrow, 1983.
69. Kanter, 1983, p. 353.
70. Skinner, 1984.
71. Skinner, 1984.
72. Skinner, 1980.
73. Leonard and Sasser, 1982.
74. Garvin, 1983.
75. Flaherty, 1982.
76. Jaikumar and Bohn, 1983.
77. Lawrence and Dyer, 1983.
78. Kaplan, 1983.
79. Kaplan, 1983.
80. A description of the research methodology and questionnaire is available from the author.
81. McCaskey, 1982.
82. Stevenson, 1983.
83. Blau, 1965, p. 61.
84. Peters and Waterman, 1982.
85. Federal Writers Project, WPA, 1939.
86. Farnham, 1921.
87. Davidson, 1984.
88. Lodge, McCormick, and Zuboff, 1983.
89. Kaplan, 1983.
90. Lodge, 1980.
91. Lodge, 1982.

REFERENCES

Abernathy, William J. *The Productivity Dilemma*. Baltimore: John Hopkins Press, 1977.

Abernathy, William J., Clark, Kim B., and Kantrow, Alan M. *Industrial Renaissance*. New York: Basic Books, 1983.

Abernathy, William J., Clark, Kim B., and Kantrow, Alan M. "The New Industrial Competition." *Harvard Business Review*, 1981.

Abernathy, William J., and Corcoran, John E. "Relearning from the Old Masters: Lessons of the American System of Manufacturing." *Journal of Operations Management*, Vol. 3, No. 4 (August 1983).

Adam, Everett E., Jr. "Towards a Typology of Production and Operations Management Systems." *Academy of Management Review*, Vol. 8, No. 3 (1983), pp. 365–375.

Baranson, Jack. *The Japanese Challenge to U.S. Industry*. Lexington, Mass.: D.C. Heath, 1981.

Bernard, J.E. "Science in History." Vol. 2, *The Scientific and Industrial Revolutions*. Cambridge, Mass.: MIT Press, 1971.

Blau, Peter M. *Bureaucracy and Modern Society*. New York: Random House; 1956.

Blau, Peter M. *The Dynamics of Bureaucracy*. Chicago, Ill.: University of Chicago Press, 1965.

Chandler, Alfred D., Jr. *Samuel Slater, Francis Cabot Lowell, and the Beginnings of the Factory System in the United States*. Harvard Business School. Case 9-377-222, Rev. 7/83.

Chandler, Alfred D., Jr. *The Visible Hand*. Cambridge, Mass. and London, England: Belknap Press, 1977.

Clawson, Dan. "Bureaucracy and the Labor Process—The Transformation of U.S. Industry, 1860–1920." *Monthly Business Review*, New York, 1980.

Davidson, William H. *The Amazing Race: Winning the Technorivalry with Japan*. New York: John Wiley & Sons, 1984.

Deutsch, Claudia H. "Productivity: The Difficulty of Even Defining the Problem." *Business Week*, June 9, 1980, pp. 52–53.

Douglas, Elisha P. *The Coming of Age of American Business*. Chapel Hill: University of North Carolina Press, 1971, pp. 81–81.

Farnham, Dwight. *America vs. Europe in Industry*. New York: Ronald Press, 1921.

Federal Writers' Project, WPA. *These Are Our Lives*. New York: Norton, 1939.

Flaherty, M.T. "Market Share, Technology Leadership and Competition in International Semiconductor Markets," in *Research in Technological Innovation Management and Policy*, Vol. 1. Edited by R. S. Rosenbloom. Greenwich, Conn.: JAI Press, 1982.

Fong, Hsien-T'Ing, *The Triumph of the Factory System in England*. Philadelphia, Penn.: Porcupine Press, 1930.

Garvin, David. "Quality on the Line." *Harvard Business Review*, September–October, 1983, pp. 64–75.

Glover, John G., and Corvell, William B. *The Development of American Industries*. New York: Prentice-Hall, 1936.

Grayson, C. Jackson. "Emphasizing Capital Investment is a Mistake." *Wall Street Journal—Manager's Journal*, October 11, 1982.

Gutman, Herbert G. *Work, Culture, and Society in Industrializing America*. New York: Random House, 1977.

Hammond, John Winthrop. *Men and Volts: the Story of General Electric*. Philadelphia, Penn.: J.B. Lippincott, 1941.

Hayes, Robert. "Why Japanese Factories Work." *Harvard Business Review*, July–August 1981, pp. 56–66.

Hayes, Robert, and Abernathy, William. "Managing Our Way to Economic Decline." *Harvard Business Review*, July–August 1980, pp. 67–77.

Jaikumar, Ramchandran, and Bohn, Roger. *Some New Approaches to Production Management*. Discussion draft. Harvard Business School, 1983.

Kanter, Rosabeth. *The Change Masters*. New York: Simon & Shuster, 1983.

Kaplan, Robert S. *The Evolution of Management Accounting*. Address to American Accounting Association. New Orleans, August 23, 1983.

Kaplan, Robert S. "Measuring Manufacturing Performance: A New Challenge for Managerial Accounting Research." *The Accounting Review*, Vol. LVIII, No. 4, October 1983.

Kearney, A.T. *Managing for Excellence: A research study of the state-of-the-art of productivity programs in the United States.* Chicago: A.T. Kearney, 1982.

Lansburgh, Richard H. *Industrial Management.* New York: John Wiley & Sons, 1928.

Lawrence, Paul R., and Dyer, Davis. *Renewing American Industry.* New York: Free Press, 1983.

Leonard, Frank, and Sasser, W. Earl. "The Incline of Quality." *Harvard Business Review*, September–October, 1982, pp. 163–171.

Lodge, George C. "Ideological Implications of Changes in Human Resource Management." Drawn from *The American Disease.* New York: Alfred Knopf, 1984.

Lodge, George C. *The New American Ideology.* New York: Alfred Knopf, 1980.

Lodge, George C. *The Uses of Ideology for Managers.* Harvard Business School, 380-021, 1982.

Lodge, George, C. McCormick Janice, and Zuboff, Shoshana. *Sources and Patterns of Management Authority.* Harvard Business School, 0-484-039, 1983.

"Manufacturing Technology." *Dun's Business Month,* February 1984, p. 26.

Marsland, Stephen, and Beer, Michael. "The Evolution of Japanese Management: Lessons for U.S. Managers." *Organizational Dynamics,* Winter 1983.

McCaskey, Michael B. *The Executive Challenge: Managing Change and Ambiguity.* Boston: Pitman, 1982.

National Academy of Engineering. *U.S. Leadership in Manufacturing.* Washington, D.C.: National Academy Press, 1983.

Nelson, Daniel. *Managers and Workers: Origins of the New Factory System in the United States, 1880–1920.* Madison, WI: University of Wisconsin Press, 1975.

Peters, Thomas J., and Waterman, Robert H., Jr. *In Search of Excellence.* New York: Harper and Row, 1982.

Pollard, Sidney. *The Genesis of Modern Management.* Cambridge, Mass.: Harvard University Press, 1965.

"The Reindustrialization of America." *Business Week,* June 30, 1980, pp. 55–138.

"The Revival of Productivity." *Business Week,* January 13, 1984, pp. 92–100.

Rosenberg, Nathan (ed). *The American System of Manufacturing.* Edinburgh: Edinburgh University Press, 1969.

Rosenbloom, Richard S. "Men and Machines: Some 19th-Century Analyses of Mechanization." *Technology and Culture,* Vol V, No. 4, Fall 1984.

Schonberger, Richard J. *Japanese Manufacturing Techniques.* New York: Free Press, 1982.

Skinner, Wickham. "The Factory of The Future: Always in the Future?" In *Towards the Factory in the future,* edited by L. Kops. Chicago: American Society of Mechanical Engineers, 1980.

Skinner, Wickham. "Getting Physical": New Strategic Leverage from Operations." *Journal of Business Strategy,* Vol. 3, No. 4, Spring 1984, pp. 74–79.

Skinner, Wickham. "The Productivity Disease." In *The Princeton Papers.* Missassagua, Ontario: Northern Telecom, 1984.

Skinner, Wickham. "Reinventing the Factory: A Manufacturing Strategy Response to Industrial Malaise." In *The Latest Advances in Strategic Management,* edited by R. Lamb. Englewood Cliffs, NJ: Prentice-Hall, 1984.

Skinner, Wickham. *The Stubborn Infrastructure of the Factory.* Harvard Business School. Working Paper, 1968.

Smith, Meritt Roe. *Harpers Ferry Armory and the New Technology.* Ithaca, NY: Cornell University Press, 1977.

Stevenson, Howard. *A New Paradigm for Entrepreneurial Management.* Harvard Business School Working Paper, 1983.

Stobaugh, R., and Telesio, P. "Match Manufacturing Policies and Product Strategy." *Harvard Business Review,* March–April, 1983, pp. 113–120.

Taylor, Frederick B. *A Piece Rate System: A Step Toward Partial Solution of the Labor Problem.* ASME Transactions 16 (1895) 856–893.

Taylor, R. Whately Cooke. *Introduction to a History of the Factory System.* London: Richard Bentley & Son, 1886.

Taylor, R. Whately Cooke. *The Modern Factory System.* London: Kegan Paul Trench Trubner & Co., 1891.

Thompson, E. P. *The Making of the English Working Class.* New York: Random House, 1963.

Thompson, E. P. *Time, Work, Discipline and Industrial Capitalism.* New York: Panther Press, 1967.

Toynbee, Arnold. *The Industrial Revolution of the Eighteenth Century in England.* London: Longmars, Green & Co., 1972. (First edition, 1884.)

Ure, Andrew. *The Philosophy of Manufactures of An Exposition of the Scientific, Moral, and Commercial Economy of the Factory System of Great Britain.* (2nd ed.) London: Charles Knight, 1835.

Wells, David A. *Recent Changes.* New York: Appleton, 1890.

Wheelwright, S. C. "Japan—Where Operations Really are Strategic." *Harvard Business Review,* July August 1981.

Index